THE OTHER FACE OF BATTLE

THE OTHER FACE
OF BATTLE

AMERICA'S FORGOTTEN WARS AND THE
EXPERIENCE OF COMBAT

WAYNE E. LEE, ANTHONY E. CARLSON,
DAVID L. PRESTON, & DAVID SILBEY

OXFORD
UNIVERSITY PRESS

OXFORD
UNIVERSITY PRESS

Oxford University Press is a department of the University of Oxford. It furthers the University's objective of excellence in research, scholarship, and education by publishing worldwide. Oxford is a registered trade mark of Oxford University Press in the UK and certain other countries.

Published in the United States of America by Oxford University Press
198 Madison Avenue, New York, NY 10016, United States of America.

CIP data is on file at Library of Congress
ISBN 978–0–19–092064–7

DOI: 10.1093/oso/9780190920647.001.0001

1 3 5 7 9 8 6 4 2

Printed by Sheridan Books, Inc., United States of America

Contents

Maps and Figures

Preface

Over the course of the last two decades the study of war has changed profoundly, becoming more demanding and more sophisticated. War can be studied at its different levels of strategy, operations, and tactics, or one can turn to logistics, home front effects, institutions, mobilizations, technology, and more. Inevitably, none of those can truly be dealt with in isolation, and yet each exists within its own chronological, geographic, and cultural context. *The Other Face of Battle* seeks to capture the personal experience of combat across a wide spectrum of American history, and particularly to highlight how that experience was (and is) affected by combat across cultural boundaries. To do this we chose to write this book together, taking advantage of our separate expertise in different conflicts and periods and yet hoping to tell a single story about the American experience of war. Over its history, the country has fought enemies from many different cultures. Ultimately, we argue that this not only made the wars different but also changed the experience of *battle*. That difference affected strategic outcomes, and it affected the men and women who experienced it and then returned home bearing its scars.

Good history speaks to the present. We seek to remind our fellow citizens of the costs of combat—costs that persist well past its nominal ending. The United States currently deploys more force abroad than any other nation on earth; the nation must take responsibility for that, and for the men and women we send out. Finally, we seek to highlight the very strong likelihood that whatever conflict we fight next is not likely to be the one we expect. That disconnect has had, and will have, implications for American soldiers in combat.

Wayne Lee writes: I am grateful to the many scholars who have helped along the way, notably Greg Daddis, Jim Lacey, and Rhonda Lee. My fellow authors in this volume have been models of how to cooperate and get things done.

David Preston writes: I am grateful to my coauthors and will always treasure our collaboration and friendships. LTC Jason Warren and his outstanding J5 team at Joint Force Headquarters provided enormously helpful insights during our staff ride of Braddock's Expedition in 2018, as did Ed Lengel and Jack Giblin at a roundtable presentation on Braddock's Defeat at the U.S. Army Heritage and Education Center. I remain ever grateful to friends and colleagues at George Washington's Mount Vernon, including Doug Bradburn, Kevin Butterfield, Stephen McLeod, and Joe Stoltz. I am also thankful to board members of the Braddock's Battlefield History Center and the Braddock Road Preservation Association and colleagues at the Fort Necessity National Battlefield as we advance the preservation and interpretation of the French and Indian War era. Many other colleagues have provided support, insight, inspiration, and friendship: Norman Baker, Walter and Nancy Bunt, Jason Cherry, Doug Cubbison, Matt Davenport, Christian Fearer, Joseph Gagné, Alan Gutchess, Rick Herrera, Paul Johstono, Matthew Kutilek, James Kirby Martin, Bob Nipar, Erica Nuckles, Walter Powell, Rob Shenk, Kyle Sinisi, Bruce and Lynne Venter, and Jim Wordsworth. I am grateful to my Citadel colleagues and especially to The Citadel Foundation, which has generously provided my research support for this volume. Finally, my wife and family have my eternal thanks and love for how they keep me grounded on what truly matters in life.

David Silbey writes: This work would not have been possible without the loving support of my wife, Mari, and my daughter, Madeline. They've heard enough war stories to write a book of their own. The support and advice of my parents was also crucial: my dad, who was there for the start of the project but did not live to see the end, and my mom, who carried him further than it seemed possible. My part of this project is for them.

Tony Carlson writes: I am particularly grateful to Wayne Lee for the invitation to contribute to this book. I also extend my hearty thanks to my coauthors and fellow bourbon connoisseurs for their constructive criticism of my work and equally valuable friendships. Tim Bent and the staff at Oxford have earned my highest praise as well. Rick Herrera, Don Wright, Tom Hanson, Kevin Hymel, Jacob Stoil, Bruce Stanley, and Yannick Michaud read and commented on earlier drafts, sharpening my prose and improving my ideas. I, too, am indebted to the leadership and staff at the School of Advanced Military Studies, specifically Scott Gorman, Rich Dixon, Kirk Dorr, Candi Hamm, and Anna White, for their invaluable, enthusiastic support. The soldiers of the 2nd Brigade Combat Team, 101st

Airborne Division (Air Assault) who fought in Zhari and generously sat for oral history interviews and answered countless nagging emails and texts have made this study unique and possible. I can never repay them. Mom and Dad, thanks for believing in me. I would be nowhere professionally without the sage advice, wisdom, and generosity of Don Pisani, and I thank him for being an inestimable mentor. Finally, Tera knows her innumerable contributions and sacrifices, and I appreciate her more than she knows. The opinions and views expressed throughout are mine alone and do not reflect the position of the U.S. government, the Department of Defense, or the army.

We are all grateful to Tim Bent, our editor at Oxford, for his support and guidance in this project; it has been a pleasure working with him. Matilde Grimaldi prepared all the maps with remarkable speed and precision.

I

Introduction

Enemies of Another Sort

The familiar snap of flags in the breeze mixed uneasily with the distant sound of enemy laughter, and the discordance unsettled and irritated Captain John Underhill. Underhill, a professional soldier hired to advise the Massachusetts Bay colonists, was trained in the cutting-edge discipline that was characteristic of the Dutch army. Enemy laughter on the eve of battle was not something he was used to hearing, and it suggested a level of enemy confidence that he found disconcerting. Beginning in 1630 he had lived with and trained the settlers for some seven years, using the standard English militia practices of the era, no doubt infused with his own love of order and spectacle as he had experienced it in the Prince of Orange's guard. Despite their frequent tensions with Native Americans, which had sometimes produced violent moments, the colonists had thus far avoided outright war with their near neighbors.

In 1637, however, Massachusetts had gone to war with the Pequots and with the Indians of Block Island.[1] Underhill may or may not have understood the deeper roots of the conflict—which stemmed essentially from the colonists' desire for more land on the Connecticut River—but he did understand the nature of his mission. He and the men with him had been dispatched to demand justice for the murder of a trader named John Oldham, killed by the Block Island Indians. Underhill accepted this story and later wrote that the "blood of the innocent called for vengeance." Under the overall command of Captain John Endecott, Underhill was one of four captains leading a hundred men—far more officers than the usual European practice. This, Underhill later explained, was in response to Indian tactics. Although his men had not yet warred against them, Underhill had learned that the "Indians' fight far differs from the

Christian practice; for they most commonly divide themselves into small bodies, so that we are forced to neglect our usual way, and to subdivide our divisions to answer theirs."[2]

After one raid into Block Island, Endecott's expedition landed on the mainland in Pequot territory to demand the persons responsible for the killing of yet another trader, one named John Stone. This was merely a pretense: the colonial government had despised John Stone when he was alive, and a full year had elapsed since his death. The Pequots, perhaps equally confused, stalled, and may or may not have intended an honest parlay. In any case, they were likely unwilling or unable simply to hand over one or more of their own to English justice. In response, according to Underhill's account, the Massachusetts militia formed up "in battalia" and then marched to the top of a ridge to await events. Ultimately, frustrated by delay, the Englishmen "rather chose to beat up the drum and bid them battle. Marching into the champaign [open] field we displayed our colors." The Pequots ignored the provocation and instead, "standing remotely off[,] did laugh at us for our patience."[3] The English might want to fight, but that did not mean the Pequots had to oblige them.

Underhill's predecessors at Jamestown, in the Virginia colony, had an experience that similarly confounded their expectations. Focused on the possibility of Spanish attack, the colonists' sponsors back in England had instructed them to find someplace "a hundred miles from the Rivers mouth," as being more defensible against a seaborne enemy. The Spanish threat was real; the planners in England reminded the colonists that the Spanish had destroyed without mercy a French colony in Florida. As further security against such an attack, the planners recommended that in addition to their main fort, they should build a small entrenchment (a "Little Sconce") at the river's mouth equipped with a small boat that could be dispatched to warn the settlement.[4]

Instead of fighting other Europeans, however, the Jamestown colonists immediately found themselves locked in conflict and ultimately outright war with the Native Americans. These conflicts were mostly generated by English desperation and greed, but they were real enough and bloody enough, continuing on and off for much of the next thirty years, briefly interrupted only by the truce brokered with the marriage of Pocahontas and John Rolfe in 1614. The wars were characterized by confusion, helplessness, and even paranoia, the fear of the knife in the dark and the enemies among the trees—but above all the sense of alienness. They were fighting enemies of another sort, and this led to more violent and more destructive forms of warfare.[5]

Underhill's experience, and that of the Jamestown colonists, reflects the key themes of this book. Americans in combat, from their colonial experiences to the present day, have almost always faced unexpected enemies—foes from different cultural backgrounds, who fought in unfamiliar ways, and against whom they were not prepared to fight. *The Other Face of Battle* is about that jarring encounter when the face of the enemy is that of the "other," and frequently that "otherness" has included a form of combat that seemed or felt "asymmetrical"—a term referring to the frequent resort of non-state or overmatched opponents to strategies and tactics that avoid usual American advantages in firepower and economic capacity. (We will explore the meaning of "symmetrical warfare" in greater depth later, but in general the term "refers to the situation where both sides have the same general goals, organize and equip their forces in similar ways, and operate through similar strategies and according to similar rules of engagement and standards of acceptable conduct.")[6] Quite often, asymmetric warfare emerged from intercultural violence, when the enemy had different modes of recruitment, equipment, engagement, and notions of acceptable conduct. In some ways the periodic and numerous confrontations with unexpected enemies should have been foreseeable. America, after all, contrary to our own mythology of only fighting wars in support of liberty and democracy, has long been an empire.[7] Settlers moved first across the Atlantic Ocean, then across the continent, and then across new oceans. When the frontiers of empires shift, they create new foes.

To illuminate this aspect of American military history (although the phenomenon is by no means confined to the American experience), we examine three battles across two and a half centuries: British and colonial American forces against the French and Indians at Monongahela in 1755—a battle also known as Braddock's Defeat; American volunteers and professional soldiers versus Filipinos at Manila in 1899; and a wide assortment of professional soldiers, marines, airmen, and sailors against the Taliban at the village of Makuan in southern Afghanistan in 2010. These are not battles that feature prominently in our national lore, but that is the point. They have been forgotten, sometimes (as we will see) deliberately so. Each battle will be narrated and analyzed from the soldiers' perspective, seeking to reveal the human experience of combat. At the same time, this book situates each battle within developments over three centuries, and thus also tells a broader story about how the American way of war has evolved and adjusted, or not.

Choosing forgotten battles in small wars is not to ignore or downplay the significance of the big wars in American history.[8] Despite all of the big wars also featuring asymmetrical components, the War of Independence, the War of 1812, the war with Mexico, the Civil War, the Spanish–American War, World Wars I and II, and Korea were dominated by "conventional" combat, meaning fighting that engaged in familiar forms that were recognizable to all parties. Our intent is not to declare one type of war easier or harder to prepare for or win than another, or to say that one type of war is acceptable and another not. It is instead to assess the comparative and qualitative difference in the nature of battle within those wars and then to explore what that difference means.

We also do not intend that the "forgotten wars" in the subtitle of this book should be taken literally. Most wars are not forgotten. They live in the memories of those who fought them and their families and descendants. But in many ways the human element of these wars has become lost to public memory. Most of our histories, movies, novels, and public commemorations focus on the big wars.[9] This is so in part because those wars seemed more existentially threatening. However, it is also because the accounts of their veterans are threaded with a comfortably familiar language. To take an example from the Civil War, in this case Confederate Private Alexander Hunter's description of a Union charge:

> Then our Colonel said in a quiet calm tone, that was heard by all, "steady lads, steady! Seventeenth, don't fire until they get above the hill." . . . The first thing we saw appear was the gilt eagle that surmounted the pole, then the top of the flag, next the flutter of the Stars and Stripes itself slowly mounting—up it rose; then their hats came into sight; still rising, the faces emerged; next a range of curious eyes appeared, then such a hurrah as only the Yankee troops could give broke the stillness, and they surged towards us.[10]

Private Hunter's story would have resonated with a veteran of the Continental Army or with a recruit preparing for war in Europe in 1941. It has calm officers, steady troops, clear instructions, fluttering standards, and perhaps above all an obvious target. Claiming that a narrative like Hunter's is reassuringly familiar, however, is not to dwell on romanticized stories about fraternization between the lines or snowball fights during Christmas truces. As James McPherson has argued, dehumanization of the enemy during the Civil War was more common than fraternization.[11] In a letter home, sixteen-year-old Private William Brearley, who enlisted to fight in the Civil War in the 17th Michigan, offered to his family that pictures he had seen of soldiers "in line, all standing in a nice level field fighting, a number of ladies taking care of the wounded, &c &c." just weren't true.[12] All war, symmetrical or otherwise, is hell.

Even so, America's forgotten wars usually offered less clarity to its soldiers, both in the sense of what was being fought for and how it was being fought. Duncan Cameron, a British soldier at Monongahela in 1755, the first of the case studies in this book, later recalled the extremity of that battle, deeming it "the most shocking I was ever in."[13] This from a man who had already served in the Battles of Cartagena, Dettingen, Fontenoy, and Culloden. And Fontenoy, fought between the British and French armies, was one of the bloodiest until World War I: some 18,000 men of 100,000 on both sides were killed or wounded on that single day in 1745. Yet, for Cameron, Monongahela was worse, not because of the sheer number of men killed or wounded but because of the setting. War wasn't just in front of you or waiting for you at the top of a hill marked by an enemy standard. It was everywhere and nowhere: it was the seemingly primeval forest, the enemies' ululating war cries, the flickering of deadly shadows moving and firing among the trees, combined with the agonized pleas of the wounded and dying men, some scalped, who were littered along the line of the march.

Soldiers in later wars with unexpected enemies made similar observations about their experience. Sergeant L. C. Peters of the 1st Nebraska, a soldier in the Battle of Manila, denigrated the "thoroughly fanatical" insurgents, who believed their leader, Emilio Aguinaldo, to be some sort of "tin god" whose talismans would protect them from American bullets.[14] There is no question of Peters's deeply embedded racist and anti-Catholic views of the Filipinos, but they shaped his experience of combat, and would influence the choices he made therein. Wayne Smith, an African American combat medic in the 9th Infantry Division in Vietnam in 1969–1970, conveyed in just a few sentences how the pressures of combat transformed everything into a nightmare world of dehumanization, and how those beliefs then shaped behavior:

> I wasn't raised to kill. But when I was in combat I was tainted by this blood lust and I, too, became a combat soldier. There was blood on my hands. I wanted to kill the enemy and I even wanted to lie and exaggerate my desire to kill the enemy. I never participated in any mutilation, but I did violate one

line. All through training, and even my first six or seven months in Vietnam, I never called the Vietnamese gooks because I knew intuitively that it would be the same as saying nigger. And it was. Yet in combat I began to call them gooks. I did not believe my country was capable of going in and killing people and counting their bodies and claiming a victory because we killed more of them than they did of us. But there was a real incentivizing of death and it just fucked with our value system. In our unit guys who got confirmed kills would get a three-day in-country R and R. . . . And the easiest way to confirm a kill was to cut off an ear or a thumb.[15]

Duncan Cameron, L. C. Peters, and Wayne Smith all experienced combat in ways that differed qualitatively and tactically from the experiences of soldiers in other American wars. They saw the other face of battle.

This difference affects how we understand and explain the past, and how we craft strategy for the future. At Jamestown, the Spanish threat was real, and therefore preparing for it was logical. In 2021, fears of losing a "big battle" against a conventional enemy such as Russia or China are equally real and equally logical. Indeed, for centuries, military planners in America, Europe, and elsewhere have been drawn to and planned for a decisive battle and a short war, usually against the expected enemy.[16] But often the focus on those big threats was also about facing what was familiar rather than what was likely. If history is any guide, the other face of battle, the one we are almost always unprepared to face, will reemerge. As we explore in this book, after each irregular, uncomfortable, often (though not always) indecisive "other" war, the nation and the institutional military quickly forgot or rejected its lessons. Even now, American institutional and cultural discomfort with that form of war, and especially with that form of combat and its strategic inconclusiveness, is leading the army to deemphasize the small wars of American history in its education, training, doctrine, and procurement. It is not the first time. In 1989, Americans were still coming to terms with defeat in Vietnam as the Soviets withdrew from their own ten-year ordeal in Afghanistan. They would not have predicted that the United States would be militarily engaged in Afghanistan for nearly twice as long (so far).

Most of America's wars have been neither big nor conventional. The American experience of battle, therefore, has usually been asymmetrical. The American military, however, has usually prepared for symmetrical combat against a roughly technologically and sociologically equivalent foe. The result has been that we have nearly always been unprepared for the next war, leading to flawed tactics or strategies. Flawed strategy has led to frustration. Frustration has led either to greater levels of uncontrolled violence in combat or to prolonged unsatisfying stalemate. John Underhill's men opted for the former in 1637. Humiliated by the Indians' laughter and frustrated by the enemy's elusiveness, the colonists persuaded their Narragansett allies to lead them by night to the Pequot village of Mystic. Underhill and his men, "being bereaved of pity, fell upon the work without compassion," ultimately setting fire to the village and killing the Indians as they fled—men, women, and children—in the hundreds. Underhill briefly fretted in his memoir about his fellow Christians' judgment of this seeming mercilessness, but, having turned to scripture, he concluded, "We had a sufficient light from the word of God for our proceedings."[17] American soldiers in asymmetrical combat in Afghanistan have experienced similar frustrations but have avoided retaliatory massacre. Instead, frustration has been drawn out into a seemingly endless war, explained neatly by Taylor Murphy, a young second lieutenant in the U.S. Army from our third case study, set in Afghanistan in 2010:

> Between the terrain and the unconventional tactics used by the insurgents in Zhari District [in southern Afghanistan], we experienced several extreme frustrations. The IED techniques prevented us from attacking the enemy in a traditional fashion. And it made it nearly impossible for us to fix and destroy them. The IED threat and the cumbersome nature of our equipment slowed us down, while our enemies experienced unencumbered movement, passive support from the populace, an ability to blend in, and an intricate cache system for weapons following engagements.[18]

With equal wisdom but fewer words, an American enlisted soldier in the Zhari operation admitted that "we have air support. The Taliban has IEDs."[19]

★ ★ ★

Lieutenant Murphy was pining for a "conventional" form of combat; a form that provides a kind of clarity in fighting an enemy who fights back the same way. Such combat involves a symmetry of action, reaction, and mutual apprehension. Or at least this is how we in the modern world imagine the duels of swordsmen or of fighter pilots, or even the "duel" of tanks and infantry in massed divisions fighting each other across an open landscape. This desire for the so-called honest battle with a clear outcome is deeply rooted in Western culture. At the end of the Battle of Agincourt in Shakespeare's *Henry V*, King Henry reflects on marvel of the outcome, in which the English had won such a great victory, with little loss, and "without Strategem, but in plain shock and even play of battle."[20] In reality, however, strategem is common and the balance of forces imaginary. There is nothing "symmetrical" about the impact of an exploding bomb or artillery shell on human flesh. And conventional combatants actively seek potentially decisive transitory moments of "asymmetry" to achieve success, whether it is an archer against the knight bogged down in mud, the horseman running down fleeing musketeers, or the tank against infantrymen.

But fighting an enemy who systematically refuses to engage on the same terms; who uses different weapons; who is guided by different sounds, cries, or dances; and who above all is guided by a different set of ethics makes the "even play of battle" feel uneven. To them, of course, we are the asymmetrical ones. The "other" is only and ever the "other" to the "other." It is we who are strange and different and uneven. There is no universal right or wrong here—although either side may impose such a judgment afterward. Even in America's most recent war, the Taliban have denigrated Americans' courage for their way of fighting from a distance and for how they cry out in combat, a behavior they deem cowardly.[21]

None of this is to claim that "symmetrical" combat isn't complicated, bloody, and destructive. Arguably, symmetry inspires ever greater efforts and ever greater ingenuity in the quest to destroy one's opponent—more troops, heavier armor, more guns, bigger bombs, faster planes, more bullets per second, multi-domain operations, cyber and electromagnetic tactics, and so on.[22] Very often in American history, however, the contest has been asymmetrical, and equally often piling on more does not always translate into victory. It is in the very nature of asymmetric warfare to deflect if not defeat technological superiority, whether using loose formations of accurately firing Indians against columns of infantry or planting IEDs against insufficiently armored and road-bound vehicles. Above all, however, it is frequently the case that the enemy simply has a different standard of victory.

There are a host of issues to confront before we turn to specific cases. What is symmetrical warfare? Why should cultural difference affect combat? How can anyone convey the experience of violence? How can we know the "other's" mind? What examples will best serve our purpose? These questions are central to this book, and they require some initial explanation and definition.

The first issue, as we've been suggesting, involves defining what we mean by "intercultural" and "asymmetrical." History tells us that battles take their shape from the imaginations of those fighting them. External factors—weapons technologies and local topography, for example—create the stage, but what happens on that stage turns on the moral force binding the combatants to each other and to their purpose. Victory and defeat ultimately reside in the mind and are culturally derived. Weapons, ideas about their deployment, and even the moral force are all inherently cultural, based upon attitudes shaped and transmitted over generations. Intercultural warfare is a clash of mindsets as much as weapons. A primary purpose of this book is to explore what that clash produces. Intercultural combat is unpredictable, as are its implications. Vocabularies shift. One side's claim of victory might be challenged by another's definition of the word. Or it might cease to have meaning.

So, too, with terms such as "symmetry" and "cultural." Is a group of Spanish irregulars fighting Napoleon's army in Spain in 1813—the origin of the term "guerrillas"—asymmetrical but intracultural? Is an artillery barrage against an infantry platoon a symmetrical fight? Is it intracultural? What if the artillerymen are Japanese and the infantrymen American? In one sense, "symmetrical" or "asymmetrical" corresponds roughly to the old chestnut from Supreme Court associate justice Potter Stewart's working definition of obscenity: he could not precisely define it, but "I know it when I see it." In military history circles, the term "asymmetrical" is applied to conflicts in which one combatant is uniformed and trained and raised by a state, while the other is not. Not all intercultural conflicts have been asymmetrical. The fighting in the Pacific during World War II was intercultural but not asymmetrical. The Battle of Manila, narrated in this book, was deliberately chosen to illuminate this type of case. Combats since World War II have been characterized by a widening spectrum of combinations of different levels and kinds of intercultural and asymmetrical conflict. The Makuan case study will examine, among other things, how the experience of having cultural others fighting on one's own side informs the experience of combat.

Ultimately, our argument is that cultural difference has shaped the experience of combat, generating new and unexpected forms of combat stress, which has had different strategic, historical, and personal consequences. Every account of the institutional development of the U.S. Army after

Vietnam, for example, highlights how wartime frustrations among midlevel officers drove them to reform the army as they rose through the ranks in the years after 1973. Their frustration arose not just from the war's outcome, but also from its conduct. What was it about their combat experience that led them to this rejection? What were the unique stresses and dislocations generated by intercultural combat?

To begin to answer those questions, consider that winning a battle of any sort has always been more about instilling fear in one's opponents and breaking their will to resist than it has been about killing or wounding them—in this sense the body count has never mattered, except as it to contributes to undermining enemy will. At its core, combat presents a theater dominated by shifting spectra of fear, rage, and despair, and cannot be reduced to a single metric of success or failure. To explain the will to fight, the term "morale" is often used, but it implies a simplistic quantifiable binary of high or low. It is also generally individualistic, as if morale were a simple sum of individuals' willingness to fight and go on. Combat, however, involves a much more complex emotional dynamic that depends on camaraderie, training, experience, and psychological resiliency. Combat is immediate and visceral, its demands intense and unrelenting. When battle is also intercultural and/or asymmetrical, it intensifies the pressures on soldiers in virtually every way—fear, rage, and despair are amplified. By its very nature, asymmetry seeks to scramble the rules and expectations of combat. Scalping or drone strikes, acceptable to one side, are abhorrent and terrifying to the other.[23]

The nature of the intercultural combat experience quickly assumes strategic significance, because it does not just affect the means of combat; it is about the *meaning* of combat. The very assumption that battles are what produce victory in war is culturally derived. As former British officer (Royal Gurkha Rifles) and historian Emile Simpson reminds us in *War from the Ground Up: Twenty-First Century Combat as Politics*, "Force is simply another way to communicate meaning, another language." Within that language "the meaning of an action in war (the outcome of a battle, for example) may be mutually recognized, just as two people may well agree on the meaning of a text or speech." Or they may not agree. Battles can define wars only if their combatants define battles that way. If one side refuses to accept battles as the defining component of war, the strategic competition becomes asymmetric, and instead "both sides are now in competition to construct more appealing strategic narratives of what the conflict is about." War then requires a strategy of persuasion, and destruction of the enemy armed forces becomes merely one line of argument.[24]

By studying battles with another sort of enemy, we can gain a better sense of why Americans have so often struggled to achieve success on their own terms. Part of the problem, as we will see, is simply in what we mean by "success," and defining it illuminates assumptions that have rarely served the country well.

Assumptions have enormous power. Civilians and professional soldiers alike have almost always prepared for the next war based *not* on the last war (despite the popular adage) but on the assumption that the next war will involve someone like themselves. Techniques, tactics, weapons acquisition programs, and, most crucially, expectations have all been built on an assumption of cultural *and* tactical symmetry. In the 1980s, for example, instead of learning and institutionalizing what it meant to fight an insurgent enemy in Vietnam while propping up an unpopular government, the American military prepared to meet the Soviets on the plains of Germany.[25]

The irony in all this is that most American wars have been intercultural, and therefore asymmetrical. Slighted in the usual popular narratives of our history were the conflicts with many different Native American nations, Filipinos, Haitians, Dominicans, Iraqis, Afghans, Somalis, Colombians, and more. Of the roughly 100 wars or interventions involving U.S. military forces since 1775, only nine can be thought of as primarily symmetrical and only seven as primarily against states with similar cultural backgrounds.[26] And even within those seven, most included intercultural or asymmetrical components, including against the Creeks and the nations of Tecumseh's Ohio Confederation during the War of 1812, the guerrilla fighting embedded within the American Civil War, and of course the brutal combat of World War II in the Pacific. There were countless smaller conflicts with Native Americans in the colonial era and afterward that, as we shall see, shaped the American experience of war.[27]

Not always, however, the military establishment. Two decades and counting into a conflict against assorted kinds of terrorists and their supporters, the U.S. military continues to send mixed messages about how it perceives that conflict and how to fight it. On one hand, the U.S. Army has created new security force assistance brigades (SFABs), built around experienced officers and non-commissioned officers and designed to provide training and state-building capabilities to host nations facing an insurgency.[28] On the other, recent years have seen a distinctive shift in the tone of U.S. Army mission statements, doctrine, and even the design of some officer education programs, markedly deemphasizing the counterinsurgency mission in favor of preparing for a symmetrical conflict with a more familiar enemy such as Russia—a type of conflict now referred to as large-scale combat operations or LSCO.[29] There is a sound logic in reemphasizing such conventional missions, given the long focus on counterinsurgency in Iraq and Afghanistan, and Russia now poses a different threat in Ukraine and other places than it did in years past. Furthermore, it is true that the new Army Field Manual 3-0 *Operations*, made public in late 2017, admits the need for all sorts of operations, including country "stabilization" missions. If one follows the money, however, one finds the equipment, education, and training that the army is now prioritizing to be mainly predicated on a symmetrical foe. The army's "Big Eight" modernization program, for example, which covers a wide range of capabilities, is justified as designed to "enhance the army's ability to conduct joint combined arms maneuver warfare, wide area security, and air and ground reconnaissance operations against advanced adversaries."[30]

The authors of this book work with the U.S. military in various ways, whether in uniform or through research and teaching. We recognize that American military leaders take seriously their responsibility to defend the nation and to prioritize truly existential threats. Past experience, especially recent experience, however, suggests that asymmetric battle with non-state actors and cultural "others" will likely define the next war.

That form of combat is increasingly unfamiliar to the American public, most of whom neither serve in the armed forces nor engage deeply with its experiences. Americans generally have become less and less familiar with the realities of combat in any form. They were arguably most familiar with those realities during World War II, by the end of which some 10 percent of the U.S. population was serving in uniform. Yet even during that conflict, the largest in which the country has been engaged, only a small minority of American men actually experienced ground combat. Vast numbers of men and women served in the Navy, in the Air Force, and in ground support roles, but exchange of live fire in ground combat was limited to army regimental combat teams and Marine infantry regiments.[31]

After World War II, direct experience with the military has continued to fall. In 2015, only about 0.4 percent of the population served on active duty, and only some 6.5 percent of the population had *ever* served in the military. By 2015, 2.5 million Americans had served in one of the wars in Iraq or Afghanistan, but even of that large number only a fraction experienced ground combat.[32]

This detachment from battle has not always been the case. When Thucydides wrote his massive history of the Peloponnesian War he did not need to dwell on the intricacies of combat because his audience took them for granted. Even Julius Caesar only offered details in his writings to the extent that doing so amplified his own role. The actual experiences of war mattered only to the degree that they reflected glory on him. A variety of consequences follow from Americans' modern distance from battle, including and especially (for the purposes of this book) unfamiliarity with the kinds of combat in which its armed forces are engaged around the world.

To counter modern ignorance of combat, in 1976 British historian John Keegan published *The Face of Battle*. Keegan argued that traditional narrations of battle ignored the human experience of combat and preferred metaphor to realistic description. He critiqued narratives in which blocks of undifferentiated soldiers moved, charged, or, in one notorious example, dissolved "like a loosened cliff."[33] Keegan suggested a new approach, one that acknowledged the individual soldier and his mental, physiological, and moral capacity to withstand the stresses of combat. Furthermore, to account for how the experience of combat has changed over time in response to technology and the social processes of mobilization (that is, the selection and provision of soldiers to the army), he used three examples of Britons in combat at Agincourt (1415), Waterloo (1815), and the Somme (1916). Following a narrative to set the scene, he zoomed down to the soldier's eye level, often via paired combatant types such as archer versus knight, or infantry square versus artillery. In addition to representing an iconic moment in British history, each battle had generated a relative wealth of soldiers' accounts. Keegan's book leaned on those soldiers' accounts but also explored the "physics" of the battlefield, importing other forms of evidence to answer questions such as what happens when a running horse confronts a line of men or when piles of dead bodies form barriers. Keegan's model has inspired two generations of historians to attend to the soldiers—to explore and express the humanity of their experience and to connect that humanity to individual choices and collective outcomes.[34]

Historians now write much better battle narratives, in that they view combat not in a detached way as a game of pawns but with greater awareness of human suffering. Nonetheless, they still struggle with non-traditional battle. Studies of combat in Vietnam, for example, are now usually told through the lens Keegan urged, but they do not always confront how the battle experience itself was affected by asymmetry and cultural alienation. Many books acknowledge how soldiers—many of whom were farm kids who had never been to a large city, let alone a subtropical jungle—confronted the foreignness of Vietnam during the course of the war, or during an individual's tour of duty, but a firefight itself is often recounted clinically, as an issue of space, time, cover, firepower, and resources. Keegan's formula of using paired combatants (e.g., machine gun versus infantry at the Somme) was relatively straightforward and compelling precisely because both sides defined victory in roughly the same way. Their cultural expectations of battle were mutual and their weapons matched. Our case studies follow Keegan's model in seeking the human experience, and we also use pairings to explore that experience, but often the pairings instead highlight the asymmetry. Chapter 2, for example, will examine Native American fighters versus British heavy infantry, while Chapter 6 explores the technological contest between mine-clearing line charges (MICLICs) and improvised explosive devices (IEDs). Such pairings make for a narrative that is viscerally real, and we hope they will truly evoke intimacy and the searingly human experience of those moments.

In the battles explored here we also try to evoke the motivations, expectations, and experiences of the other side. It is no longer helpful, if it ever was, to write history—especially military history—from a one-sided perspective. The enemy's perspective must be considered. This is not something that Keegan even really attempted—he focused on his British combatants. In part this approach worked because the enemies, Frenchmen and Germans, were from the same cultural sphere. Keegan's deeper insight, however, was that what battle has in common across time is that it hinges on universal human reactions to violence, wounds, and fear. And above all, it hinges on the *interaction* of the two sides' will to combat. To truly discern that interaction, we must enter into the minds of both sides.

Having said that, we must acknowledge the limitations of available sources. Sources for the other side are weak at best, and further made suspect by the means of collection.[35] Native American voices from the colonial period, for example, nearly always survive via translation and transmission by European colonists and soldiers (there are other sources of evidence for Native American society in general, but not for any specific battle). Some of the Filipino accounts are from those who survived what became a grinding guerrilla war; some are from Filipinos who had come over to the American side during the war; some are accounts from the battle itself, and all are subject to the normal distortions of memory. All of these factors likely altered their view of what had happened in the conventional fight around Manila that began the conflict. The same problem applies to the Taliban fighters in Afghanistan. We occasionally get somewhat suspect glimpses of their attitudes, including one memorable claim that they thought the American soldiers looked like "Martians," made alien by their "elaborate equipment, their menacing body armour, and their impenetrable Ray-Bans." This perception had strategic implications. They saw the Americans as only "briefly emerg[ing] from the high walls behind which they barricaded themselves," and unlike their old Russian opponents, as one Taliban fighter put it, "the Americans were afraid to fight on the ground and their bombing was indiscriminate."[36] Some of this was surely hyperbole and myth-building, and may not have been widely shared, but it suggests how much better we need to be at conceptualizing the human experience of combat on both sides. Unfortunately, although interviews about the Taliban's more general motives and methods exist, Taliban accounts of the specific battle at Makuan are vanishingly rare.

Why, then, choose Monongahela, Manila, and Makuan from the vast array of intercultural battles within American history? Almost by definition, intercultural and asymmetrical wars often lack "iconic" battles, with a few exceptions like Little Bighorn or Iwo Jima. Even when Americans remember their irregular wars, they tend to focus on the largest engagements (for example, the fight at Ia Drang or Hue in Vietnam) or the most spectacular defeats. The three under scrutiny here serve a variety of purposes. Although Monongahela is not widely remembered now, to eighteenth-century American colonists, including George Washington, who fought in it, the battle was a major event, a turning point. Their British commanders expected harassing raids from small Indian war parties but never credited the Indians (intellectually, culturally, or militarily) with the capacity to demolish a regular European force. Afterward, the colonists chose to believe that had the Virginia provincial forces been better prepared, and had the British officers only listened to the colonials, then all would have been well. This belief would help define the American approach to manning and fighting for another 150 years.

The second case, the Battle of Manila in 1898, provides a case of an intercultural fight that at least began with relatively symmetrically armed and equipped forces. There were 14,000 American troops and 11,000 Filipino militiamen, and both sides were equipped with rapid-firing rifles and artillery. Here, as would happen again against Japan in World War II, technologically similar but culturally different foes generated a unique experience of combat. Ultimately, apparent American success on this battlefield was confounded by the Filipinos' reaction. They rejected the supposed meaning of battle, and their defeat led not to surrender but to a long and painful guerrilla war.

That political and military lesson about the false decisiveness of battle in intercultural wars was then lost in the crucible of the total wars of World War I and II. The lesson was painfully relearned in Vietnam, and then lost again in the aftermath. After 2001, when America once again found itself fighting culturally alien guerrilla forces in Iraq and Afghanistan, the relearning was slow and painful. Although not widely known, the engagement at Makuan, part of the larger Operation Dragon Strike in 2010, is one of the most well-studied small-unit actions of the war in Afghanistan, revealing the experiences of the combatants in visceral immediacy. Together, the three battles give a sense of the consistently unpredictable nature of intercultural war, and of the stresses of combat in it.

★ ★ ★

Heroism and atrocity, courage and stalemate walk hand in hand through these pages. Comprehending the full range of the human experience of battle is part of our duty as historians and as citizens. In a 2019 essay in the *New York Times Magazine*, Marine veteran Russell Worth Parker joined a long line of veteran authors who have struggled to explain their experiences of combat, in his case in Iraq in the early 2000s. He acknowledged the difficulties not only in explaining his experiences but also in getting his audiences, even close friends, to hear him. His essay pleads for a "common understanding" of war, something that he says "is both the thing we most need from each other as veterans and the thing that keeps some of us from effectively reconnecting with civilians, a critical factor as we become civilians ourselves."[37] This book cannot alone bridge that gap, but perhaps by glimpsing the other face of battle we can learn to better hear.

Map 2.1 Braddock's March and Beaujeu's Voyage. (Map by Matilde Grimaldi)

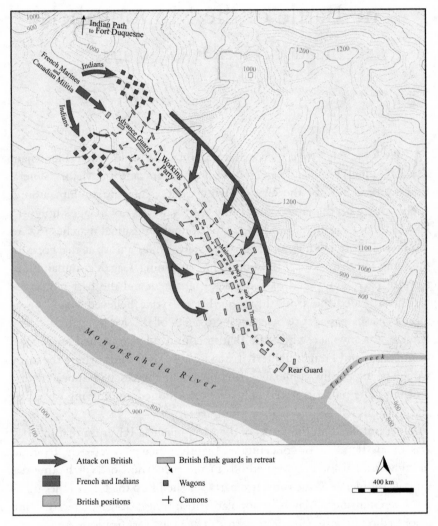

Map 2.2 The Battle of the Monongahela. (Map by Matilde Grimaldi)

2

The Battle of the Monongahela

Braddock's Defeat, July 9, 1755

March on until three o'clock. Those were the orders that Lieutenant Colonel Thomas Gage received when an aide of Major General Edward Braddock of the British Army came riding up to him around twelve-thirty on the afternoon of July 9, 1755. It was now Gage's honor to lead Braddock's army of nearly 1,500 personnel on its final marches toward the French Fort Duquesne, lying only twelve miles ahead, at the Forks of the Ohio in what is today Pittsburgh. That morning, Gage's command—an advance party composed of 300 crack grenadiers and the best regulars—had spearheaded the army through what everyone believed would be its most perilous passage: two separate crossings of the Monongahela River. If there was anyplace where the British commanders expected an ambush from Indian and French fighters, it was at those river fords, where the army would be especially vulnerable. But no enemy forces had appeared that morning. The redcoats noted only a few abandoned, smoldering campfires and weapons left behind with seeming haste.[1]

What unfolded on the banks of the Monongahela River on that July day was a majestic scene of concentrated British military power—the triumph of conventional forces and methods in the wilderness of North America. Full of confidence, Gage's advance party splashed into the ford to the strains of "The Grenadiers' March," a popular British tune that celebrated the elite troops who flung grenades as they stormed enemy fortifications. An eyewitness recalled how the troops appeared "in the greatest order, with bayonets fixed, Colors flying, and Drums and Fifes beating and playing." Twenty-three-year-old George Washington, acting as a volunteer aide to General Braddock, was also struck by the "beautiful spectacle" as he beheld it from his saddle. Having secured the north shore, Gage sent word to Braddock that he had executed his orders without any enemy opposition, as he covered the remainder of the army until it had all crossed.[2]

Braddock's army had managed that passage as it had every conceivable obstacle during the campaign, whether political, logistical, military, or geographical. Lieutenant Colonel Gage, of the 44th Regiment of Foot, had seen far worse in fifteen years of service to His Majesty in numerous campaigns in Europe and Scotland. Born in 1719 as the second son of an Irish viscount, Gage had been predestined for military life. He had witnessed the slaughter at the 1745 Battle of Fontenoy, where at least 15,000 British, French, Dutch, and German soldiers became casualties. The next year he fought in the climactic Battle of Culloden in the Scottish Highlands, where British forces led by King George II's son, the Duke of Cumberland, suppressed the Jacobite challenge to the Hanoverian dynasty. Gage counted himself as one of the "old Culloteners" in the ranks of the 44th Regiment, a unit that had also seen action during the Jacobite rising of 1745. During Braddock's Expedition, as it was called, Gage frequently led the advance party, which had maintained impeccable security during the rapid march over the mountains. Small French and Indian parties had shadowed the army, but not once had they seriously threatened British progress, and they melted away whenever regular troops turned out against them.[3]

With the river crossings accomplished, a short two hours' march was all that separated Gage and Braddock's army from their next encampment— and victory. If they reached it, the fate of their French adversaries at Fort Duquesne would be sealed. By the end of that two-hour march, the advance party that Gage commanded would have climbed from the banks of the Monongahela River and surmounted the high ridge looming before them. They would have then created a secure defensive perimeter, marking out the army's next encampment while the rest of the main body, with its artillery and wagons, filled the interior. As Braddock had projected in a letter dated June 21, his army would invest Fort Duquesne on July 10 and then break ground to start the siege. Incredibly, he was right on schedule. One British officer believed that operations would thenceforth become a familiar process and offer a textbook example of cutting off and besieging an enemy fortification: "[We] thought we had got over our greatest Difficulties, for we look'd upon our March through the woods to be such: We were sure we should be much above a Match for the *French*, if we got into the open Ground near the Forts, where we could use our Arms." Were the French foolish enough to remain at Fort Duquesne, a hellish iron rain would descend on them from the bores of the British 8-inch howitzers, 12-pounders, 6-pounders, and Coehorn mortars that composed their artillery train. Indeed, some officers expected to hear an explosion in the distance, already anticipating that the French would accept the inevitable and scuttle their fort. It was only a matter of time.[4]

Gage's advance party began its gradual ascent up the steep ridge with the army in its usual line of march: a well-defended convoy or column formation, fully following conventional protocols and bristling with dozens of flanking parties out in the woods that totaled one-third of Braddock's force. By the time that Gage's men were halfway up the ridge, the entire British column stretched for about one mile in length. Behind the advance party was the working party, directed by the Deputy Quarter Master General, Major Sir John St. Clair, and composed of about 200 Virginia provincials and the New York Independent Company of Captain Horatio Gates (the future American victor over the British at the Battle of Saratoga). St. Clair's party constructed the ten-foot-wide military road as they went, enabling the artillery, wagons, and pack horses of the main body directly behind them to proceed. Braddock, his aides, and his personal guards were posted at the head of the main body, consisting of at least 600 regulars. The bulk of Braddock's regulars were arrayed in two columns behind him, marching on each side of the artillery and wagon train, with plenty of flanking parties. At the tail of the column was the rear guard, to which Braddock had relegated two American companies from South Carolina and Virginia numbering 110 men in total. The commander of that Virginia company, Captain Adam Stephen, had seen action against the French and Indians in 1754 and judged the British regulars as too confident.[5]

"The Indians are upon us!" yelled the guides who were out scouting the way ahead with some Virginia light horsemen, a few hundred yards in front of Gage's advance party. The startled guides came streaming back on the vanguard, stunned by the unexpected report of massed Indian warriors coming down the forest trail to attack them. George Croghan, an Indian trader and guide, and Sub-Engineer Harry Gordon, who was with the guides marking out the road, had a "free sight of the Enemy as they approached." They noted several French officers dressed like Indians, wearing gorgets, and waving their hats at the Indians to move into the woods on the right and left.[6] Croghan and Gordon would be among the handful of British who actually laid eyes on enemy combatants during the ensuing battle. As

firing erupted at the head of the column, Braddock's soldiers began to hear
an unearthly, spine-chilling sound of Indian warriors raising their war cries.

Within the next hour, Native warriors would envelop the convoy and
collapse the entire British network of flanking parties, leaving only a slender
and immobilized column of redcoats in the woods. Within thirty minutes,
Gage's advance party would cease to exist as a coherent unit and fall back,
colliding with main body units moving forward, as the men fell into irredeemable chaos and panic. They were slaughtered en masse by enemy and
friendly fire. Two of every three soldiers who crossed the Monongahela
River on July 9, 1755, would be killed or wounded in the span of three
hours, including Braddock, who succumbed to his wounds four days later
(see Figure 2.1).

The experience of battle against skilled irregulars seared British veterans with a horror that eclipsed anything that they had experienced in
Europe. Private Duncan Cameron of the 44th Regiment, veteran of the
horrendous battles of Cartagena, Dettingen, Fontenoy, and Culloden,
believed that Monongahela "was the most shocking I was ever in." The encounter with irregular Indian and French opponents had been categorically

Figure 2.1 *The Wounding of General Braddock.* (By Robert Griffing, 2005,
courtesy of Paramount Press, Inc.)

different—from the terrifying war cries resounding in the woods to the Indian warriors' bewilderingly rapid movements along their flanks, their sniping of officers and artillerists, the horrific deaths by Indian war clubs and scalping knives, and the Indians' seemingly indiscriminate slaughter of civilians and soldiers fleeing back across the river.

Left behind on the battlefield, Private Cameron managed to escape and then struggled to rejoin the shattered army in its sixty-mile retreat to the rear division's encampment. Along the road, Cameron stumbled upon corpses, and heard deranged soldiers begging to be killed because their misery was so great. "Indeed the Horrors of a Battle are very great," Cameron mourned, "but this seem'd to be the most piercing Scene mine Eyes had ever seen."[7] Years later, Lieutenant Matthew Leslie would say that "the yell of the Indians is fresh on my ear, and the terrific sound will haunt me until the hour of my dissolution."[8]

By August 1755, the "melancholly Account of the Slaughter" of Braddock's army on the banks of the Monongahela River had spread throughout the British world. In Nova Scotia, Colonel John Winslow thought it the "Most Extraordinary thing that Ever [happened] in America and Unparalleled in History that Such a number of English regular Troops (than which there Certainly is none Better) Should be Defeated by a Handful of French & Indians, & Directly to run away." Lieutenant Governor Spencer Phips of Massachusetts believed the defeat "beyond what has ever befallen the English Arms in the Colonies since their first Settlement." Those who had witnessed the slaughter—and survived—were especially shocked. George Washington reflected to a friend upon returning to Mount Vernon following the battle: "I join very heartily with you in believing that when this story comes to be related in future Annals, it will meet with unbelief & indignation; for had I not been witness to the fact on that fatal Day, I should scarce have given credit to it even now."[9]

Many American colonists faulted British regulars for their complacency about French and Indian irregulars. A writer from Boston admonished, "This is, and always will be the Consequence of Old England Officers and Soldiers being sent to America; they have neither Skill nor Courage for this Method of Fighting, for the Indians will kill them as fast as Pigeons." Contemporaries—in the colonies and in Britain—were stunned by initial reports that a mere 300 French and Indians had defeated nearly 1,500 British troops bristling with firepower. Casting about for metaphors, contemporaries compared the action to the infamous destruction of

Quinctilius Varus's three Roman legions by Germanic tribesmen in the Teutoburger Forest in AD 9.[10]

The Campaign

By the middle of the eighteenth century, imperial rivalry in North America between Britain and France had centered on control of the strategic Ohio River (*la belle rivière*, as the French referred to it). New France had become the dominant colonial empire in North America, due to its continental network of alliances with Native Americans, military superiority over the English colonists, and access to interior waterways. Although New France had largely ceased to be economically profitable for the crown, its value in imperial strategy was containment of the expansive British colonies. The rugged Appalachian Mountains were also a formidable aid to the French and their Native allies. They hemmed in the more numerous British settlers—the largest number of which were in Virginia and Pennsylvania—who viewed the Ohio Valley as their gateway to western trade and settlement. Cascading actions and incidents drew the British and French crowns deeper into North American affairs, even as the ink had barely dried on the 1748 Peace of Aix-la-Chapelle, which had ended the War of Austrian Succession (1744–1748). During the war, British traders had pushed into the region, which threatened to draw French allies into the British orbit. A group of land speculators who formed the Ohio Company of Virginia obtained a royal grant in 1749 to more than 200,000 acres of Ohio land in what amounted to a self-fulfilling prophecy: the grant required the investors to expand trade, build outposts, and plant settlers in the Ohio Country. The French, in turn, envisioned a chain of substantial fortifications in the Ohio Valley to anchor their regional claims and to reinforce their network of Native alliances.[11]

Both France and Great Britain had blithely played a game of reckless escalation, gambling that each could achieve de facto control of the Ohio Valley without alienating its Indian owners or provoking a general war in America or in Europe. In 1753, the Marquis Duquesne—the governor general of New France—sent to the Ohio Valley 2,600 men led by the veteran officer Captain Paul Marin de La Malgue, who was to build the forts and garrison them. It was the largest European force ever seen west of the St. Lawrence Valley at that time. Duquesne had acknowledged in a 1752 letter the "extreme boldness" of his plan but believed that the French must "seize and establish ourselves on the Belle Rivière, which we are on the verge of losing if I do not make this hasty but indispensable effort." Natives in the region bristled at the display of French military power. However, the British had given them ample reason to acquiesce to the French presence. The Ohio Indians knew that French forts did not attract swarms of colonists, as British ones usually did. By the end of 1753, the French had established two forts to secure the Lake Erie portage from Presque Isle over to a tributary of *la belle rivière* known as *la rivière au boeuf*. George Washington, sent by the Virginia government in 1753 to demand the cessation of French fort building in the region, would name it French Creek. His odyssey from Williamsburg, Virginia, to Fort Le Boeuf in the middle of the winter revealed a young officer with superb powers of observation. Washington's map and journal of his journey provided the British with the best intelligence picture of French activities in the Ohio Country.[12]

For their part, the French received the young Washington with civility but quickly rebuffed Virginia's summons to depart. When the ice melted the following spring, the French completed their invasion of the upper Ohio Valley, much as Washington had predicted. In April 1754, another veteran French officer, Captain Claude-Pierre Pécaudy de Contrecoeur, led 600 troops with artillery southward and bloodlessly conquered the Forks of the Ohio—the strategic junction of the Allegheny, Monongahela, and Ohio Rivers. A few dozen Virginians had been there since February, hastily constructing a small stockade fortification known as Fort Prince George, or Trent's Fort. The sight of French cannons drawn up against their fort induced them to surrender. The French soon began the construction of Fort Duquesne, the centerpiece of their fortification chain. It was an imposing square fort with four artillery bastions, well engineered using the art and science of the great French master of siege warfare and fortification, Sébastien Le Prestre de Vauban.[13]

Contrecoeur's conquest of Trent's Fort was viewed by the British as an open act of war. News of its surrender reached Washington, now the lieutenant colonel of the Virginia Regiment, as he was leading the regiment's advance westward over the mountains. When his Ohio Iroquois allies warned that a menacing French party was approaching him, Washington participated in an ambush of the small French force as it was encamped in a ravine. The action became known as the Jumonville Affair, after the killing of Ensign Joseph Coulon de Villiers de Jumonville by one of Washington's Indian allies following the battle. That in turn led to a reprisal attack by the French, who considered Jumonville a diplomatic emissary and his killing an assassination. In July 1754, Virginia and South Carolina forces led by Washington capitulated to a larger French and Indian force at the Battle of Fort Necessity and were paroled back to Virginia. It was the point of no return in the escalation toward open war between Britain and France.[14]

When news of French offensives and Washington's surrender reached London in September 1754, the British government decided to intervene directly, sending professional soldiers to accomplish what the colonials seemingly could not. Fully accepting the risk of declared war with France, the British planned four preemptive expeditions aimed at key French fortifications located on contested territories in North America: Fort Beauséjour in Nova Scotia, Fort St. Frédéric in the Champlain Valley, Fort Niagara on Lake Ontario, and Fort Duquesne. King George II appointed General Braddock as commander in chief of all British forces in North America. British officials expected that Braddock would not only restrain French territorial encroachments but also curb the thirteen colonies' growing independence. As a career officer with an unblemished if unremarkable record, Braddock would personally lead the expedition to seize Fort Duquesne.[15]

The British ministry's operational planning, however, betrayed a woeful ignorance of the geography of North America and the capabilities of the British American colonies. The Duke of Cumberland, the Duke of Newcastle, and other leading ministers had defined the basic parameters of the expedition in September 1754, even before Braddock himself could be recalled from Gibraltar, where he had charge of one of Britain's most important possessions. When Braddock returned to England in November 1754, he learned the details of the "Expedition to Virginia," as it was called. Braddock's orders required him to land in Virginia and advance up the Potomac Valley before marching across the Appalachians. He did not have discretionary authority to land in Philadelphia, as later pundits claimed he should have done, for its better resources. Astonishingly, the British ministry expected Braddock—in a single campaigning season—to capture Fort Duquesne, advance up the Ohio River to Lake Erie and collapse the network of French forts there, construct boats, and then go across Lake Erie to attack Fort Niagara: a march of more than six hundred miles through mountainous country and hazardous waterways with no improved roads.[16]

Britain's ability to project such transoceanic power drew upon the growing amphibious capabilities of the eighteenth-century Royal Navy. Commodore Augustus Keppel and Captain Hugh Palliser transported Braddock and his expeditionary force from Ireland across the Atlantic in January 1755, and most of the ships had reached Virginia by late February. Once arrived, Braddock was taken aback by the challenges facing British forces in America during the war against the French—challenges that would recur during the War for American Independence twenty years later. War in America was different. Braddock's contentious dealings with stingy colonial assemblies and his inability to acquire adequate recruits, supplies, horses, and wagons from seemingly recalcitrant colonists were also notable. His reports hardened British officials' views of American colonists, whose seeming in-gratitude and republican legislatures threatened to unhinge the political constitution of the British Empire. The general also found that the colonists' western land-grabbing had alienated Indian nations and foreclosed on his considerable and earnest efforts to cultivate Indian allies—who he thought would "be very usefull to me in the Course of the Expedition."

In addition to the colonial legislatures' lack of cooperation, the logistical challenges of campaigning in North America stunned Braddock and his officers. There were few improved roads leading westward from Alexandria and virtually no infrastructure in the countryside, meaning no supply depots, magazines, or barracks. All of those would have to be assembled and constructed during the campaign. British officers railed against the min-istry "for ignorantly landing them in a Country destitute of the Means of conveying their Stores, Baggage, etc."[17]

The Forces

Braddock's Expedition was not the first time that British regulars had operated in North America. The British Army and the Royal Navy were no strangers to expeditionary warfare—or "conjunct expeditions," as eighteenth-century commentators referred to joint army-navy ventures. English regulars had been dispatched to Virginia to quell Bacon's Rebellion in 1676. During Queen Anne's War (1702–1713), an army of 7,000 regulars under General John Hill attempted to conquer Québec—an ef-fort that ended in nautical disaster and hundreds of redcoats drowned in the St. Lawrence River. In 1740, British regulars under the command of General James Oglethorpe had unsuccessfully besieged the Spanish Castillo de San Marcos at St. Augustine, Florida, while Royal Navy warships had supported an expedition of New Englanders who captured Fortress Louisbourg on Île Royale (modern Cape Breton Island) in 1745.[18]

What all those shared was being restricted to the navigable Atlantic coastline and being utterly dependent upon naval support. Braddock's Expedition was unprecedented in two respects: it was the first time that the British crown had appointed a commander in chief with such expansive powers over the thirteen colonies, and Braddock would be the very first commander in the history of English America to project a large conventional force with artillery hundreds of miles inland—in his case, across the Appalachian Mountains, over which not a single improved wagon road existed. Every previous attempt by English intercolonial armies to advance from Albany to Montréal using the Hudson River–Lake Champlain corridor—in 1690, 1692, 1709, 1711, and 1747—had either never even gotten off the ground or ended in abject failure from a lack of supply and disease.

The officer selected by the British government to lead that expedition has been one of the most maligned and mythologized generals in all of American history. Braddock was portrayed after his death as brash, arrogant, and inexperienced, and his stubborn adherence to conventional tactics supposedly led to his defeat. Subsequent historians have largely accepted that caricature, ignoring much archival and contemporary evidence that contradicts it. Braddock more than merited his selection as commander in chief of His Majesty's forces in North America, as his career had equipped him well for his mission, which was a literally groundbreaking achievement, bringing his army to its target in a march of astonishing speed. Twenty years later, a British newspaper still extolled the "incredibly rapid, nay unparalleled marches of Braddock."[19]

Born around 1694, Edward Braddock III came from a family distinguished by its generations of service to the monarchy. In 1710, he gained a commission in the Coldstream Guards—a unit of the elite foot guards that protected the monarch and his household—and his career was characterized by competent service and steady advancement. Although Braddock was never engaged in combat prior to coming to America, he participated in a campaign in the Low Countries in 1747. His connections to key members of the British government led to a colonelcy of the 14th Regiment of Foot in 1753. Shortly thereafter, and with sufficient faith in Braddock's abilities, the royal government entrusted him with command of Gibraltar—one of Britain's most important and heavily defended overseas possessions.[20]

As lieutenant governor and commander in chief of the garrison, Braddock acted in both a political and a military capacity, and he garnered praise all around for his conduct. His civil-military abilities, heightened by his service at Gibraltar, equipped him for a similar role in North America. Gibraltar's multi-ethnic environment and logistical weaknesses, requiring constant diplomatic negotiation, also prepared Braddock to deal with those same conditions in America. His command of a garrison boasting more than two hundred artillery pieces and elaborate fortifications imparted a deep understanding of siege warfare. It was likely for all those reasons that the Duke of Cumberland thought Braddock "the properest person to command the troops in North America."[21]

The British government's planning for the expedition was premised upon the ability of regular, professional soldiers to accomplish the task in North America. The eighteenth-century British Army had achieved a growing reputation as a disciplined and professional standing army, especially after the Duke of Marlborough's epic campaigns in Europe during the War of Spanish Succession (1702–1713). Reliant upon strict discipline among the enlisted men and the absolute authority of officers drawn from the gentry or aristocracy, the British Army mirrored the country's social structure. British redcoats, armed with a .75 caliber Long Land Pattern flintlock musket (known as the Brown Bess), were indeed a formidable opponent on a linear battlefield. The musket's effective range of about a hundred yards necessitated a close-quarters engagement against a clearly visible enemy line. With plumes of white smoke produced by muskets quickly obscuring a battlefield, the madder-red regimental coats with distinctive facings and lace patterns aided officers in effective command and control. Using the platoon system of firing, a British infantry battalion could deliver an alternating, controlled, and continuous volume of firepower, then close upon an enemy unit with the shock force of the bayonet. Cumberland's regulars had demonstrated that lethal effectiveness at the 1746 Battle of Culloden, inflicting at least 1,500 casualties upon their 6,000 Jacobite opponents.[22]

But the regulars that Cumberland selected for Braddock's Expedition—the 44th and 48th Regiments of Foot—were not the fittest for service in North America, notwithstanding his assumption that professional troops would readily accomplish a conventional mission of besieging French fortifications. As historian John Houlding has demonstrated, the British Army's hard-earned wartime proficiency and its battle readiness were eroded by what he called the "friction of peace." In peacetime, the army reverted to a constabulary role with a trio of duties—garrisoning posts in the British Isles and elsewhere, suppressing rebellions and riots, and controlling smugglers. The readiness and quality of regiments also varied greatly depending on whether they were maintained on the English or Irish establishment (with different administration and funding via the English and Irish parliaments). Both the 44th and 48th Regiments were understrength units drawn from garrison duty in the Irish establishment, each numbering 374 officers and men and commanded, respectively, by Colonel Sir Peter Halkett and Colonel Thomas Dunbar. Units in Ireland struggled to maintain even basic proficiencies in drill. With their small garrisons scattered across the countryside, few soldiers ever trained in formations larger than a regiment. Firearms training emphasized the manual of arms and did not include firing at marks or routinely practicing with live ammunition. Bringing the two regiments up to full strength (around 1,000 each) required drafts of questionable quality from other regiments. When the fleet departed Cork, Ireland, in January 1755, the total embarkation number of the two regiments was 1,332 officers and men. With additional recruiting done in the American colonies, Braddock's regulars were conglomerates at best. Their red coats and regularity belied their poor unit cohesion and identity.[23]

These conventional troops would prove utterly unprepared for the irregular warfare they would face. In eighteenth-century Europe, irregular or unconventional warfare was often known as small war (or *la petite guerre*) to distinguish it from the large-scale battles, campaigns, and sieges between armies and nations (*la grande guerre*). Irregular warfare encompassed a range of conflicts, including peasant and political rebellions, and a range for forces, from individual rebels to militia bands and even light troops (often known as partisans) that functioned as auxiliaries to a regular army. Indeed, the 1779 *Universal Military Dictionary* by Captain George Smith, inspector of the Royal Military Academy at Woolwich, defined *la petite guerre* as "carried on by a light party, commanded by an expert partisan, and which should be from 1000 to 2000 men, separated from the army." Some have tried to claim that the British Army came to America with experience against irregulars in Scotland and on the continent of Europe in the wars of the 1740s and was therefore prepared for the American warfare they encountered. The evidence, however, suggests otherwise.[24]

Braddock's 44th and 48th Regiments had both campaigned in Scotland's Highlands and on Flanders's plains during the 1745 Jacobite uprising and the War of Austrian Succession. The Jacobites did not consider themselves to be irregulars, however, as they were organized into regiments and constituted a royal army of the sovereign whom they believed to be the legitimate king. They engaged Hanoverian armies with muskets in conventional line-of-battle formations on open fields at Prestonpans and Culloden. As terrifying as Highlander opponents may have been, they cannot be equated to Indian war parties, whose tactics, organization, methods, and mobility in a mountainous environment were completely foreign to Braddock's regulars. The 48th Regiment's subsequent service in Flanders in 1747 was purely conventional, as the unit was involved in urban warfare at the Battle of Lauffeld. In short, before 1755, the British Army had no formalized training in irregular warfare or common procedures for how to fight irregulars in the woods. It had yet to develop any theory or practice of *la petite guerre*, and it lagged far behind the French army's development of light infantry and methods of combatting irregulars.[25]

There was also no basic continuity in the officer corps of either regiment between the 1740s and 1755. Turnover and attrition diminished the institutional memory of previous wars and the experience gained thereby. The testimony of numerous British officers makes this clear. They perceived American warfare and its operational environment as different from anything they had experienced in Europe. John Campbell, 4th Earl of Loudoun, thought the logistical challenges facing an army quartermaster "more than in any Service I ever was in." The officer in Braddock's army who was most experienced with mountain warfare and irregulars was Sir John St. Clair, who had fought with the Austrian field marshal Count von Browne in the Appenines and Alps, and had even commanded parties of Croatian and Hussar irregulars in 1747. Yet St. Clair maintained that "the War in North America differs widely from that in Europe."[26]

The British rank and file most likely had pre-formed assumptions of Native American "savagery." Once in America, they imbibed certain ideas about warfare from their colonial brethren, who seemed eager to tell stories "in regard to their [Indians'] scalping and Mawhawking," including that they would receive no quarter if captured and would suffer horrendous torture. Some British officers attributed the regulars' panic during the battle to the "frequent Conversations of the Provincial Troops and Country People was that if they engaged the Indians in their European manner of fighting they would be Beat."[27]

The presence of provincial units from Virginia, Maryland, and North Carolina not only created friction with the regulars but also raised larger issues about the status of British Americans within the empire. Indeed, the ministry's decision to send Braddock's regulars from Ireland reflected a fundamental distrust of the colonists' military abilities. In 1754, there had been considerable debate within the British ministry over whether to mobilize patriotic colonists into their own royal regiment, as had been done in the Cartagena Expedition in 1741. George Washington's older brother had once held a royal officer's commission as a captain in the 43rd, or American Regiment, in that expedition. By the 1750s, that same route to personal and military advancement was completely closed to George Washington, whose provincial commission from Virginia's governor was deemed inferior to a royal one. British imperial authorities' resolve to commit British Army regulars to America reflected disdain for the Americans' military capabilities. But it also reflected their wariness over the growing independence of the thirteen colonies and a desire to reform their political constitutions.[28]

The advent of open conflict with New France had further revealed significant weaknesses in Virginia's and Maryland's military preparedness. The political strife between the governors and assemblies over the military funding and supply—and the disunity it produced in joint colonial ventures—all seemed to highlight the colonists' military incompetence vis-à-vis the French. Unlike their more veteran New England counterparts—which had fought more frequently against Native and French opponents—the southern colonies' militias were ill-trained and inexperienced. George Washington characterized Virginia as "a Country young in War. Until the breaking out of these Disturbances [it] has Lived in the most profound, and Tranquil Peace; never studying War or Warfare." Militia were by definition called forth for short terms of defensive service against invasions or insurrections, and some Virginians were wary of enlisting in a war that they perceived as advancing the narrow interests of Ohio Company investors.[29]

In 1754, the Virginia government had organized a provincial unit, the Virginia Regiment, to sustain expeditions and long-term conflict against the French. Soldiers of that regiment were defined as provincials, not militia, and more akin to colonial regulars who enlisted for longer periods with promises of land bounties for their service. Virginia provincials had fought under the command of Colonel Washington at Fort Necessity, sharing in that humiliating disaster, which had left the Ohio Valley firmly in French hands. The British government's decision to send regulars to America also came with a price for provincial officers, whose commissions derived from colonial governors. By rule, a royal officer's commission would supersede the authority of any provincial officer; even a colonial general or a field-grade officer such as Washington "shall have no Rank" with their regular counterparts. To avoid a "great Feud" between royal and provincial officers, Governor Dinwiddie in late 1754 broke the Virginia Regiment into in-dependent companies (commanded by captains, who would always be in a subordinate position to British officers). Washington lost his regimental command and resigned his colonelcy, brooding over the discriminatory policies that had rendered him and his men second-class subjects. Still, Washington hoped for preferment as a royal officer, and it was with that expectation that he accepted Braddock's invitation to serve as a gentleman volunteer in his headquarters—an invitation that recognized Washington's singular knowledge of the Ohio Country as well as his ambition.[30]

By the spring of 1755, the colonies had supplied nearly 900 troops to Braddock's Expedition. None of those soldiers were militia—they were pro-vincial companies specifically raised by Virginia, Maryland, and North Carolina for long-term service on the frontiers. While very few of them had any ex-pertise with Indian warfare, Virginia had a number of veteran soldiers of fron-tier fighting. The independent companies of the broken Virginia Regiment still retained many of the same officers and men who had fought during the 1754 campaign at Fort Necessity, including captains Adam Stephen and William Polson. Additional forces were drawn from the British Army's own independent companies stationed in North America. In 1754, the British government had ordered three independent companies—weak garrison troops stationed in the colonies of New York and South Carolina—to bolster Virginia's defenses (the South Carolina Independents, for example, had also fought with Washington at Fort Necessity). Those unregimented companies containing around 100 redcoats were technically regulars, part of the British establishment, led by British officers bearing royal commissions, and filled with elderly colonial recruits. Regular British officers viewed the American colonists as less than British, and they disdained the Independents and espe-cially the irregular provincials, whom one British officer described as "languid, spiritless, and unsoldierlike." While the more experienced Virginia companies might have been employed as scouts or rangers, they were instead relegated to manual labor and road work for the duration of the campaign. In all of these ways, Braddock's Expedition helped to reveal an emerging American martial identity—one that emphasized the perception and nature of colonials' military service and the distinct contributions they could make fighting against their very formidable opponents.[31]

By the 1750s, French Canadian marines and militia—particularly their officers—outclassed their British foes both militarily and in their ability to move forces on the continent. North American warfare was qualitatively different from irregular warfare or *la petite guerre* seen in eighteenth-century Europe. It was a kind of warfare so entrenched in Native American strategy, tactics, and rituals that Canadians knew it as *la guerre sauvage*, while British contemporaries variously called it the "Indian manner," "the Indian mode of warfare," or the "art of bush fighting." *La guerre sauvage* reflected a larger Native strategy aimed at an enemy's society, economy, and morale. It featured devastating ambushes of enemy forces and terrifying hit-and-run attacks on vulnerable British colonists along their settlement frontiers and towns: the storming of Schenectady, New York, in 1690 and the destruction of Deerfield, Massachusetts, in 1704 are notable examples. With great economy of force—raiding parties ranged from only a few dozen to a few hundred—the French and their extensive network of Indian allies could depopulate entire frontiers. The tactics of *la guerre sauvage* included Native rituals of scalping, torture of prisoners, and mutilation of enemy dead to sow terror and dread. Settlers' families were killed before their eyes, their homes, barns, and crops torched, and livestock shot in the fields and left to rot. Typically, Native warriors took more settlers captive than they killed, fulfilling Native ritual practices of adoption to replace deceased members of a community (some captives were also held until redeemed by the French or British in return for payment). The flight of thousands of civilians from the frontiers to the seaboard often created refugee crises for the English, and the scorched-earth landscape left on the frontier made it all the more difficult for any advancing English army to find sustenance.[32]

By the eighteenth century, military strategy and practice in New France had come to depend heavily upon *la guerre sauvage* and the coalition warfare that it truly represented. Indeed, when French army regulars arrived in Canada in 1755 and 1756, their officers found that Indians were "so necessary to the war effort that they rivaled French officers as *the* defenders of France," as historian Julia Osman has written.[33] For the Canadians who had learned the art of Native American warfare, it was an education and a reliance born of necessity. Since the early 1600s, the small size of the French population in North America had initially rendered them as vulnerable to Indian dangers in addition to Dutch and English threats. They had learned *la guerre sauvage* in part by being victims of it. Over the course of the seventeenth century, chronic warfare with the Five Nations (also known as the Haudenosaunee or Iroquois Confederacy) had brought the colony to the brink of disaster. Alliances with other Native nations located in Canada and the Great Lakes region were the means of French survival, as was the Great Peace of 1701 that brought the long century of war with the Five Nations to an end. Thereafter, the Haudenosaunee maintained a policy of neutrality vis-à-vis the French and British, one that enhanced their strategic importance, power, and numbers (the Five Nations became the Six Nations in the 1720s when the Tuscaroras rejoined their Haudenosaunee brethren).[34]

But the British threat remained. By the 1750s, New France's population had grown to over 50,000 souls stretched across the continent from the Gulf of St. Lawrence to the Gulf of Mexico, with most concentrated in Canada, Acadia, and Louisiana. The French, therefore, necessarily relied on Native American allies to contain the much larger British colonial population of around 1.5 million. Over time, the French and many Native nations developed alliances based upon mutual dependence and structured by Native diplomatic protocols. The Indians called the French governor "Onontio," or "great mountain," a reference to the area of Montréal, where they frequently met for conferences. But that title also connoted the role of a benevolent and generous Indian father, a role that they expected the governor and his representatives to play. Bonds of Indian alliance with the French were manifold: personal ties to Canadian officials and traders, a shared if syncretic Catholic faith, and prior service against mutual English enemies all explain their motivation. As one Kahnawake warrior explained, "The French & we are one Blood & where they are to dye we must dye also. We are linked together in each others Arms & where the French go we must go also."[35]

The strategy of *la guerre sauvage* also enabled the Indians and the French to achieve mutually compatible objectives—what historian Peter MacLeod has termed "parallel warfare." While the French sought military conquest of English forts or settlements, Native peoples fought for their own objectives in war, even as they fulfilled an obligation of their alliance with the French. Warriors who came to the Ohio Valley in 1755, for example, sought tangible symbols of military victory such as enemy scalps, war matériel that enriched their communities, and captives who would be adopted in the place of deceased kin. Often outnumbered in their joint expeditions with Indian allies, French officers were well aware that success entailed a constant process of negotiation with leading Indian war captains. They had to be diplomats as well as commanders, often bending to Native determinations about the objective, the route, and the plan of the attack. Natives expected quick action and would brook no prolonged campaign or costly attacks that would result in high casualties. And they always held the trump card—they could go home at any time.[36]

Captain Daniel-Marie Hyacinthe Liénard de Beaujeu personified how the French Canadians gained such deep experience in diplomacy and military operations with Native allies. Beaujeu is one of the most remarkable yet underappreciated figures in early American military history. Not a single British colonial, let alone a regular officer, could match his level of experience in war and diplomacy. Unlike the British imperial system, which devalued its colonists' military worth, the French crown commissioned Canadians as royal officers in the *troupes de la marine*, or *troupes du Canada*. They were organized into independent marine companies (*compagnies franches de la marine*) and functioned as the regular troops garrisoning various forts across New France. The marine companies often functioned as cadres for the more numerous Canadian militia drawn from the *habitants*, whose quality was uneven. While the status of "being Americans" deprived many ambitious colonials, including George Washington, of gaining commissions in the regular British Army, the French Canadian elite served for the honor of their king, advanced their personal and familial prestige, and reaped economic profit through military service. Those martial ambitions often culminated in the king's bestowal of the Croix de Saint-Louis, and knighthood in the military order to which Canadian officers zealously aspired.[37]

Born in 1711 in Montréal, Beaujeu entered the ranks at a young age, serving first as a cadet in the *troupes de la marine* before gaining his ensign's commission. With a force composed of Canadian marines and militia, Nipissings, Canadian Iroquois, and Abenakis, Beaujeu participated in the devastating raid against the Anglo-Dutch frontier settlement of Saratoga, New York, in 1745, led by Lieutenant Paul Marin de La Malgue—the same officer who would lead the French foray into the Ohio Valley in 1753. The French and Indian victors not only destroyed a wealthy frontier community and its resources but also took captive fifty Anglo-Dutch settlers and sixty African slaves (some of whom were adopted by Indians, while others became slaves in Montréal households). The destruction of Saratoga had been so spectacular that it virtually paralyzed the New York colonial government and put the colony on the defensive for the remainder of the war. The following year, Beaujeu demonstrated his instincts as a combat leader. Acting as the brigade major, he led from the front, personally killing a British sentry. The attack faltered when the French commander, Nicolas-Antoine Coulon de Villiers, was seriously wounded (Nicolas-Antoine was the elder brother of Joseph Coulon de Villiers de Jumonville, who was killed during Washington's ambush in 1754). But Beaujeu rallied the French and went "aux coups de fusils que nous entendions"—toward the sound of the musketry. Promoted to captain in 1748, he served as the commandant of Fort Niagara, on the shores of Lake Ontario, from 1749 to 1751. The fort's location in Seneca Haudenosaunee territory and its function as a fur trading destination for western nations only enhanced Beaujeu's ability to conduct diplomacy with Indian allies.[38]

Beaujeu was hardly exceptional among the concentration of veteran French Canadian officers posted in the Ohio Valley in 1754 and 1755. A list of officers and cadets present at Monongahela enables a full reconstruction of French leadership in 1755 and the broad experience in irregular warfare that they brought to their eventual confrontation with Braddock's army. Officers such as Jean-Baptiste Philippe Testard de Montigny and François-Marie Le Marchand de Lignery were already veterans of la guerre sauvage, having recently fought against the British in Acadia or raided the frontiers of New York and New England. Most all of them had been stationed at various forts and posts across New France that were mere islands amid Indian worlds. That in turn required a thorough grounding in a sort of realpolitik defined by Indian power and independence. Many officers learned Native diplomatic and military rituals and particular Native languages as they became attached to particular communities through personal or economic ties. They had become, in short, masters of coalition warfare in America.[39]

By midsummer of 1755, due to effective French diplomacy, between 600 and 700 Indian warriors had assembled at Fort Duquesne, drawn from twenty different nations or communities, all ready to fight in alliance with their French father Onontio. Ohio Indians, such as Delawares, Shawnees, and Senecas represented as much as one-quarter of the entire force; these had suffered the most from British colonial expansion and were motivated to strike back in defense of their lands. Warriors from the St. Lawrence Valley composed about one-third of the Native coalition—Canadian Iroquois from Kahnawake and Kanesetake, Abenakis from Odanak and Wôlinak, and Hurons from Lorette. They were the most resolute of all French allies, as they lived intermixed with French colonists in the St. Lawrence Valley. One example was a young Kahnawake Mohawk warrior named Atiatoharongwen, who had been taken as a captive from Saratoga in the 1745 raid in which Beaujeu had participated. The offspring of an African slave and an Abenaki woman, Atiatoharongwen was adopted into the Kahnawake Mohawk community near Montreal. Around half of the warriors came from the *pays d'en haut*, or Great Lakes country—Anishinaabeg (Odawas, Ojibwas, and Potawatomis), Mississaugas, and Wyandots, as well as Sac, Fox, and Osage Indians from the Mississippi Valley. The British remained oblivious to fact that these historical French and Indian alliances could field such a large coalition—in fact, the largest Native coalition ever assembled at that time.[40]

Logistics

Major William Sparke, the brigade major of the 48th Regiment, marveled at the strange environment that he encountered in 1755 when he landed in America. "We began our March," he recalled in a letter after the expedition, "but surely such a one was never undertaken before. . . . I apprehend [it] will be look'd upon as Romantick by those who did not see, and therefore cannot comprehend the difficulties of that March." Sparke's appreciation of the unprecedented nature of Braddock's march is all the more remarkable given his previous experience campaigning in the Highlands of Scotland and at the Battle of Culloden. For many British soldiers, the American wilderness seemed an utterly foreign landscape. Lieutenant Charles Lee of the 44th Regiment, who hailed from a prominent gentry family in Cheshire, England, was awed by the "magnificence and greatness through the immense extent (which we have seen of this Continent) not equal'd in any part of Europe." He was also struck by the "darkness and thickness of the woods." Another British officer wrote that "the very Face of the Country is enough to strike a Damp in the most resolute Mind," as if a strange pall hung over it. A sense of isolation and distance increased once the army began to venture deeper into the vast wilderness, closer to possible encounters with enemy forces.[41]

Even before they left, the army's encampment in Alexandria in March and early April 1755 had immediately revealed the political and logistical trials of an American campaign. At a congress with five royal governors at merchant John Carlyle's stately Georgian house, Braddock coordinated the four campaigns moving forward against French targets. He was bitterly disappointed, however, when the governors informed him that intransigent colonial assemblies would balk at contributing any money to a "common fund" under Braddock's control. Individual colonial governments promised Braddock recruits, supplies, wagons, horses, and quarters—then could not deliver enough of them. Braddock demonstrated an uncommon regard for his soldiers in his efforts, and in how he adapted the uniforms and regulations for American conditions before leaving Alexandria. He was far from being a devotee to "Hyde Park discipline"—a reference to the strict regulations and punishments imposed when the Foot Guards drilled in London's Hyde Park. Braddock increased the amount of their daily rations, substituted cooler osnaburg linen breeches and waistcoats for the red woolen ones, and lightened their load by dispensing with heavy cartridge box straps, belts, and ornamental short swords.[42]

The lack of sufficient wagons and horses forced Braddock to divide the army's westward march across both Virginia and Maryland along roads that were barely improved. Colonel Halkett's regiment and the artillery train proceeded northwest from Alexandria, over the Blue Ridge Mountains, toward the small frontier town of Winchester. To access horses and wagons, Colonel Dunbar's 48th Regiment had to advance through Maryland and then cross the Potomac River back into Virginia, marching southward toward Winchester. North of town, both columns took the same road leading northwest to Fort Cumberland (in western Maryland)—one that Sir John St. Clair called the "worst Road I ever travelled," marveling that it literally went "in the Channels of the Rivers" multiple times. During his journey through Maryland, Braddock received an urgent report from St. Clair: unless more horses and wagons could be acquired, "our expedition must be at a stop."[43]

Benjamin Franklin, who was visiting Braddock's headquarters in his capacity as the deputy postmaster general in America, lamented that the British had not landed in Pennsylvania, where "almost every Farmer had his Waggon." Upon hearing Franklin's hint, Braddock immediately empowered Franklin and entrusted him with £800 to contract for a corps of 150 wagons, 1,500 horses, and teamsters. One of the teamsters who joined Braddock's Expedition was a young Virginian named Daniel Morgan, who later became a Revolutionary War general. A few weeks later, the industrious Franklin not only delivered the goods (including baskets of delicacies for the officers) but virtually rescued the entire campaign. By the end of May 1755, the British regulars and provincial American troops were all staged at Fort Cumberland for the most difficult part of their passage.[44]

It was a testament to Braddock's determination that he overcame so many political and logistical roadblocks and nearly accomplished his mission. His march across the Appalachian Mountains was a tremendous logistical and engineering feat. Braddock's engineers carved a ten-foot-wide military road out of the wilderness, capable of transporting heavy artillery and wagons through some of the most rugged and forbidding terrain. The army's initial progress upon leaving Fort Cumberland was grinding. On any given day, St. Clair's working party (always composed of American provincials) would venture ahead to clear the road—an ordeal of cutting old-growth timber, hacking through thickets of dense mountain laurel, digging the roadbed, blasting enormous boulders, and bridging swampy areas. A small detachment of thirty-five Royal Navy sailors, led by Lieutenant Charles Spendelowe of HMS *Centurion*, also accompanied the expedition, charged with constructing any boats needed and assisting the movement of artillery up and down steep grades using block and tackle. The ascent of Big Savage Mountain on June 14–15, 1755—a 9 percent grade over a distance of two miles—brought the army and animals to the breaking point. And the British still had nearly a hundred miles of road to build, five more perilous ridges to cross, and three major river crossings.[45]

Movements of French forces from Canada to Fort Duquesne, meanwhile, were equally treacherous and labor-intensive, despite the troops' ability to use interior waterways. In the spring of 1755, the Marquis Duquesne sent convoys of reinforcements and supplies to Fort Duquesne and encouraged support from Native allies. On April 23, 1755, Captain Beaujeu departed Montréal with a large convoy consisting of forty fully laden riverboats known as *bateaux*. Other, smaller convoys followed in Beaujeu's wake in May 1755. The French and their Native allies had to navigate the treacherous rapids and currents of the upper St. Lawrence River. The journey on Lake Ontario, from Fort Frontenac over to Fort Niagara, was also fraught with risk due to frequent storms and squalls. French crews then had to portage *bateaux*, canoes, and heavy cargoes around Niagara Falls—an exhausting process compounded by a lack of horses and carts. After another passage along the south shore of Lake Erie, Beaujeu's convoy finally arrived at Fort Presque Isle on June 8.[46]

It had taken seven weeks for Beaujeu's convoy to move from Montréal to Fort Presque Isle, covering a distance of slightly over five hundred miles. Yet it would take an additional four weeks to cover less than two hundred miles from Fort Le Boeuf down to Fort Duquesne. French movements virtually ground to a halt at the Presque Isle portage. The sixteen-mile portage road over to Fort Le Boeuf went through muddy and swampy terrain that drained the men and horses of strength. Upon reaching Fort Le Boeuf, the French relied upon canoes and pirogues (dugouts) to transport men and goods down the shallow and rocky streambed. The water level on *la rivière au boeuf* was becoming perilously low; by summer's end, the waterway would be virtually dry and closed to navigation. When the French reached Venango, or Camp Machault, at the river's junction with the Allegheny River, the latter's fast-moving current greatly eased the rest of the journey. Beaujeu and his convoys arrived only a few days before Braddock's army crossed the Monongahela River.[47]

The logistical odysseys of the hundreds of Indian combatants were equally astounding. Unencumbered by wagons, horses, or huge cargoes, Native warriors enjoyed greater strategic mobility than either of their European counterparts. Their lightweight and durable canoes enabled them to ply the waters and portages of North America with comparative ease. In the seventeenth and eighteenth centuries, Native nations carried on wars across enormous distances—such as the incessant battling between the Haudenosaunee and southern Indians such as the Cherokees and Catawbas, separated by eight hundred miles. In the summer of 1755, Ojibwas journeyed nearly a thousand miles to reach Fort Duquesne. Warriors sustained themselves by hunting or by obtaining provisions from allied communities through which they passed—and expected their French father to supply their needs upon reaching Fort Duquesne. The convergence of French convoys and hundreds of Indian allies there in early July 1755 strained French supplies to the breaking point. The French knew that concentration of force could only be maintained for a narrow window of time—but it proved to be enough.[48]

Military Intelligence

In 1765, a decade after Braddock's defeat, a French officer, the Chevalier de Johnstone, reflected on the North American ways of war that he had experienced in the 1750s (though born in Scotland, Johnstone served under the French general the Marquis de Montcalm). His draft narrative, *A Dialogue in Hades*, featured an imaginative conversation between the ghosts of Montcalm and James Wolfe—the rival French and British commanders who had been mortally wounded at the Battle of the Plains of Abraham at Québec in 1759. Montcalm's ghost emphasized that in the woodlands of America, "there cannot be a greater advantage for a General than the entire knowledge of the country—the seat of war: without this, he must always grope in the dark—be foiled in his operations—rest often inactive, uncertain in his projects; and be only inactive and on the defensive." Braddock's expedition, too, had featured two forces groping in the dark—both uncertain of the other's location and forced to rely upon uncertain and limited military intelligence in a state of general geographic ignorance.[49]

Braddock's best intelligence of his target was a detailed scale map of Fort Duquesne drawn and smuggled out by Robert Stobo, a Virginia officer who had been held there as a hostage as part of the surrender terms following Washington's defeat at Fort Necessity the previous year. It confirmed that Braddock would indeed require siege artillery to capture this Vaubanian outpost in the wilderness. Braddock also fully realized—in his own words—the danger of "Surprize from the Indian Parties, which is always very much to be feared, notwithstanding all the Precautions that can be taken." That is perhaps a far more reliable assessment of Braddock's mindset than Benjamin Franklin's pithy comment written thirty years later, that Braddock scoffed at the threat of irregulars, supposedly insisting that "Savages may indeed be a formidable Enemy to your raw American Militia; but, upon the King's regular and disciplin'd Troops, Sir, it is impossible they should make any Impression." In fact, Braddock recognized the need for Native American support, and he made considerable effort to reach out to potential allies. The vast majority of contemporary evidence from 1755 shows that Braddock did not disdain or alienate potential Indian allies, as many have charged. His own speeches—some of which were drafted by Indian agent William Johnson—declared his intent to restore the Indians' lands to them by ejecting the French from the Ohio Country. Despite Braddock's earnest efforts, he had entered a geopolitical environment shaped by American colonists who had either outright dispossessed or alienated Native nations along their frontiers.[50]

Only a handful of Ohio Iroquois allies, numbering eight warriors in all, joined the British Army for the duration of the campaign (sixteen more were en route to the army by early July). Discord had beset Braddock's relations with his few scouts, although he was no different from other British generals of that era who experienced friction with Indian allies. Sometime later, the Haudenosaunee leader Scaroyady (Monacatootha) allegedly stated that Braddock "looked upon us as dogs, and would never hear any thing what was said to him." Braddock certainly doubted their efficacy. On two occasions, he requested that his Ohio Iroquois allies scout ahead. They produced no actionable intelligence of the actual numbers or movements of French and Indian forces. Even a scouting party that Braddock dispatched in early July, just days before the battle, did not return any accurate information of enemy activity. Moreover, their reconnaissance of Fort Duquesne managed to miss the presence of hundreds of Native warriors massing in the vicinity. Significantly, not a single French deserter or prisoner was taken by Braddock's army during the entire expedition, depriving the British of vital human intelligence.[51]

The most actionable information that Braddock received came from the New York colony, where British officers at Fort Oswego on Lake Ontario had noted the passage of French convoys in May 1755. They had also ascertained from a French trader that there was only a small number of troops at Fort Duquesne, as reinforcements were stalled at the Presque Isle portage and along *la rivière au boeuf*, which the French used to access the Allegheny River. A drought that year had significantly lowered levels on the region's waterways, slowing the French advance to a crawl but enabling Braddock's army to cross larger rivers with ease. George Washington, who had traveled along French Creek in 1753, believed that French reinforcements would be delayed "during the continuation of the Drought which we were then experiencing." When consulted by Braddock, Washington recommended pushing forward with a "small but chosen Band"—a faster, lighter, and less encumbered force that could win the race to Fort Duquesne against those French reinforcements.[52]

Washington's recommendation and Braddock's decision to split the army were militarily sound. Such a *coup de main* was perfectly in keeping with what British officers understood about expeditionary warfare in the eighteenth century: "the very name of an expedition implies risk, hazard, precarious warfare, and a critical operation," observed George Smith, in his 1779 dictionary.[53] For his own *coup de main* against Fort Duquesne, Braddock would trade logistical security for time. On June 18, 1755, he split the army, leaving Colonel Thomas Dunbar of the 48th Regiment in charge of the 2nd Division. Dunbar would bring up that rear column and also coordinate the movement of supplies coming in from Pennsylvania via Burd's Road, which was under construction.

Braddock's march was not burdened with heavy baggage and civilian contingents that "would have serv'd an Army of 20,000 in Flanders," as one officer scurrilously reported afterward.[54] His artillery train was actually exceedingly light: two 6-pounders, four 12-pounders, four 8-inch howitzers, and three portable Coehorn mortars. These were more than enough to accomplish the destruction of Fort Duquesne (by contrast, in 1777, Major General John Burgoyne's army was burdened in its advance through the Champlain and Hudson Valleys with nearly forty guns of far heavier caliber and weight).[55] Braddock's novel use of pack horses to transport supplies also speeded the advance and lessened his dependence upon wagons. In fact, Braddock achieved one of the most rapid marches in early American warfare and was set to invest Fort Duquesne, as he had predicted, on July 10. Braddock had achieved the very thing that his French adversaries believed impossible: marching a large army with siege artillery across the Appalachian Mountains.[56]

The French commandant at Fort Duquesne, Captain Contrecoeur, praised Braddock for the vigilance and security of his march. In a letter to Pierre de Rigaud, Marquis de Vaudreuil (the governor general of New France), he admitted that "these troops [Braddock's] maintained themselves so well on their guard, always marching in order of battle, that all the efforts the detachments made against them became useless." In May and June 1755, Contrecoeur had ordered dozens of joint French-Indian scouting parties—amounting to nearly 600 men—to attack or harass the British column. The French knew quite early when the British had departed Fort Cumberland and had reasonable estimates of their numbers and artillery.[57]

The French also had far better human intelligence, in the form of a handful of British deserters—including one of Braddock's Indian scouts, a Delaware or Tuscarora warrior named Skowonidous (known to the British as "Jerry"), who deserted the army in mid-June. These deserters undoubtedly provided crucial information on the size and organization of Braddock's force. Yet the arrival of Braddock's army in the Monongahela Valley in early July seems to have taken the French command by surprise, despite the frequent scouting missions. It was a measure of how difficult it was to pinpoint an adversary's location in the immense woods.[58]

The Indians' non-compliance with Contrecoeur's order that they attack the British column suggests that they indeed had other goals and motives in their scouting parties. On June 19, as Braddock's army ascended a ridge nearly three thousand feet in elevation, a French and Native scouting party managed to capture Scaroyady, the leader of the eight Ohio Iroquois warriors who had accompanied the British. Two French cadets, Joseph Godefroy de Normanville and René-Marie Pécaudy de Contrecoeur (son of the fort commandant), bound Scaroyady to a tree. The cadets called upon the others to kill the influential warrior, but were refused. Instead, the allied warriors used the opportunity to interrogate Scaroyady about the numbers and organization of Braddock's column and then released him. In the same manner, when a Native war party captured James Smith, a young Pennsylvania colonist working on Burd's Road , the warriors questioned him after bringing him back to Fort Duquesne. An English-speaking Delaware Indian told Smith, as he later wrote, that "the Indians spied on [Braddock's army] every day, and he showed me by making marks on the ground with a stick, that Braddock's army was advancing in very close order, and that the Indians would surround them, take the trees, and (as he expressed it), *shoot em down all one pigeon.*"[59]

Yet for all their prowess, neither the French nor the Indians had ever engaged a well-defended British column formation bristling with artillery and flanking parties. Their scouting therefore enabled them to study the British column over several weeks, testing its reflexes and determining how best to attack it—if at all. During that first week of July 1755, there was still considerable uncertainty in the French and Indian camps in and around Fort Duquesne. The arrival of Beaujeu's reinforcements beginning on July 2 certainly strengthened the French position, and provided Captain Contrecoeur with sufficient force to strike Braddock's column. Whether his Indian allies would fight, however, was still unclear. The largest Indian coalition yet fielded in an Anglo-French war was yet to become unified.

The Battlefield

As July 9 dawned at Fort Duquesne, Captain Beaujeu was at confession with Father Denys Baron, the *aumonier* or chaplain of the French detachment. Beaujeu's spiritual devotions that morning formed part of his preparations to do battle with the approaching British force. Weeks earlier, on June 14, an urgent letter from Captain Contrecoeur had found Beaujeu while he was at Camp Machault. Contrecoeur alerted his "dear friend" that Braddock's army was closer than they had realized. He cautioned Beaujeu to conceal from his soldiers the significant artillery that the British were carrying. Upon his arrival at Fort Duquesne on June 27, Beaujeu had time to assess the situation, gather information from Indian scouts and British deserters and prisoners, and rally the Native allies. On June 21, Contrecoeur had written to Governor Vaudreuil that "if we are besieged, I plan to put all our savages outside. They will have the woods to themselves, with the French to guide them, in order to strike behind the army day and night." Due to Contrecoeur's poor health, Beaujeu was selected to lead a spoiling attack against the British. Senior French officers knew that Fort Duquesne was powerful enough to require an enemy to break ground with siege artillery, but it was "too small to be able to sustain a siege," in one French engineer's terse estimation. Beaujeu's reinforcements swelled the garrison to a few hundred men—who could not all fit in the small fort. Everything therefore depended upon the success of Beaujeu's attack, and that in turn depended entirely upon the Indian allies.[60]

Contrary to legend, Captain Beaujeu did not rally supposedly reluctant Native warriors on the morning of the battle. For weeks, Contrecoeur, Beaujeu, and other French officers had worked to strengthen the coalition. July 8, 1755, was the day given to "assembling all the Indian nations into one body"—and it was then that Beaujeu sang the war song. "I am determined to confront the enemy," he told his allies. "What—would you let your father go alone? I am certain to defeat him!" The assembled Natives "immediately joined" Beaujeu, with the exception of the Potawatomis, who wished to delay the march until the next day. The commissary officer at Fort Duquesne, Jean-Marie Landrière des Bordes, supplied great quantities of powder, ball, and flints to Onontio's allies, who gathered around the large kegs and barrels to equip themselves for battle.[61]

Around 8:00 a.m. on July 9, 1755, the allied French and Native force departed Fort Duquesne. It consisted of 108 officers, cadets, and men of the *troupes de la marine*, 146 Canadian militia, and 600 to 700 Native warriors, advancing in three parallel columns through the woods. The route that they took to the field of battle, their organization, and their exact tactical decisions have never been studied in any detail. But a 1755 French account of the battle recently discovered in the Archives du Calvados in Caen, along with French and British maps of the period, sheds light on all of these. The newly unearthed French account was written by Michel-Pierre-Augustin-Thomas Le Courtois des Bourbes to his cousin in France. Le Courtois was a French officer at the Louisbourg garrison, but his October 1755 letter is based upon eyewitness testimony and provides the most detailed account of the battle of any contemporary or eyewitness French source. The initial plan had been to ambush the British at the Monongahela crossing—until the Native scouts Beaujeu had sent out brought back the news that the British column had already crossed the river. The scouts also provided a precise description of the column's disposition, including the fact that fifteen grenadiers were marching abreast at the head of the column with two artillery pieces behind them.[62]

Monongahela was no meeting engagement or blind collision of two forces. The French and Native advance brought them northwest, along the Allegheny River, to Shannopin's Town, a Delaware settlement just a few miles upriver from the fort. There they turned due south on a trading path that linked Shannopin's Town to the junction of Turtle Creek and the Monongahela River. It was the same path that the British were taking to reach Shannopin's Town. A map captured from Braddock's headquarters papers reveals that the British intended to seal off Fort Duquesne on the peninsula, cross the Allegheny at a ford near Shannopin's, and invest Fort Duquesne from the north and east. The path leading north toward the Allegheny River also allowed the British to access higher and safer ground known as the "ridge route" for their final advance upon the Forks of the Ohio.[63]

"Certain of the enemy's position," as Le Courtois relates, Beaujeu organized what is today called a hasty ambush (a tactical movement, not a classic lying-in-wait ambush). Beaujeu's tactics reflected decades of experience that had defined commonly understood procedures for allied French and Indian combatants. He embedded in each Indian nation "an officer or cadet who spoke the language." Lieutenant Jacques-François Legardeur de Croisille de Courtemanche, for example, had accompanied the Lorette Hurons—"his savages," as a French document referred to them—all the way from Québec to Fort Duquesne in 1755. While those French officers never commanded their allies in any direct way, they facilitated effective coordination of the entire coalition. As they advanced down from the heights, they were finally sighted by the startled British scouts and light horsemen. Beaujeu enjoined the allies to fan out on the left and right, with instructions to conceal themselves and withhold fire until he launched a direct attack with the main French column in the center. It was probably Beaujeu or another senior French captain who caught the attention of George Croghan

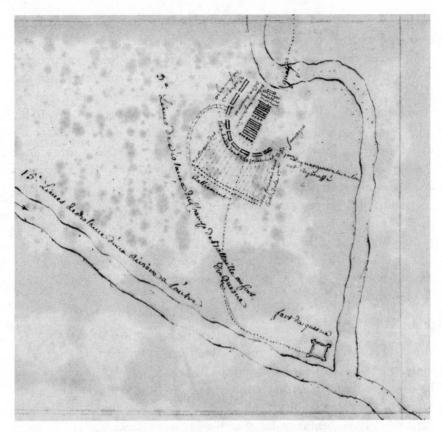

Figure 2.2 Detail of *Bataille du fort Duquesne defaitte de Bradok*, 1755, illustrates the route of the French and Native advance and the half-moon the allies formed around the British column. (Library and Archives Canada, NMC 7755)

and Harry Gordon as they scouted and marked the road ahead of Gage's advance guard (see Figure 2.2). As one British account related, the French officer was "dressed like an Indian, with a gorget on, [waving] his hat by way of signal to disperse to the Right and Left, forming a half Moon."[64]

The British Advance Guard Versus the French Column

Beaujeu's attack serendipitously unfolded at the very moment when the British were at their most vulnerable. British confidence in their inevitable victory, much enhanced by their successful river crossings, blinded them to the prospect of an unexpected battle in a bewildering place. They also had no time to prepare themselves psychologically for battle or manage a deployment into line of battle in the woods. Gage's advance party had just entered old-growth forest after going through the bottomlands nearest the river, where a British trader had cleared a small amount of land around his cabin. Enormous white and red oaks, walnuts, and hemlocks towered above the soldiers and created a dense canopy blocking light to a forest floor that was largely free from any undergrowth. Only a few rock outcroppings and large fallen timbers interrupted a view that Sir John St. Clair later characterized as "so open the Carridges Could have been drove in any part of it." Under this deep shade the British army stretched out for nearly a mile as the working party built a road paralleling the contours of a huge ridge for an easier ascent. The army's route did not proceed along the Monongahela River but rather headed due north, following the Indian path overland toward Shannopin's.[65]

Gage did not bypass any hill or violate conventional protocols, as some have misleadingly charged. He was ascending a ridge whose elevation was comparable to that of the Plains of Abraham at Québec. The absence of long-range reconnaissance was perhaps Braddock's greatest failure. He did have scouts ahead of the army, but they were too close to provide any timely warning. With contact made, his defense would rely upon the flanking parties—fully one-third of his force—who were screening the column's advance through the woods.

As firing erupted, the British tactical challenge centered on how to defend a convoy on the side of a steep wooded ridge (see Figure 2.3). The artillery and wagon trains had to be defended at all costs. The column could not press through the ambush, as the wagon road was unbuilt, and the French blocked the way ahead. Nor could Braddock easily extricate himself with an orderly movement back across the river while under attack. The only choice was to fight it out in the woods, where the trees and steep terrain made it difficult for soldiers to deploy and fight in line of battle, and for artillery to have its maximum effect.[66]

As the guides came back spreading the alarm, Gage later related that his vanguard of about twenty grenadiers also "came to the Right about" and turned back toward the main British column. Gage and other officers prevailed upon the grenadiers to face the enemy, and rallied them in a line of battle upon the edge of a ravine running perpendicular to their line of

Figure 2.3 Robert Orme, *A Plan of the Disposition of the Advanced Party*, 1758. (Map reproduction from the Richard H. Brown Revolutionary War Era Maps Collection of the Norman B. Leventhal Map Center, Boston Public Library)

march. The officers' resolve steeled their grenadiers, as did their orders to fix bayonets and load their muskets. The British also quickly brought into action two 6-pounder cannons. Beaujeu had formed his French troops in a massed column (fifteen men abreast, fifteen ranks deep), roughly the same length as the British grenadiers, and "attacked them with intrepid courage," as Le Courtois related. But the British grenadiers had rallied on the high ground at the eastern edge of the steep ravine, crying out "God save the king!" A French officer named Godefroy, who was either at Fort Duquesne or an eyewitness of the battle, related that the British "struck back from the high ground, which was very disadvantageous to us." Volleys of musketry ripped through the forest between the French and British ranks. The third British volley killed Captain Beaujeu, who fell dead into the ravine separating the two lines of battle.

The experience of standing in ranks and firing punishing volleys of lead was part of the moral force that cohered the British rank and file in combat. Relying on drill that had rendered the process second nature, soldiers ripped open cartridges, primed their pans, charged powder and ball with ramrods, and fired on command at the French line. British artillery was also beginning to take effect, heightening morale. Thunderous booms of cannons and ripping volleys from muskets accentuated the immense firepower that British soldiers knew was their greatest advantage. The grenadiers were fighting with such order and discipline, as Le Courtois related in his letter, that they "opened their ranks after every discharge to the right and to the left to leave a free passage to the cannons that they concealed, charged with grapeshot." British gunners sent as many as a hundred rounds of those "Tin Cases fill'd with Iron shot" toward the French and Indians, shattering not only trees but the attack itself. The British had repulsed Beaujeu's attack, as Captain Jean-Daniel Dumas bravely rallied the retreating French troops. Around a hundred Canadian militia fled the field entirely, shouting "Sauve qui peut!" (every man for himself). The first phase of Beaujeu's plan, with massed French troops attacking line abreast, was a conventional struggle. It was the kind of combat the British expected—won or lost in a few minutes, and decided by massed volleys and artillery fire. And they had stood their ground.[67]

Native Light Infantry Versus British Heavy Infantry

The British repulse of Beaujeu's attack, combined with the French retreat and flight of at least some of the Canadian militia, rapidly transformed the battle into a confrontation between British heavy infantry and Native American light infantry, with the French now acting more like auxiliaries of a largely Indian army (see Map 2.2). "The Indians instantly set up the Warr Cry as is their Custom," one Frenchman reported. British soldiers later described the sound as a "violent and horrid scream," and "perhaps the most horrid sound that can be imagined." An American officer a few decades later described it as an "infinitude of horse bells"—a ringing sound that magnified the numbers of Indians in the woods. Combatants in nearly every human society have used shouts, screams, cries, and even music as props to courage—as psychic shots of encouragement, propelling a perhaps unwilling body into combat. The Indians' war cries stoked warriors for combat and psychologically disarmed their opponents, so that "our enemies . . . are half dead before they begin to fight," as a Delaware warrior later explained to a British official. Trained to fight on open fields where their muskets would have maximum impact, British soldiers struggled to comprehend this unexpected combat in a place and with sounds completely foreign to them. With acrid smoke filling the murky woods, British soldiers could not see their enemy, only hear their strange and chilling screams echoing around them—screams that "were never heard in any European Campaign," as one contemporary reported.[68]

The coalition of Indian warriors now massed on the flanks of Gage's advance party proved to be the most disciplined force on the field. It was organized into national groups, but warriors fought in what were essentially small squads headed by a war captain who had earned both respect and consensus among his peers. One American observer of Indian warfare later noted that Shawnees on the march exercised "great regularity" and were "formed in certain squads, equal in number."[69] Each of these squads also acted with a great deal of autonomy, reflecting the social independence that Natives enjoyed in their communities, in that "every one of them is like a king and captain, and fights for himself," as a British official observed. The English captive James Smith marveled at the tactical flexibility of Native warriors, who could "perform various necessary manoevres, either slowly, or as fast as they can run," and particularly excelled in forming "a circle, or semi-circle: the circle they make use of, in order to surround their enemy, and the semi-circle, if the enemy has a river on one side of them"—or to their back, in the case of Braddock's army.[70]

So it was that Monongahela became "a kind of running fight," as a British contemporary described it. Native warriors formed a half-moon around the enemy column, collapsing the Redcoats' flank parties and inexorably wresting the initiative from the British. Given how consensus governed Native warriors in a coalition-type war, it defies logic to say that there was nothing premeditated about their tactics. For two months they had scouted the British column, studying its organization and numbers, and they un-doubtedly discussed around campfires how they might attack it. Many of them also knew the terrain, having used the trail from Shannopin's to the Monongahela fords. As many as three or four Native warriors could take cover behind just one of the mammoth trees, whose diameters were meas-ured in several feet. From these sylvan bulwarks, they sensed that this was a battle of opportunity—else they would have disengaged after the French retreat—and could discern the great vulnerability of the British position.[71]

The elite grenadier and regular companies of Gage's advance party were the first to experience the Natives' devastating onslaught and terrifying tac-tics and methods. Following the French repulse, Indians who had been readying themselves behind the cover of trees unleashed volleys of their own, "a discharge all the more terrible as their fire was continual," a French account related. The fight had shifted, as war parties began to attack the small British flanking parties posted up to a hundred yards from the main column in the woods. Untrained as light infantry and lacking resolve to stand against Indians at close quarters, the redcoat flankers either were killed in place with tomahawks or clubs or fell back upon the main column, sowing terror wherever they ran. Some, like Captain Charles Tatton of the 44th Regiment, a veteran of the 1745 Battle of Prestonpans, were felled by friendly fire. The British perceived that the Indians were running along their flanks, and became terrified at the prospect of being encircled and cut off. Gage's column instinctively turned away from the French to their front and faced to the right and to the left. The Natives' actions afforded their French allies time to rally and re-form under Captain Dumas and then reenter the fight.[72]

A thin, immobile red line was all that remained as Gage's advance party ceased to exist as an organized unit. Lieutenant William Dunbar, in the gren-adier company of the 44th Regiment, related how soldiers began to lose discipline and "throw away their fire," discharging their muskets at imagined threats or from nervous compulsion. Some of their own flanking parties were killed by the column as they ran in on it. The soldiers and especially the officers "dropped like Leaves in Autumn," one eyewitness remembered, and Indians had silenced the crews manning the two 6-pounders. A con-stant and heavy volume of Native gunfire whistled around; bullets struck human flesh with a dull thud, splintering bones. Incredibly, Gage remained on horseback, suffering only a grazing wound, and encouraged his men to stand their ground and re-form their line, even as smoke and confusion enshrouded his command. Although he was praised for his bravery by contemporaries, it was ineffectual; no officer, however brave, was capable of maintaining a viable unit in the face of the Indians' barrage of musketry—a fire so devastating, as Lieutenant Dunbar recalled, that "most of our advanced Party were laid sprawling on the ground" before any reinforcement came forward. Fifteen of eighteen officers in the advance party were either killed or wounded, and any effective command and control vanished. As the remnants of Gage's advance party fell back by degrees upon the working party, discipline and unit cohesion completely broke down. Only thirteen of seventy men of the 44th's grenadiers and eleven of seventy-eight men of the 48th's grenadiers escaped the slaughter of that day.[73]

General Braddock, who had been at the head of the main body when the firing began, immediately sent forward one of his aides de camp to reconnoiter. The aide did not return. Instead, Sir John St. Clair came up to his commander covered in blood and gasping from a chest wound. He provided Braddock with his initial sense of the battlefield, urging him "for God-Sake to gain the riseing ground on our Right to prevent our being Totally Surrounded" (despite the desperation of the moment, it was a plea that St. Clair may have spoken in Italian so that bystanders would not hear his foreboding assessment). Braddock then rode forward himself, making several important decisions that shaped the battlefield. He ordered Sir Peter Halkett of the 44th Regiment to take command of the artillery and wagon trains, which were brought into a more compact linear formation within the protection of flanking parties. That enabled Braddock to free the bulk of regulars alongside the train to move forward in support of the advance party and presumably to form in line of battle. He also deployed three 12-pounder pieces on his left to anchor that flank as he attempted to gain the rising ground on his right flank.[74]

But Native warriors were enveloping the column with incredible speed and bringing the fight to its rear, even as Braddock responded to the firing at the vanguard. They sowed disorder and panic among the wagon train and its civilian component, including the young Daniel Boone, a teamster from North Carolina who thought the better part of valor was to cut a horse out of its harness and flee the field. Natives extending the kill zone along the length of the column also complicated Braddock's movement of his regulars from the main body. Under the command of Lieutenant Colonel Ralph Burton of the 48th Regiment, the regulars who had been deployed in column on either side of the train moved forward to reinforce the advance party and working party and clear the rising ground on the right. They ran a gauntlet of fire so severe that there was some question as to whether they had become disorganized while moving forward. Regardless, the timing could not have been worse, as the remnants of Gage's advance party fell back and collided with Burton's reinforcements. Few actions in battle produce more devastating consequences to organization, and especially soldiers' morale, than the backward flight of terrified comrades. Not only did the retreating soldiers break whatever organization and formation of Burton's men existed, but they instilled panic and fear wherever they went. Braddock's regulars either had been put *hors de combat* or had crowded together like a mob. "Blue, buff and yellow were intermix'd," one officer reported, referencing the different-colored facings of the provincials and the 48th and 44th Regiments. The crowding was so dense that some officers reported it to be twenty or thirty ranks deep—like sheep in a slaughter pen. Braddock's aide de camp Captain Robert Orme remarked that "from this time all was anarchy, no order, no discipline, no subordination."[75]

Discipline and Panic

British officers would later blame their enlisted soldiers for the disaster, equating their panicked state with cowardice and disobedience. Gage remarked that "a visible Terror and Confusion appeared amongst the Men" under his command. Soldiers lost fire discipline ("threw away their fire," as Lieutenant Dunbar complained), refused to heed the orders and entreaties of their officers, shot down their own comrades, and were gripped with such palpable fear that all attempts to restore order were doomed. Captain Orme bitterly charged that officers "got themselves murder'd by distinguishing themselves in leading their men on."[76]

Panic had long been a phenomenon of warfare, and it was common to European battlefields with their shock power of massed muskets and bayonet charges. Indeed, British contemporaries had falsely criticized the 44th Regiment for panicking and running off the battlefield at Prestonpans during the 1745 Jacobite rising. But panic took on a new dimension at Monongahela. "The novelty of such fighting struck our Troops with amazement and terror, [and] they found themselves destroyed by an invisible Enemy," Governor Horatio Sharpe of Maryland later commented. The regulars had steadily been imbibing fears of Indian warfare and "savagery" from their British American allies. Following the battle, Gage and Burton surveyed the enlisted survivors, who remarked that "the frequent Conversations of the Provincial Troops and Country People was that if they engaged the Indians in their European manner of fighting they would be Beat." One British officer commented that his men were "pannick struck" "from what storys they had heard of the Indians in regard to their scalping and Mawhawking." During the army's march the Indians had killed and scalped a few wagon drivers and left ominous carvings on trees, only reinforcing British fears of their shadowy foes.[77]

What particularly eroded British confidence in their conventional prowess was fighting against a seemingly invisible enemy—one whose tactical skill and lethality seemed to them utterly diabolical. Gage and other officers insisted that the "greatest part [of the soldiers] never saw a Single man of the Enemy," which ran against any expectations of facing enemies on an open field. Officers and artillerists were picked off with chilling accuracy. Even if soldiers saw a target, the Indians were "changing their places as soon as they have fired, creeping or laying upon the Ground while they Load which they do very quick and are good marksmen," as Major William Sparke affirmed. A fellow officer noted how disconcerting it was that the Indians "from their irregular method of fighting by running from one place to another obliged us to wheel from right to left, to desert the guns and then hastily return & cover them." While British soldiers could never fix on an enemy position, Native warriors hit their human targets with the same ease displayed during their hunting of whitetail deer, a cultural practice that rendered second nature the techniques of breathing, aiming, and squeezing the trigger to fire an accurate shot. Leaning on the giant trees gave them stability for each shot, and they made each one count. One British officer noted his Indian foes "kept an incessant fire on the Guns & killed ye Men very fast"—silencing not only the guns but also the confidence that British soldiers placed in the dominance of their artillery. The casualty rate of the Royal Navy detachment that assisted in servicing the guns was 52 percent, and this included the mortal wounding of its commander, Lieutenant Spendelowe.[78]

British officers in battle were expected not only to keep control of their men but also to lead from the front and to inspire by their sangfroid—a steely disregard of enemy bullets. But, knowing the importance of officers in European armies, the invisible enemy cut down them down relentlessly, leaving the rank and file confounded and disorganized. Those few moments when regulars did see their enemies were traumatic. Using the concealment of heavy white smoke, Native warriors stealthily moved forward to fire at officers or, in acts of bravado, to lift their scalps in plain view of the enlisted soldiers.[79] Captain Robert Cholmley of the 48th Regiment was killed during the mauling of Gage's advance party early in the battle. After he was shot, his regulars stood aghast as two Indian warriors rushed in, scalped him as he lay wounded, and bashed his skull with tomahawks or war clubs. The British newspaper account reported a gruesome detail, perhaps embellished, that the warriors "took out his Brains, and rubbed their Joints with them."[80] The Tuscarora deserter Skowonidous, now fighting with the French, was seen scalping soldiers of the 44th Regiment. Warriors also targeted Colonel Halkett, whose coolness under fire had thus far steadied his soldiers. Halkett was killed at close range, before George Croghan could reload his weapon and kill the enemy assailant. A moment later, his son Lieutenant James Halkett was shot dead by Indian gunfire as he rushed in to attend to his father. Braddock's aides had also come under heavy enemy fire and were "prettily pickled," as Orme lamented. William Shirley Jr., the son of Massachusetts royal governor William Shirley, had been shot through the head and died instantly around the time that the Halketts were killed. Captain Roger Morris of the 48th Regiment received a painful facial wound, having been grazed on the nose, according to one account. Captain Orme received a gunshot to his leg, slightly above the knee. George Washington was the general's sole unwounded aide by the end of the battle, but his aide's role as messenger was rendered moot—there were precious few officers to whom Braddock could dispense orders.[81]

The battle evolved in a way that fundamentally undermined British soldiers' expectations: they were men trained to fight in line of battle, obey the orders of their officers, and deliver volleys at a discernable enemy line. Blasts of cannon and dozens of rounds of musketry in a concentrated space quickly enveloped the British ranks amid impenetrable white smoke, trapped beneath the forest canopy. Many could see only the flashes of French or Indian muzzles through the smoke. As Lieutenant Dunbar explained it, his men, being "unaccustomed to that way of fighting, were quite confounded & behaved like Poltroons."[82] The contest between British regulars and Indian warriors revealed two varieties of eighteenth-century martial discipline—one an external discipline demanding subordination and enforced by regulations and punishments, and the other an internal discipline characterized by individual initiative and motivation. Native and French combatants had only to fire into the mass of British humanity to create chaos, using the smoke as concealment to gain a specific target. Rank-and-file British regulars had no other response than to crowd together—some as a survival instinct, some reflexively trying to maintain a kind of linear formation.

With no training for this combat or understanding of their commander's intent, officers were as perplexed as their enlisted soldiers. They attempted to sort out the mob of intermixed soldiers by advancing the "king's colour" of the 44th Regiment and the 48th's regimental flag, a tactic that did not solve the problem. Officers complained that soldiers indiscriminately fired into the air, at trees, and into the ground; cravenly refused to obey their commands and to follow them; and, worse yet, shot at their own comrades. Yet despite what British contemporaries and modern historians have argued, panic was not the primary cause of British defeat. "Something besides Cowardice," Sir John St. Clair wrote in the aftermath, "must be attributed to a Body of men, who will suffer the one half to be diminished by Fire without being pursued in their Retreat." Some regulars fought on with courage, knowing that "it was in vain to stand and spend their ammunition to no purpose against trees and bushes, but that if they could have sight of the enemy, they would fight him," as some of them informed their officers after the battle. Many of the behaviors that officers condemned as disobedience were in fact typical physiological responses to combat. Soldiers with tunnel vision could become fixated on a target to such a degree that they could not see friendly forces in their line of fire. Terrified regulars were deaf to their officers' commands not from cowardice but from auditory exclusion. Some, knowing that they were going to die, had faces that were white from vasoconstriction. Yet some British soldiers stood their ground and bravely fought on rather than perish by a scalping knife or tomahawk. "If it was not for their Barbaras Usage which we knew they would treat us, we should Never have fought them as long as we did," as Cholmley's servant observed of the regulars' three-hour stand in a hopeless situation.[83]

Indeed, some British units fought on with cohesion and discipline—particularly the American companies that composed the working party as well as the rear guard. St. Clair normally held no brief for colonials, but he praised the conduct of the Virginia provincial companies in his working party. Captain William Polson's company, he believed, "did their work better than any people I ever saw," and "they were much Readier to fight than to work." He credited Polson and his officers for "this kind of spirit," one "that Rose at the heads and Communicated downwards." The sturdiness of Virginia provincials owed something to the soldiers and officers in the ranks who had fought at Fort Necessity against the French and Indians a year earlier. Having seen what could happen when surrounded, and with St. Clair wounded and unconscious, the Virginians independently began to take to the trees, and their officers coordinated attacks up the rising ground to clear their right flank. Fearing that such actions would stoke cowardice and disorganization, Braddock "discountenanced" them, according to George Washington. Private Martin Lucorney, a Hungarian-born recruit in the New York Independent Company of Captain Horatio Gates, was one of several regulars who followed the Virginians' example. Seeing that the battle was going against them, he encouraged Corporal Andrew Holmes to take to the trees, shouting, "The English be all killed!" As many observers reported, the Americans who fought behind trees did so bravely, and at an exceedingly high cost. Captain Polson valiantly led efforts to clear the rising ground on the British right, though he and the Virginians, caught in a crossfire between the British regulars and enemy forces, suffered severe casualties from before and behind.[84] Polson was killed and his company lost two-thirds of its strength, while Gates's New York Independents suffered a staggering 78 percent casualty rate: forty-five of fifty-seven men were killed or wounded. Private Lucorney was one of the lucky survivors.[85]

George Washington had barely escaped the melee as well, having multiple bullet holes through his clothes, one through his hat, and two horses shot from under him as he performed his duties as Braddock's aide de camp. He later claimed that he pleaded with Braddock to let the Virginians fight in the "Indian manner." Seeing the Virginians' noble efforts as the battle slipped away, Washington asked for command "before it was *too late*, & the confusion general . . . to head the Provincials, & engage the enemy in their own way," as he recalled. Although some have assumed this was Washington inventing his own mythology, there are several corroborating sources from participants in 1755 to indicate that some kind of discussion occurred along those lines.[86]

Braddock, however, put his faith in Burton's regulars to attack up the rising ground while others pushed ahead to regain the two 6-pounders that the advance party had earlier abandoned. Burton organized around 150 men in line of battle and led them forward up the steep slope even as their order was broken by boulders, fallen timbers, and the bodies of Virginians. Native warriors met Burton's assault by absorbing it—"always giving way," all the while maintaining an accurate fire (wounding Burton in the process), then counterattacking the isolated and disorganized British. The redcoats fled back down the hill, disregarding their officers' commands to stand fast.[87]

Braddock's reliance upon heavy infantry did not prevail against Native opponents, who proved to be the most disciplined force on the battlefield. From their terrifying war cries, which psychologically disarmed their foes, to their accurate and well-timed musketry, which gutted the British officer corps, and their ability to wrest all initiative from the British convoy, Native light infantry had brought a professional European army to the brink of destruction.

The Wounded and the Dead

By 4:00 p.m., the British forces were approaching the point of dissolution, fighting more as a mob than as an organized force. Most of the British officers had been killed or wounded, and Washington, as noted, was the sole member of the general's staff who had escaped death or wounds. British attacks had accomplished nothing, and as soldiers exhausted their ammunition, their muskets became more difficult to load and fire from the accumulated fouling in their barrels and on flints and frizzens. Soldiers nursed debilitating musket wounds that had shattered shoulders, arms, legs, and knees. Thomas King of the 44th Regiment, a thirty-one-year-old carpenter from Yardington, England, with fifteen years' service, lost his left arm at Monongahela, while his comrade Timothy Crawley of the 48th Regiment suffered permanent disability in his left shoulder as a result of his wounds. Braddock's dauntless courage had symbolized the dogged stand of the British infantry amid the slaughter. Four horses had been shot from under him during the battle's course, and he was mounting his fifth steed when a bullet ripped through his arm and lung, creating (most likely) the sucking chest wound that claimed his life four days later. He attempted an orderly retreat, but the soldiers only huddled around the wagon train. French officers including Lieutenant Jacques-François Legardeur de Croisille de Courtemanche—who later received the Croix de Saint-Louis—pressed the attack, encouraging the warriors to prevent any English rally. For a brief moment in the battle's fourth hour, an eerie silence descended on the battlefield. But it was only a pause, during which the French and Indians prepared to fall upon the surviving British with tomahawks and war clubs. "As if by beat of Drumm," one redcoat officer avowed, the rank and file did a collective right-about-face and fled in terror.[88]

Braddock's rear guard of 110 men was all that stood between the enemy and possible annihilation of the entire army. Composed of Captain Adam Stephen's Virginia provincials and a South Carolina Independent Company detachment, these Americans had been relegated to the task of defending the rear from attack—one that British officers probably thought a super-fluous formality. But, again, many in those units had been surrounded by the French and Indians at Fort Necessity—and when the firing commenced on July 9, they dispersed behind the cover of trees. In their desperate stand, at least one-third of the American rear guard became casualties. They also blocked the movements of Indian parties toward the river crossing and "preserved the pass" for the British forces, and as a result, they saved the army from potential destruction.[89]

Native warriors pursued the British survivors to the banks of the Monongahela River, staining it with streams of blood as they shot down fleeing soldiers and civilians in the ford, tomahawked them, or scalped them. "How brilliant the morning,—how melancholy the evening!" one partic-ipant later remembered, highlighting the stark contrast between the two British crossings that day. Indeed, two of every three British and American soldiers who had crossed the Monongahela that morning were killed or wounded in the space of four hours. According to one return done in late July 1755, 976 British were killed or wounded out of 1,476 who entered the fight. The French and Indians had achieved this monumental victory at the cost of only a few dozen casualties. Had they sought to annihilate the British, Native warriors could have easily done so, by cutting off the army from either the lower or upper fords. But their lack of pursuit was wholly in keeping with their military objectives, which remained on the field— Braddock's abandoned supply wagons and the scalps and trophies lifted from the hundreds of British dead and wounded who lay scattered through the woods. Pennsylvania captive James Smith, still at Fort Duquesne, heard the scalp halloos of triumphant warriors streaming back, and saw them bearing scalps, regimental coats, grenadier caps, horses, and a few captives who were ritually tortured to death within sight of the French fort.[90]

Private Duncan Cameron, who, as noted, had survived Fontenoy and other killing fields, witnessed the orgy of destruction and scalping that made this battle the "most shocking." After making his escape, he struggled to rejoin the army, which was in full retreat back to Colonel Dunbar's base

camp on Chestnut Ridge, nearly sixty miles away. Washington, who had
vainly attempted to rally the fleeing British and safely escorted his wounded
commander off the field, had been ordered to ride through the night back
to Dunbar's command to secure supplies and aid. He and other soldiers
struggled to find the road during the pitch-black night as they felt the trees
for the road builders' hatchet marks. The "shocking Scenes" that Washington
saw along the road forever seared him—"the dead—the dying—the
groans—lamentation—and crys along the Road of the wounded for help .
. . were enough to pierce a heart of adamant," he remembered decades later.
Among the dying was Washington's comrade and friend Captain William La
Péronie, a French Huguenot and Virginia provincial officer who had fought
with him at Fort Necessity. Mortally wounded at Monongahela, La Péronie
died on July 13, 1755, at Dunbar's camp.[91]

The British Army's unpreparedness for a major battle extended to its lack
of medical treatment. The vast scope of casualties was simply far beyond
the ability of a few regimental surgeons and surgeon's mates to handle. Dr.
Robert McKinley, the 44th Regiment's surgeon, had lost his equipment
and medicines on the battlefield, along with everything else. The general
hospital established at Fort Cumberland at the beginning of the expedition
was more than a hundred miles from the field of battle. Like many of his
men lacking adequate treatment, Braddock succumbed to his wounds on
July 13, as the remnants of his army struggled back across the Appalachian
Mountains to Fort Cumberland. The army's sense of humiliation increased
as they burned or abandoned their valuable stores and buried their dead
commander in his eponymous road. The wounded were heaped into
wagons and bumped and jostled along the same roads and ridgelines that
they had marched over the month earlier. Maggots were feasting in their
wounds by the time they arrived at Fort Cumberland on July 22—thirteen
days after the battle. Braddock's successor, Colonel Dunbar, completed the
British Army's disgrace by abandoning the frontier altogether and going
into winter quarters in Philadelphia—in August.[92]

Braddock bore the weight and the responsibility of a catastrophe rooted
in British imperial shortcomings. It was an age when distance made theater
commanders such as Braddock all the more autonomous—and singularly
responsible for victory or defeat. Contemporaries, including as an anonymous British pamphleteer who could not fathom how a regular army
could be "totally routed by a handful of invisible Savages," accused the
dead general of every wrongdoing. Subsequent historians have followed

the Anglocentric conceit that the battle was Braddock's to lose, while also generally ignoring French-language sources and Indian perspectives. Monongahela was not lost because Braddock was arrogant, or had alienated potential Indian allies, or had failed to follow conventional protocols for security, or had rejected Americans' advice to fight in the "Indian manner."[93] Even so, his troops were singularly unprepared for this other face of battle, represented by the formidable military power of Indian nations and their practice of irregular warfare, which yielded immense military and geopolitical advantages. That realization led James Smith, who would remain a captive among Ohio Indians for the next four years, to extol the Indians' ways of war: "Could it be supposed that undisciplined troops could defeat Generals Braddock, Grant, &c.?" He observed that "Indian discipline is as well calculated to answer the purpose in the woods of America, as the British discipline in Flanders: and British discipline, in the woods, is the way to have men slaughtered, with scarcely any chance of defending themselves." For the British, fighting in Flanders had been the face of battle. The woods presented another story.[94]

The Legacy

Few battles in world history have had such enormous consequences as Monongahela, in part because—as has often been the case with first engagements in a war—it defined the basic character of the ensuing conflict. Lexington and Concord, St. Clair's Defeat, First Bull Run, Kasserine Pass, Task Force Smith at Osan, Ia Drang, and Operation Anaconda—all of them revealed a combination of technological, tactical, or training deficiencies on the part of American soldiers, or dashed their assumptions about the enemy and expectations of easy victory. In the same way, Monongahela was distinguished by far more than battlefield slaughter. It has come to symbolize the clash of conventional and unconventional warfare in North America. While it was one of the worst disasters in the entire history of the British Army, it was among the greatest victories ever achieved by Native Americans, who constituted two-thirds of the French and Indian coalition. The Battle of the Monongahela dramatically escalated the war in America, which in turn became the global conflict known as the Seven Years' War (1756–1763), involving Britain, France, Prussia, Hanover, Austria, Russia, Sweden, and eventually Spain.

For days and weeks following the battle, the French hauled off Braddock's captured artillery and supplies, even as the stench of bloating and unburied corpses of hundreds of British soldiers covered the battlefield—yet another instance of the cruel face of war in America. The materiel that the British had abandoned proved crucial in escalating the war and shifting strategic momentum to the other side. Braddock's captured headquarters papers were a diplomatic and propaganda coup for the French, who translated and published some of them. They revealed how leading British ministers of state had plotted war against France in a time of actual peace, and justified the French counterdeclaration of war in 1756. The French eventually hauled off ten field guns, eleven mortars, and a vast amount of ammunition, tools, wagons, and supplies from Braddock's army.

For Native Americans, the Monongahela represented the greatest victory they had yet achieved over a European force. As noted, it satisfied their primary objectives in war: producing an abundance of captured war matériel and trophies of war such as scalps, uniforms, weapons, flags, and horses. After the war, one British officer traveling through the Maumee Valley in 1764 noted "an Indian on a handsome white horse, which had been General Braddock's, and had been taken ten years before when that General was killed on his march to Fort du Quesne" (see Figure 2.4). All of those objects and their stories sustained the memory of Monongahela among Indian nations. The victory had also imbued warriors with a sense of British armies as "a Parcel of old Women for that they could not travel without loaded Horses and Waggons full of Provisions and a great deal of Baggage," as a Delaware warrior named Lamullock joked. In the aftermath, Native warriors entered the war as French allies in far greater numbers than ever before, hoping to replicate their success at the Monongahela. They not only joined French expeditions across northeastern North America but unleashed *la guerre sauvage* on the frontiers of Pennsylvania, Maryland, and Virginia. Their wide-ranging attacks rendered those populous and wealthy colonies impotent for much of the war. French and Indian war parties departing Fort Duquesne often used Braddock's Road in reverse, as a highway leading to the heart of British colonial settlements.[95]

The cascade of British defeats in America and in Europe from 1755 to 1757 not only placed them on the strategic defensive but imbued their soldiery with a fear of the wilderness and of their enemies' prowess. Using some of Braddock's captured artillery and ammunition, the French besieged and captured two key British outposts: Fort Oswego on Lake Ontario in

Figure 2.4 An Indian warrior displays General Braddock's white horse captured at Monongahela in 1755. (Robert Griffing, 2017, *He Said It Was General Braddock's Horse*. Courtesy of Paramount Press, Inc.)

1756 and Fort William Henry on Lake George in 1757. While the French and British commanders arranged conventional European protocols for surrender, victorious Indian warriors were determined to obtain their own honors of war. They attacked and killed some of the British garrisons after their formal surrenders, and took many captives and much matériel back home. British contemporaries labeled these incidents "massacres"—ones that highlighted French and Indian treachery in this other face of surrender. Fear of Indian threats was again palpable during the 1758 expedition to Fort Ticonderoga, in which the largest British force ever fielded in North American history at the time (over 17,000) was defeated by a French force of around 3,000 under the Marquis de Montcalm. General James Abercromby, the British commander, threw his regulars against strong French field fortifications in a series of costly frontal attacks. After suffering around 2,000 casualties in a single day's action, the British were seized with an inordinate fear of fighting invisible French and Indian foes. The British abandoned the expedition and fled southward up Lake George to their base camp—on July

9, 1758, the anniversary of Braddock's Defeat. As Montcalm's ghost tells his adversary James Wolfe in the Chevalier de Johnstone's imagined narrative, "Your army was always so struck with terror and dread, that, constantly blinded with fear, the shadow of an Indian set them a trembling."[96]

Memories of the Monongahela catastrophe and its carnage fundamentally changed the character of the war for the British. Instead of a limited war aimed at rolling back French territorial encroachments, it became a war of vengeance whose goal was nothing less than the absolute conquest of New France. Memories of Monongahela also merged with those of the 1756 and 1757 "massacres" of British troops following their surrender at Forts Oswego and William Henry, all of which justified in British minds a more total war against the Canadians and Indians. In addition, Monongahela was the touchstone for all future British efforts to adapt to American warfare and the threat of Canadian and Native irregulars. As Washington rightly observed, with the wisdom of hindsight, "The folly & consequence of opposing compact bodies to the sparse manner of Indian fighting, in woods, which had in a manner been predicted, was now so clearly verified that from hence forward another mode obtained in all future operations." That other mode was a larger British institutional adaptation to campaigning in America. Major General John Campbell, 4th Earl of Loudoun, the commander in chief in America from 1756 to early 1758, recognized that because "in Effect we have no Indians, it is impossible for an Army to act in this Country, without *Rangers*; and there ought to be a considerable body of them."[97]

That sense of operational dependence upon irregulars led Lord Loudoun to establish independent ranger companies (generally known as Robert Rogers's Rangers) to conduct long reconnaissance and strike missions. The British Army in America also began to designate a light infantry company in every regiment that could screen an army's advance through the woods and skirmish with enemy forces. British and American troops, including Ensign Thomas Gist of Virginia, increasingly learned "the art of bush fighting," trained to fire at marks, and wore camouflaged or lighter weight clothing. Officers developed formations better designed for marching large armies through the forests and procedures for fighting against French and Indian irregulars.[98]

Veterans of Braddock's Expedition were conspicuous in that transformation. Thomas Gage created the British Army's first light infantry unit—the 80th Regiment of Light Armed Foot—for the express purpose of adaptation;

Captains Quintin Kennedy and Charles Lee of the 44th Regiment went even further in their responses, immersing themselves in Native diplomacy and culture and dressing as Indian warriors during campaigns on the New York frontier. Far from being militarily conservative, George Washington also trained his Virginia Regiment in light infantry tactics, occasionally outfitted his soldiers as Indians, and frequently deployed them to fight as irregulars alongside Cherokee and Catawba allies. The Virginia provincials "knew the parade as well as the Prussians, and the fighting in a Close Country as well as Tartars [i.e., partisans]," according to Adam Stephen, who became the lieutenant colonel of the Virginia Regiment following the Monongahela. The Seven Years' War and the American Revolution beyond always had a compound quality—a hybrid of conventional and unconventional forces and practices.[99]

Captain Richard Bayly, of the 44th Regiment of Foot, who survived three of the greatest disasters of the French and Indian War, personified the British Army's perseverance (see Figure 2.5). Bayly had been part of Braddock's Expedition and was among the small percentage of officers who emerged from Monongahela unwounded. He witnessed another crushing defeat of British arms at the Battle of Carillon (Ticonderoga) on July 8, 1758, and was listed as wounded in action (one of the more than 20 percent casualties his regiment suffered). Happily for Bayly, the third disaster he experienced was one that he helped to inflict on French forces, at the Battle of La Belle Famille in 1759, which sealed the fate of the French garrison at Fort Niagara on Lake Ontario. Many of the French Canadian forces, including their commander, Captain François-Marie Le Marchand de Lignery, had been drawn from Fort Duquesne and had fought at Monongahela in 1755. This time, however, Captain Bayly and the 44th Regiment's light infantry inflicted heavy losses on the French and gained a measure of revenge.

Over the course of the war, the British and Americans developed an unprecedented ability to strike deep into the interior of the continent, counteracting the strategic mobility that the French and Indians had always enjoyed. The supply shortfalls that Braddock experienced motivated subsequent British commanders' efforts to build a strong logistical foundation for the more than 40,000 provincial and regular soldiers who were ultimately fielded by 1758. During his tenure as commander in chief, Lord Loudoun pioneered the construction of bateaux, roads, wagons, fortifications, and storehouses necessary to project and to sustain multiple British armies

Figure 2.5 Captain Richard Bayly of the 44th Regiment was a veteran of the Battles of the Monongahela, Ticonderoga, and La Belle Famille. (Portrait by Joseph Wright of Derby, Derby, England, 1760-1761, oil on canvas, accession #2018-284, A&B, image #D2019-JBC-0116-0005. Courtesy of the Colonial Williamsburg Foundation. Museum Purchase, Friends of the Colonial Williamsburg Foundation Collections Fund)

operating in North America. What had been impossible in the century prior to the 1750s had become possible.[100]

The Monongahela had ultimately changed *how* war was fought and *where* war was fought in North America. The British Army thus fulfilled Braddock's prophetic words that "we shall better know how to deal with them another time." In 1758, General John Forbes conducted a brilliant campaign that finally resulted in the French abandonment of the Ohio Valley. Forbes led an expedition of around 7,000 British, American, and Indian forces that corrected in every respect the challenges or errors witnessed during the 1755 expedition. Lieutenant Colonel Henry Bouquet, Forbes's most trusted lieutenant, underscored that the "obstacles which he had to surmount were immense, 200 miles of wild and unknown country to cross, obliged to open a road through woods, mountains, and swamps; to build forts along our lines of march for the security of our convoys, and with an active and enterprising enemy in front of us." It cost "infinite trouble" but was worth the effort. Forbes's soldiers eventually constructed a new military road across Pennsylvania to the Forks of the Ohio, as well as a network of fortifications and supply bases to anchor the British presence beyond the Appalachian Mountains. Indeed, Braddock's and Forbes's roads had become crucial in shifting military operations from the seaboard to the interior. Those military roads also cemented British control of the Ohio Valley, as they became the conduits for thousands of colonists to enter the region in the decades following the war. Forbes's victory marked the beginning of a permanent British and American presence in the trans-Appalachian west and the ability to project power into the continent's interior.[101]

By war's end, the British cry "Carthago delenda est" had been fulfilled—and Monongahela avenged—in the expulsion of thousands of French Acadians from Nova Scotia, the scorched-earth campaign aimed at Québec's *habitants* in 1759, and the convergence of three separate British armies upon the last French bastion, Montréal, in 1760. Britain's global triumphs over France as well as Spain extended to the Caribbean, West Africa, India, and the Philippines—victories that helped to consolidate the first British Empire following the Treaty of Paris in 1763. Despite the triumphs of British arms, however, those global victories contained the seeds of bitter defeat in the future. Britain's decision to garrison in America a peacetime regular army of more than 7,000 men was completely unprecedented—and expensive. And as numerous French officials predicted, saddling Britain with Canada and its attendant expenses as an occupying power would drive a wedge between Britain and its subjects in North America—Indian as well as colonial.

Although the British had conquered the French, they had not conquered the Native peoples of the Ohio Valley and the Great Lakes region. Resentful of British military occupation, hubris, and restrictions on trade, much of the same Native coalition that had defeated Braddock went to war against the British Empire. As if to underscore that Native nations retained their independence, fighting erupted in 1763 as the ink dried on the Treaty of

Paris, which supposedly brought the Seven Years' War to a close. Warriors dismantled much of the British military network in the west, capturing nine outposts across the Ohio and Great Lakes region and besieging Forts Detroit, Pitt, and Niagara. What was called Pontiac's War lasted from 1763 to 1765, during which warriors again devastated large sections of the Pennsylvania, Maryland, and Virginia frontiers.

The British Army was in a far weaker state in 1763 but still able to strike back. Colonel Henry Bouquet's effective adaptation of Native American tactics and psychology at the Battle of Bushy Run in 1763 was a demonstration of just how far the British Army in America had evolved since 1755. Marching westward from Philadelphia along Forbes's Road, Bouquet led a small force to Fort Pitt to relieve the Indian siege of that garrison. At a way station called Bushy Run, Bouquet's regulars were encircled by Native warriors in what appeared to be a repetition of Monongahela. But with veteran, disciplined troops who had fought under him during Forbes's campaign, Bouquet pulled his light infantry companies out of his perimeter, feigning a retreat and creating a false sense of confidence among the Indians. Meanwhile, his reformed light infantry companies unleashed a shocking assault on the Natives' right flank, in which the bayonet triumphed for once over the tomahawk in close combat. Despite Bouquet's tactical masterpiece and his relief of Fort Pitt, the war ended not with British military triumph over the warring Natives but rather with a negotiated settlement in 1764 and 1765—the Indians remained unconquered and had forced a political equilibrium with the British Empire.[102]

As historian Stephen Brumwell has observed, Britain's "American army" was a casualty of its own successes, owing to its severe attrition over nearly ten years of war and occupation. That was part of the reason the army's hard-earned prowess and expertise in fighting North American irregulars failed to register a lasting doctrinal impression upon the British Army. Although light infantry companies were retained in British regiments following the war, the post-1763 army had lost some of its finest practitioners and theorists of irregular warfare, such as Lord Augustus Howe, Quintin Kennedy, John Forbes, and Henry Bouquet, who died of a fever in Pensacola, Florida, in 1765. Had they lived, their "art of bush fighting," elaborate diagrams of orders of march, and standard procedures on fighting irregulars in the woods—the lessons of Monongahela that had helped to secure victory for British arms in North America—might have been more than short-term adaptations and have become more fully institutionalized in the postwar army. As a result, when it was charged with suppressing the American rebellion in 1776, the British Army would have to relearn many of the lessons gained through hard experience and blood in the Seven Years' War in America.[103]

For decades to come, the Battle of the Monongahela resonated with mythological as well as military importance for Americans. In contrast to the post-1763 British Army, a generation of American frontier colonists preserved more of their experience in frontier warfare through conflicts such as the Cherokee War (1759–1761), Pontiac's War, and Dunmore's War (1774). Monongahela had been central in creating a distinctly American identity, and especially in many colonials' self-conception as proficient Indian fighters. Many colonists were awakened to a sense of "being Americans"—as George Washington expressed it—as they campaigned with British regulars who often denigrated their military abilities and provincial status.[104] In rhetorical self-defense against such slights, Americans celebrated the conduct of Washington and the effectiveness of the Virginia provincials at Monongahela, as well as other victories distinguished by American contributions.

Following the war, Braddock's field remained a macabre scene of scattered skulls and bones—an American Golgotha that supposedly symbolized the downfall of an arrogant general who led his army to disaster and slaughter in the wilderness.[105] When the War for American Independence broke out, twenty years after Monongahela, revolutionaries remembered it as evidence that trained British regulars could be defeated and that American provincials had fought there with greater effectiveness. Indeed, the first Continental Army units ever created by the Continental Congress were not line infantry regiments but light infantry companies of "expert riflemen" drawn from Virginia, Maryland, and Pennsylvania, many of whom arrived at the Siege of Boston dressed and equipped like Indian warriors. The veterans of Braddock's Expedition who became generals in the Continental Army— George Washington, Horatio Gates, Charles Lee, Adam Stephen, and Daniel Morgan—carried its legacies into the Revolutionary War.[106]

However, even as Monongahela shaped the broader trajectories of eighteenth-century warfare and fueled a mythology of the American militia's prowess in wilderness warfare, its challenges and lessons had to be relearned—most often painfully—by subsequent generations. In 1788, the newly appointed governor of the Northwest Territory, Arthur St. Clair—a former British officer and veteran of the French and Indian War—journeyed to Pittsburgh with Lieutenant Ebenezer Denny of the recently formed 1st American Regiment of the United States Army. Together, they "visited the remains of poor Braddock's soldiers" at Monongahela, still visible on the battlefield thirty years later. And three years hence, they too would experience the other face of battle against Native forces along the Wabash River.[107]

3

Interlude I

An American Army of Expansion

Despite Braddock's disaster and its lessons, the ensuing years of the Seven Years' War and the course of the American War of Independence suggested that not just one type of war but several lay in the future of North America. Braddock's experience and subsequent American myth-making seemed to suggest that the ability to fight in the wilderness, to accommodate one's forces to the landscape, and to fight in irregular formations would solve the puzzle of war in the New World. The significant British victories from 1758 to 1760, however, were won primarily through conventional fighting against uniformed French forces, in conjunction with naval and amphibious power, and through the sieges of cities and fortifications.

Similarly, during the American Revolution, George Washington struggled to create a conventional army with which to confront his British adversary. Washington's experience at Monongahela, and even his belief in the superior performance there of the Virginia provincials, did not dissuade him from his desire for an army trained to fight in a linear fashion, delivering volleys of fire at a nearby enemy behaving in the same manner. He was not wrong. Ultimate American victory in the war depended not just on fighting the way that the British did but on creating a "respectable army"—one that accorded with the international community's opinion as to what an army should be.[1] The final victory at Yorktown was a conventional siege conducted alongside a European ally and in coordination with naval forces. Most Americans, however, remained persuaded that the key to victory had been their spirited citizenry, fighting as amateurs, generally in an irregular manner, chasing off the British columns at Concord in 1775, devastating them at Bunker Hill that same year, and rallying to Washington's ragtag forces when most needed throughout the war, most notably the decisive victory at Saratoga in 1777.

Like most myths, the ones surrounding the American frontier fighter were only partly true. Colonial militias were often poorly disciplined and fared badly in the woods, though, as we've seen, the colonists had also learned to create "ranger" units designed to mimic Indian tactics and to be able to remain longer in the wilderness in a self-sustaining way. Robert Rogers's Rangers, serving with the British Army in the Seven Years' War, were only the most well known. Gorham's Rangers, from Massachusetts, fought across several of the eighteenth-century wars, and South Carolina's rangers were key supports to British expeditions against the Cherokees in the 1760s. During the Revolution, rebel partisan units fought the British, especially in the southern colonies, helping to bring about the ultimate American victory.[2] The seeming efficacy of rangers and partisans combined with a populace disinclined to invest in a standing regular army. Not only were Americans ideologically averse to standing armies, but the young nation lacked the financial wherewithal to pay for one. Furthermore, fear of renewed war with Britain suggested investing in coastal defenses and some form of expandable army. From early in the life of the United States, the nation fortified key harbors, and periodically renewed or replaced them as technology changed and the nation's budgetary situation improved.[3] Fort McHenry, outside Baltimore, was only one of many, though it would be made famous as the subject of the verses of "The Star-Spangled Banner" during the War of 1812.

As for the troops themselves, the same war that saw the British attack Fort McHenry also seemed to validate—at least to the public—the sense of relying on the militia, although now in the form of "volunteer" regiments, raised by the states, that could be sent on expeditionary missions outside state boundaries (a long-standing limitation on traditional militia forces). After the war, the notion of a small standing force to be expanded in wartime, heavy with officers as a cadre, supplemented by state regiments of volunteers, became the de facto policy, although it was never officially approved by Congress.[4] This system structured the forces raised for the war against Mexico from 1846 to 1848, as well the Civil War from 1861 to 1865—with conscription added late and controversially to the latter conflict.

Both before and after the cataclysm of the Civil War, however, the vast majority of conflicts that the United States engaged in were against Native Americans. For such wars, neither the coastal forts nor the expandable army was particularly suitable. This is not to say that conventionally trained regulars were not useful or adaptable—quite the reverse. The freshly raised and poorly trained troops of the American "regular" army, buttressed by local militias, were destroyed by a confederacy of Ohio Indians in Harmar's Defeat in 1790 and what became known as St. Clair's Defeat in 1791. The latter was the worst battlefield defeat ever suffered by the U.S. Army in its many Indian wars—far worse than George Armstrong Custer's more famous debacle at Little Big Horn.[5] More careful training and better pre-battle preparation eventually brought victory to a third American army at the Battle of Fallen Timbers in 1794, leading to the Treaty of Greenville and the cession of most of Ohio. The duration of that conflict and the ultimately successful preparations made by the army under General Anthony Wayne spoke to the larger pattern of wars against Native Americans. In most cases, defeating them demanded converging columns moving over great distances (usually guided by other Native Americans), year-round and multi-year operations, and ultimately systematic attacks on their subsistence.

Such operations characterized not only many of the earlier colonial wars but also the Second Seminole War from 1835 to 1842 and numerous campaigns against the Plains Indians from the 1850s to the 1890s.[6] The skills, persistence, and logistical resources necessary for such operations could rarely be found in militia or volunteer forces. Even so, regular army officers considered "the Indians little more than a temporary nuisance" and, concludes historian Peter Maslowski, "never developed any cogent guidance for Indian fighting."[7]

That they succeeded in any case was due to strategic vulnerabilities inherent to Native American societies. As was clear in the Monongahela campaign, Indians excelled at strategic and operational mobility, and were skilled tacticians, but they could not readily sustain their forces in the field beyond a single campaigning season. The men had to return home to provide for their families, and taken as a whole, their societies lacked a subsistence buffer if crops were burned, or, in the case of the peoples on the Great Plains, if the bison were hunted out—either through governmental policy or simply through commercial hunting.[8]

Virtually all of the Indian wars were fought with very little national investment in the military. The standing army remained tiny from the 1790s through the 1890s, with only 6,000 men in 1821, still just 8,500 just prior to the war with Mexico in 1846, and a mere 27,442 in 1876, at which level it remained until the end of the century.[9] Reliance on wartime expansion through state regiments and a continued belief in coastal fortifications dominated peacetime budgetary thinking. Despite those constraints, what we now call a sense of "professionalism" among the officer corps developed, both before and especially after the Civil War.[10] Professionalism included building a body of coherent thought to guide the behavior of its members, in this case how best to ensure the nation's security against its enemies. As historian Brian Linn has pointed out, however, "those officers who served on the frontier failed to translate their experience into an organized body of military thought on warfare."[11] These men did not look to their frontier experiences as a model for their future; they worried instead about European-style armies, and looked to them as models, both institutionally and tactically. Napoleon's success recommended the French example for many years, to be succeeded by an interest in the Prussians after 1871, and then by an increasingly broad interest in whatever theater of conflict a contemporary European army became engaged in.[12] The official army establishment consistently ignored the Indian wars in its official publications, even as the officers involved in them struggled to create and pass on a set of rough-and-ready methods. Their experiences survived as part of the American army's culture, which at the end of the nineteenth century consisted, according to Andrew Birtle, of "a deep appreciation for the value of mobility; a rich heritage of small-unit leadership that stressed self-reliance; aggressive, independent action and open order tactics; [and] a near obsession with individual marksmanship."[13] The lessons American officers learned fighting Native Americans in North America went with them to the Philippines as shared experience, not as a formal doctrine.[14]

Indeed, the United States' expansion beyond the continent and across the oceans coincided with a reorganization and revitalization of the U.S. Army.[15] The army that fought the first of those wars abroad, however, against Spain in Cuba in 1898 and in the Philippines, was still built from the old model, consisting of a few small regular regiments supplemented by state regiments made up of volunteers. The senior officers in both sets of regiments were men either without experience or whose combat time had been in the Indian wars and the Civil War. As we will see in Chapter 4, one of the leading American commanders in the Philippines, General Wesley Merritt, had been a cavalry commander with Ulysses S. Grant at Appomattox. That first imperial war against Spain was the one that the Army, and the nation, expected. It was the war they had prepared for intellectually and technologically (although actual training in large unit maneuvers had not been possible since 1865). Very quickly, however, they found themselves in a war they did not expect: one against their allies in the war with Spain, the Filipinos.

As the men stepped ashore in Manila, the equipment they carried represented a vast change from that of their forebears at Monongahela. At that battle, British and American infantrymen generally stood upright in ranks, tore open black powder cartridges with their teeth, primed their lock, poured the remaining powder down the barrel, rammed a ball down after it, and then fired in volleys. In this they resembled European infantry of the seventeenth century, as well as those who would fight in the Civil War. There had obviously been substantial changes between the matchlock muskets of 1600 and the percussion-cap-fired rifled muskets of 1861. And some eighteenth-century units on some occasions had indeed learned to fight as skirmishers, forswearing line and volley tactics, and even reloading in a prone position. But for the most part, technology and technique remained fairly unchanged across that long swath of time. (The long-range capability of the rifled muskets of the 1860s was infrequently used, due to both terrain and tactics.) This technological stability meant that for this whole period there was a relative parity between the weapons of the state and the weapons available to everyone else, whether Native Americans or an insurgent citizenry. Artillery was generally confined to the forces of the state, although it could readily be captured, and the standard weapons of the infantry and cavalry (and of course the horses themselves) were easily available.

From the 1850s, however, the increasing automation of precision machining technology began to change dramatically the amount of firepower an infantryman could unleash. Precision machining allowed first for safely loading a weapon at the breech instead of the muzzle, followed within three decades by magazine-fed bolt-action rifles. To these products of industrialization was added a product of chemistry in the form of smokeless powder, first used in a rifle in France in 1885. Its chief virtue was not just its smokelessness but its much greater power and the smaller amount of residue left behind in the barrel. The greater velocity meant an equivalent stopping power from a smaller round, allowing a soldier to carry more ammunition. Ultimately, a new generation of rifles emerged from the 1880s and early 1890s, with the U.S. Army selecting the Norwegian-designed Krag-Jørgenson in 1893. Firing rates went from roughly three rounds per minute in 1861 to as many as twenty per minute. Industrial capacities and the new

powder also made possible early machine guns and, perhaps most important, artillery that was more powerful, more mobile, and quicker-firing.[16]

By 1898, for American and Filipino forces, these new capacities were still
relatively evenly distributed, though they already promised an increasing advantage for state-raised armies versus their less well-financed and organized
opponents, who would begin to find it difficult to match firepower. They
would have to adopt different tactics. What the Indians had done more
or less naturally against their American foes, other non-industrial societies
would have to learn—and in the face of an increasing disadvantage. The
more that Americans emphasized firepower, the more their opponents
would choose an asymmetrical response.

★ ★ ★

The American soldiers in the Philippines arrived expecting to fight the
Spanish. The U.S. Navy's success in Manila Bay rendered that fight mostly
unnecessary. For their part, the Filipinos sought independence and statehood,
and so they organized and presented a conventional army for the world to
see, one not unlike George Washington's Continental Army. Furthermore,
the Filipino forces had hoped to march in and occupy the capital, Manila. As
a result, the first U.S.-Filipino battle would be almost entirely conventional.

Both sides were similarly armed and organized; in combat both engaged
in volley fire and unit rushes. Even so, this was still a fight against an enemy
the Americans had not expected. Though this fight was seemingly conventional, most of the American soldiers carried their civilian attitudes and
expectations with them. Included in those attitudes was a racism that affected the strategy and tactics they adopted in the first fight, as well as their
experience of combat. Furthermore, while their infantry weapons were not
yet markedly superior to those carried by their non-state enemies, their
artillery was substantially superior—especially the shipborne guns firing in
support. Such a firepower advantage, however, would not extend to the
guerilla war that followed the Battle of Manila.

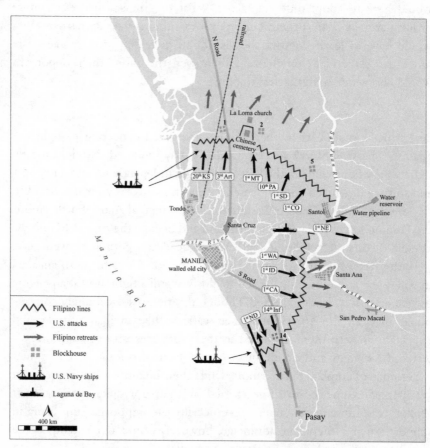

Map 4.1 The Battle of Manila. (Map by Matilde Grimaldi)

4

The Battle of Manila,
February 4–5, 1899

On the morning of Sunday, February 5, 1899, American soldiers outside of Manila rose from their trenches and strong points and launched the largest frontal assault by U.S. troops since the Civil War. The resulting engagement was an accidental battle in an accidental war. The United States had not originally intended to get involved in the Philippines when it went to war with Spain in 1898, but after the triumphant victory of Admiral George Dewey's Asiatic Squadron in Manila Bay, President William McKinley found himself the dominant power in the archipelago. The Spanish land forces were quickly forced to surrender, leaving a Filipino army of independence facing American forces around the capital city. The tense standoff turned to war on that Sunday.

The Battle of Manila was a turning point in intercultural war. A conventional battle waged using symmetrical tactics, it was one of the encounters that showed decisively that, with some exceptions, non-Western forces could no longer stand on the battlefield against a Western power. It was not just that the Filipinos were defeated at Manila; it was that they were overwhelmed. That had not necessarily been true previously, as seen at Monongahela. Now, entering the twentieth century, it was. The immediate lesson for the Filipinos, though it took some time for the leadership to absorb it, was that they needed a new approach to fighting, one that avoided the open battlefield and massed forces, instead prioritizing asymmetrical methods. The longer-term lesson of this battle (and of similar battles) was that asymmetrical approaches to warfare were essentially the only path to success against Western powers.[1]

On the American side, the initial conclusion was similar. The United States rightly believed Manila to be a crushing victory against a largely incompetent foe. They identified the source of that incompetence not in the correctable factors of training, discipline, and army organization but on the unchanging basis of race. The Americans believed that the Filipinos were racially inferior. They fit them into familiar racial categories, whether Jim Crow visions of the American South or racist and romanticized imaginings of Native Americans from the American West, using words such as "nigger" or "brave" to identify Filipino soldiers.[2] It was this racial inferiority, the Americans believed, that made the Filipinos militarily inferior, and it always would. Thus the United States would always be militarily superior.

This certainty dangerously undermined the Americans' ability to react effectively to the enemy's tactics and strategy. No military, no matter how strong, can escape the need to respect an opponent's actions and figure out how to respond to them. Hamstrung by its own racial blinders, the United States failed in this. The American way of fighting was civilized, the United States thought, and it was up to the Filipinos to accept that, not to fight back in uncivilized ways. That feeling persisted through the war in the Philippines and, for the next century, in other wars in which the United States encountered an intercultural enemy. It was an attitude that would cost the United States dearly.

But on February 5, all of that was in the future. Instead, American soldiers attacked. One of them was John Bowe, a volunteer in the 13th Minnesota Regiment. His experience highlights many of the elements of the battle and its individual and kaleidoscopic nature. Bowe had wandered off from his unit that morning with a fellow soldier—whom he knew only as "Windy Bill"—and linked up with the 10th Pennsylvania Regiment. They were climbing the hill toward the Filipino defenses, through fields full of growing rice, when "without a second's warning" the Filipinos "pumped a terrific volley into us." They lay down in the rice and waited. They were there, Bowe remembered, for two hours, with the morning sun burning down on them, unable to fire for risk of hitting their own skirmishers. The only Filipinos they could see were the officers walking back and forth on the walls protecting the rest of the Filipinos. As they lay there, thousands of shots flew over them. The Filipinos could not hit them, however, not even when one seemed to target Bowe individually. The Minnesotan could hear the bullets getting closer and even kicking dust into his eyes, but they never quite connected. After several magazines' worth of shots—"five shots would come with equal regularity, then a short time for loading, and then again"—the bullets stopped, and Bowe fell asleep. Windy Bill, who was still with him, did the same. Finally, guns from the Utah Volunteer Artillery arrived to extricate them. The guns opened up against the Filipino fortifications, and Bowe and the other soldiers charged them, led by an American officer shouting a war cry and "running in front with his hat waving over his head." They ran forward, loading, then dropped to one knee to fire. He remembered the other soldiers joking or "swearing a cuss" as they did. The attack broke the Filipino line, and the Filipinos tried to retreat over the hill behind them. Bowe and the other American soldiers slaughtered them mercilessly as they did: "Few went over that hill. At one place there were sixty dead goo-goos in that many square yards."[3]

Bowe's day was not an uncommon one. Many similar moments happened to American soldiers around the battlefield: the heavy but inaccurate Filipino fire, the frontal assault and breaking of the fortifications, and the slaughter of the defenders as they retreated. What was also common was the ground-level nature of the experience. Bowe had little idea what was happening outside his range of vision. He had no sense of how the battle was going overall, his horizon constrained by the rice fields in which he advanced, lay, and advanced again. In many ways, his experience stands in for those of all the American soldiers, a tiny part that collectively came together into a massive whole.

The assault in which Bowe was involved came after an uncertain night, with Americans and Filipino troops exchanging fire in the dark without doing much damage to each other. When morning came, no one knew if the Americans could break the heavily fortified Filipino defensive lines without being slaughtered wholesale. Civil War veterans in the American force, including the commander, General Elwell Otis, might have been forgiven for thinking of the bloody repulses at Fredericksburg, Gettysburg, or Cold Harbor.[4]

They would have worried for nothing. The American assault the morning of February 5 shattered the Filipino defensive lines, sending the Philippine Army reeling back in disarray. The Battle of Manila, the biggest show of American arms between the Civil War and World War I, was a remarkably complete victory. While the Americans emerged triumphant from that battle, the war, much to U.S. surprise, dragged on for years. Winning the field, it turned out was not enough, a lesson the United States would have to learn again and again in the future.

The Campaign

It was something of a surprise to everyone that the United States even fought at Manila. In 1898, most Americans had little idea where the Philippine islands were and less interest. Even President William McKinley struggled to locate the archipelago on a map. Americans had spent most of the post–Civil War era looking westward, thinking of Manifest Destiny and paying little attention to the rest of the world. Even the country's foreign policy crises were mostly regional ones, including an uprising in Cuba against the Spanish Empire. The Cuban War of Independence, which began in 1895, filled American newspapers with stories of Spanish atrocities. The public outrage pushed McKinley to take a hand, an effort that went badly wrong when the armored cruiser USS *Maine*, showing the flag in Cuba, blew up in Havana harbor on February 15, 1898. The explosion killed the majority of her crew, triggering a war between the two countries.[5]

The war did not remain long in the Western Hemisphere. Some Americans had an idea where the Philippines were, and one of them was Theodore Roosevelt, then the undersecretary of the navy. Roosevelt fervently believed that the best place for the United States to assert itself as a global power was in the Pacific, where the world's empires—England, France, Germany, and Russia—were busily savaging China. He ordered the American Asiatic Squadron to head to Manila and attack the Spanish. Led by Admiral George Dewey, the U.S. fleet entered Manila Bay on May 1, 1898, and engaged the defending Spanish ships. A Jesuit priest, Jose Arcilla, watched the battle from shore. After the Spanish fired, Arcilla wrote, the Americans, "haughty in their colossal barks, answered with energy, all of their cannons aimed at destroying our vessels." It was, the priest said sadly, "veritably infernal."[6]

The obsolete Spanish ships proved no match for the Americans. The American fleet swiftly sank them, and by the end of the day Dewey owned Manila Bay. Warships of other imperial powers would start prowling its waters as well, more or less respectfully. "I am here by the order of the Kaiser, Sir!" German vice admiral Otto von Diederichs snapped at Dewey in June 1898 upon arriving with his fleet, which at the time outnumbered that of the American admiral.[7] Von Diederichs was not alone: there were ships present from Britain, France, Japan, and Austria-Hungary.[8] A substantial Spanish garrison still held the city. In the countryside, a Filipino revolutionary army

made up of a wide range of ethnic groups and led by revolutionary government president Emilio Aguinaldo was marching through Luzon on the way
to Manila. Aguinaldo was a Tagalog, a member of the archipelago's dominant
economic and political group. By 1898, he had fought the Spanish, taken
bribes from them, struggled with internal political rivals, and had not quite
reached his thirtieth birthday. The messiness of Aguinaldo's contradictions
reflected a society riven by political and ethnic rivalries. The United States
encouraged him to take up the fight again to weaken the Spanish, implying
that the reward would be Filipino independence. It would not be the first or
last time that an indigenous insurgent believed American promises.

President McKinley confronted a prickly question: what to do with the
Philippines? Spain's grip had been crumbling for a while. King Alfonso
XIII of Spain was still a minor, more concerned with consolidating his
grip on the throne against his Carlist rival than with a sleepy set of islands
thousands of miles away. It was up to the Americans and Filipinos to figure
it out. McKinley equivocated at first, expressing a reluctance to annex the
Philippines, but then changed his mind and ordered American troops to
Manila. The forces he sent were largely state volunteer regiments raised to
fight in Cuba or the Caribbean; instead they got the Philippines. Mostly
from the western states, they boarded trains to the Presidio naval base in San
Francisco where ships waited to carry them across the Pacific. Coming the
farthest was one of the few non-western regiments, the 10th Pennsylvania.
The unit's trip was a public event. At a stop in Harrisburg, the state capital,
the unit's commander, Colonel Alexander Hawkins, wrote that they were
"surrounded by thousands of admiring friends, who gathered to bid them
god-speed."[9] Governor Daniel Hastings shook the hand of each man in the
regiment, and the governor's wife fed them a hot meal.[10] Across the United
States, crowds greeted the 10th with "ovations of welcome."[11]

The units assembled in San Francisco became the Eighth Army Corps,
commanded by General Wesley Merritt, a career soldier. Merritt grew up
in Illinois and went to the United States Military Academy at West Point.
He graduated in 1860 and was thrust immediately into the Civil War, where
he made a name for himself in the cavalry. He was promoted directly from
captain to brigadier general on the same day as George Armstrong Custer,
and was one of the officers at Appomattox with Ulysses S. Grant. After
the Civil War, his career encompassed the full range of responsibilities for
the peacetime army, including commanding federal troops in occupied
Louisiana during Reconstruction, being superintendent of West Point, and

"much hard marching and considerable severe fighting with hostile Indians in the Northwest," as one of his biographers noted.[12] His first wife died early in the 1890s. As one of the last things he did before taking his forces to the Philippines, Merritt, then in his sixties, married a woman forty years his junior.

The Philippines-bound military expedition was a hastily mustered affair with hurried improvisation standing in for proper organization. Much of Merritt's official briefing memoranda came directly from the *Encyclopaedia Britannica*.[13] Many of the soldiers arrived in San Francisco without uniforms—"almost naked," as Thomas Osborne, a private in the 1st Tennessee, observed in a letter home.[14] Once they were in San Francisco, poor health, substandard hygiene, and the chilly climate caused illness. Osborne remembered that at one point, 59 of the 106 men in his company were in the hospital.[15]

The journey across the Pacific did not help matters. Most of the men had never been to sea before. The 1st California suffered so badly from seasickness on their ship, *City of Peking*, that they rechristened it "City of Puking."[16] The only relief came when they stopped at islands along the way. In Hawaii, the Pennsylvanians and the Nebraskans played a game of baseball, a game won handily by the Pennsylvanians.[17]

Once arrived in the Philippines, they found a three-way standoff: between the American naval fleet in Manila Bay, the besieged Spanish garrison in Manila city, and the surrounding Philippine Army. It was not the most violent of sieges. Many Filipinos both in Manila and outside socialized with the Spanish, who had, after all, ruled them for centuries. Even insurgent officers such as General Pío del Pilar crossed the siege line to attend parties thrown by the Spanish. The son of a poor farmer and seamstress, del Pilar had been born locally in San Pedro de Macati, the area of the lines his men now occupied. Del Pilar had served for a year in the Spanish army, fighting in Mindanao, but left and joined the revolution, rising to become one of Aguinaldo's most trusted subordinates. The Filipino visits were viewed skeptically by the Spanish, as the Jesuit Arcilla noted "the friendship shown these past few days was that which his domestics feel for a dying rich man, and who seek to take possession of his riches before others come to claim them."[18]

All sides, including the United States Navy, greeted the arrival of the American forces with suspicion at first—an "entire absence of enthusiastic reception," as the official historian of the 1st Montana Infantry noted.[19] Admiral Dewey worried that the Army would steal his glory. The Filipinos hoped that the Americans had come to help them gain independence, but they remained wary, concerned, as Aguinaldo said, that the United States would "covet" the Philippines, "this very beautiful pearl of the Orient Sea."[20] The Spanish, oddly, were the most welcoming, hoping that the American soldiers would somehow save their situation.

Aguinaldo let Merritt talk him into handing over a southern stretch of the siege line. When the American soldiers came ashore, they received a friendly greeting from the ordinary Filipino soldiers, some shouting, "Americano, Filipino, amigos! Espanõl Malo!" ("Americans, Filipinos, friends! Spanish bad!")[21] This stretch was centered on the Manila suburb of Pasay, facing two of the stronger Spanish fortifications, Fort San Antonio Abad and Blockhouse 14. An attack there—if stoutly defended by the Spanish—would be costly. The Americans found out quickly, however, that the Spanish mostly wanted to go home and as soon as possible. They knew that the war was lost and Manila was running low on food. They could not simply surrender—the previous Spanish captain general there, Basilio Agustin, had suggested as much to Madrid, and had been fired by return telegram on August 5—but they could moderate their resistance. After Agustin's firing, Merritt, Dewey, and the replacement Spanish captain general, Fermín Jáudenes, discussed how to surrender Manila in a way that would allow Jáudenes to save face. Merritt and Dewey kept Aguinaldo, their supposed ally, in the dark about the discussions, and on August 13, 1898, when American forces mounted a frontal assault on the Spanish lines facing them, the Filipinos were caught by surprise.[22]

The Spanish troops resisted fiercely at first but then, as prearranged, the garrison surrendered. Edgar Sutcliffe, a company commander in the 1st California, remembered the fight as being over almost before it began: "The city was ours and very easily taken."[23] U.S. forces blocked the Filipinos from joining in the occupation of Manila. To prevent Filipino incursions into the city, Merritt initially allowed some of the Spanish troops to remain in their defensive trenches, and then eventually spread his forces out in lines on the limits of Manila proper, facing outward. The Filipinos occupied the line of old Spanish blockhouses.

The confirmation of Aguinaldo's suspicions poisoned the relationship between the two forces. As one officer in the 10th Pennsylvania remembered, "The feeling of friendship and amity so cordial heretofore was greatly changed, and discontent, dissatisfaction, and general distrust were manifested."[24] A journalist noted that when any American "strayed beyond their fortifications, the attitude of the native sentries was often violent and abusive." Eventually the Americans were not allowed out of their own lines, and "the Malay line of muskets tightened around the city like the arm of a colossal dragon."[25] The siege had not really ended. Instead, the Americans had replaced the Spanish in the Filipino noose.

Merritt was sent to Paris in late August 1898 to assist in negotiating a peace treaty with the Spanish. He was replaced by Major General Elwell Otis. Otis had not intended to be a career soldier. Born in Maryland, he had gone to the University of Rochester and then Harvard Law School, graduating in 1860. His nascent legal career was interrupted by the Civil War. He served with distinction during the war, most particularly in Grant's final drive upon Richmond and Petersburg in 1864–1865. This led him to stay in the Army after the war was over. Otis spent most of the rest of the nineteenth century in the American West, fighting Native Americans. He thought of himself as enough of an expert on the frontier to write a book, *The Indian Question* (1878), in which he wondered, "Has the American Indian the capacity and inclination to adopt the customs, and receive the faith of the white man?"[26] A Civil War wound left Otis with near-constant insomnia, and his wakefulness exacerbated natural instincts toward micromanaging. He was legendary for arriving at his desk at seven-thirty in the morning and leaving at midnight, with only a break for dinner.[27]

Otis took over the command during a phony peace: the two sides were supposed to be allies, but neither side trusted the other and violent confrontations were common. Filipino and American patrols frequently ran into each other. Sometimes fights broke out, instigated by both sides, with shouting, shoving, and the occasional shot fired. No one was killed, but there were bruises and abrasions aplenty. An officer in the 1st Washington recalled a general sense of unease. The Americans were "always on the *qui vive*. False alarms were of frequent occurrence, and more than once the regiment was assembled in East Paco ready to support the outposts should hostilities commence."[28] Edgar Sutcliffe of the 1st California wrote on December 1, 1898, that while he regretted the situation, the solution was for the Filipinos to "gracefully accept [U.S.] domination."[29] Even if they did not and instead remained "cranky," Sutcliffe was not especially worried, believing that the United States would make "short work" of them.[30]

The situation worsened in mid-December 1898 when news of the signing of the Treaty of Paris with Spain reached Manila. As part of the treaty, the United States purchased the Philippines from the Spanish for $20 million, thus shattering any lingering idea that the Americans might give the Filipinos their independence. The Filipinos and particularly Aguinaldo were indeed cranky. The Americans, Aguinaldo thought, had been revealed as just another colonial power to be resisted. The resisters would, he wrote to Otis, "fight to the death rather than be bought and sold like cattle."[31] Further, Aguinaldo wrote separately, "I denounce these acts before the world, in order that the conscience of mankind may pronounce its infallible verdict as to who are the true oppressors of nations and tormentors of human kind. Upon their heads all the blood which may be shed."[32]

The increased hostility of the Filipinos after the treaty was evident at the ground level as well. In early January, a Filipino patrol confronted an outpost of the 1st Nebraska on the San Juan Bridge. "A party of fifteen armed men came up to the bridge where outposts were stationed and attempted to drive them off, but the guards stood firm," one of the American soldiers noted. The Filipinos loaded their rifles threateningly, and it was not until a Filipino officer came up that things calmed down. But the Filipino officers were angry too. On January 10, 1899, one of them confronted an American unit just south of Manila, saying that because "McKinley opposed our independence I did not want to have dealings with any American. War, war, is what we want." "The Americans after this speech went off pale," wrote the Filipino officer to Aguinaldo later. "They said to me that America offered 30,000 men to attain their liberty. I answered that the Philippines will offer the lives of all her sons."[33]

The tension was significant enough that both sides began to prepare for war. Aguinaldo mapped out a plan that would coordinate an uprising inside Manila with a general assault on the American lines. General Arthur MacArthur Jr., who commanded the U.S. 2nd Division, prepared a counterattack to a potential Filipino assault. MacArthur, like Otis and Merritt, was a Civil War veteran. A native of Wisconsin, he had joined the 24th Wisconsin Infantry Regiment at the start of the war, age seventeen. He served valiantly, earning a Medal of Honor at the Battle of Missionary Ridge on November 25, 1863. After the war, he embarked on a law career, but abandoned it after only a few months and returned to the military. His wartime rank of colonel reverted back to captain, and MacArthur spent the next twenty years without promotion in the small and stagnant U.S. Army. As had Merritt's, his postings crossed the country, from occupying the rebellious southern states to fighting the Indian wars out west. His family moved with him, and MacArthur managed a comfortable domestic life; when he was appointed to the Department of the Dakotas, MacArthur set up house in his hometown, Milwaukee, and "commuted every weekend by train" to his headquarters in St. Paul, Minnesota.[34] When MacArthur shipped off to the Philippines, his son Douglas (whose own military career would heavily involve the Philippines) headed to West Point.

The environment did not calm down over the next month. On February 3, 1899, Otis wrote to Dewey, "There has been a great deal of friction along the lines in the past two days. . . . The city is quiet, though there is a vast amount of underlying excitement. We are constantly losing our [Filipino] employees. Yesterday seven of our men at the Malacañan quarters left us suddenly to join the Insurgents. They stole and took with them whatever they could find of value."[35] One of the items stolen was an officer's carriage, which the newly minted insurgents simply drove through the American lines. But no one was quite willing to start a war yet, so the two sides sat staring at each other in the suburbs of Manila, waiting for a blink.

The Forces

The American forces lined up outside Manila in early February consisted of a range of regiments and units. From the regular Army came the 14th United States Infantry, and there were also state volunteer regiments, including the 20th Kansas, 1st Montana, 10th Pennsylvania, 1st South Dakota, 1st Colorado, 1st Nebraska, 1st Washington, 1st Idaho, 1st California, and 1st North Dakota. Artillery units consisted of the 3rd United States Artillery Battalion, the 6th United States Artillery, and two batteries of the Utah Volunteer Artillery. They were organized into four brigades, which were sorted into two divisions. The structure allowed Otis to control his forces relatively easily because he dealt directly with only two subordinates, Major General Thomas Anderson, who commanded the 1st Division, south of Manila, and MacArthur, who commanded the 2nd Division, north of Manila.

The volunteers were mostly armed with several models of the long-serving Springfield, a single-shot breech-loading rifle firing a heavy, slow-moving .45 round. The big bullet did massive damage to whatever it hit.

A later observer wrote that "this comparatively large slug carried a tremendous shock on impact and, in most cases when an insurgent was hit, he was either disemboweled or the top of his head literally blown off."[36] But the Springfield was a "venerable antiquity"—an old design, originally from just after the Civil War—and it had major problems.[37] The rifle did not use smokeless powder, so every volley a unit fired left them "blanketed with a pall of white smoke that resembled a fierce prairie fire," as one officer put it. The low muzzle velocity of the bullet meant that it traveled on a more pronounced arc to its target, which made accuracy challenging. In addition, the heavy recoil made firing it a painful experience. William Thaddeus Sexton, who later served in the Philippines and was one of the Battle of Manila's first historians, noted that the Springfield's "severe kick encouraged flinching with its attendant poor marksmanship."[38]

The regular Army infantry units had a much better weapon than the volunteers, the new Model 1893 Krag-Jørgensen rifle. The Krag-Jørgensen used a magazine that allowed multiple shots before reloading, and it took smokeless powder, which did not give away the shooter's position. The Krag-Jørgensen also fired a lighter bullet than the Springfield, a .30 round. Its higher velocity meant that it caused the same level of damage as the Springfield, but the projectile took a flatter path, making it easier to be accurate. But the Krag-Jørgensen's magazine had to be loaded one bullet at a time, unlike the magazine of a similar weapon, the 1893 Mauser, which could be loaded with five-round clips. The result had been that Spanish soldiers armed with Mausers back in Cuba had put out a much higher volume of fire than American soldiers armed with Krag-Jørgensens.

The American artillery's two main types of weapons were larger guns, firing heavy solid shot or explosive shells, and smaller rapid-fire guns, shooting hundreds of rifle-sized bullets a minute. The heavier guns did their damage by the impact or explosion of their shells. Each could wound or kill multiple soldiers at a time. The rapid-fire guns produced wounds like those from a normal rifle, often a multiplicity of them, but perhaps their most important effect was the overwhelming nature of their firepower, which pinned down enemy soldiers and slashed away at their morale. Unlike in later wars, when such machine guns would be on the front lines, used to create mass fields of interlocking fire to slaughter attackers, in the Philippines the Army kept the rapid-fire guns as part of the artillery units. There, separate from the main infantry, the guns fired indirectly on enemy targets, sending hundreds if not thousands of rounds down in a lethal rainfall. However, the Americans had relatively few such guns, and that limited their impact.

The artillery units were the regular 6th Artillery and the Utah Volunteer Artillery (the 3rd Artillery had actually been sent without its heavy weapons, to act as infantry). The main gun for both was the 3.2-inch rifled artillery piece. This was the most modern weapon that the U.S. Army had, a breech-loader firing a 13.5-pound shell out to a range of two to three miles, though the accurate range was much less. It was an "efficient and handy weapon," Sexton noted.[39] By February, the units had acquired a random assortment of additional guns, as the official history of the Utah Volunteer Artillery catalogued: "Utah soldiers on different parts of the line manned thirty-two pieces of artillery, including 3.2-inch B.L. rifles, Hotchkiss revolving cannon, Hotchkiss mountain guns, Maxim Nordenfelts captured from the Spanish, Mortars, Colt's rapid-fire (Browning's) gun, a navy field piece, navy six-pounder and Gatling guns of various calibers."[40]

In addition to this mélange, the Americans had several aces in the hole. They had outfitted a captured riverboat, the *Laguna de Bey*, with machine guns and armor, and sent it to patrol the Pasig River. Otis and Dewey had also arranged for the admiral's ships to serve as a floating battery. The guns on those ships dwarfed almost everything ashore. The largest were the 10-inch guns on the USS *Monadnock*, which fired shells of 500 pounds each, roughly forty times the size of the 3.2-inch breech-loader's shell. The rounds traveled at more than 2,000 feet per second, well past the speed of sound, meaning that a shell exploded before the sound of its firing could be heard.

There were other differences between the regular Army units and the volunteer state units besides their weaponry. The 3rd U.S. and 14th U.S. consisted of veterans from top to bottom. The American army in the post–Civil War era was both small and stable. As seen with Arthur MacArthur, soldiers and officers spent decades in the service, often at the same rank and responsibility. That meant they were deeply experienced, professional soldiers, trained and disciplined—if also prone to alcoholism.

By contrast, the volunteer units had a wide range of experience. Some officers had a great deal of military knowledge; many of those were veterans who had gone into civilian life and reenlisted during the Spanish-American War, and others were still in the Army but had shifted to a volunteer regiment at a higher rank. John Stotsenberg of the 1st Nebraska, for example, graduated from West Point in 1881. When the war came, he was a captain in the Army, teaching military science and tactics at the University of

Nebraska. He agreed to serve in the 1st Nebraska Volunteer Regiment at the rank of major and was quickly promoted to colonel and command of the regiment. Most of the enlisted, however, were inexperienced, ordinary men who had signed up in 1898. The time between the formation of the units and combat proved fortuitous, as it gave the officers time to train and drill their men.

As noted, most of the volunteer regiments were from states west of the Mississippi, including South Dakota, Colorado, California, Utah, and Nebraska. They believed strongly in American exceptionalism, with a determined sense that U.S. history was the story of triumph over a mostly empty continent. The frontier, the historian Frederick Jackson Turner had told them in 1893, had only just closed, and the United States, especially in the West, still saw itself as a rural and outdoor society.[41] For the soldiers, this sense of national destiny was closely tied to their own sense of a masculinity that demonstrated itself publicly through physical prowess.[42] They thus connected their performance in war to being seen as a good man and a good American. Thomas Osborne of the 1st Tennessee vowed that he would rather die than "than go home and have someone say I ever failed to my duty."[43] In Osborne's mind, his behavior was not just about doing his duty but also about being known to do it. Sergeant L. C. Peters of the 1st Nebraska echoed Osborne: the unit "will do itself proud when the critical moment arrives," he said, so the people at home should "keep your eye on us."[44] Such performative phrasing illustrates a masculinity that had to be publicly seen and appreciated.

The sense of destiny and manhood was also strongly connected to their thinking about race. American soldiers—as we saw with Bowe at the start of this chapter—believed themselves a superior race, and that superiority gave them divine blessing to rule lesser peoples. The Philippines, the "splendid Asiatic archipelago," fit nicely into a narrative, part of the "responsibility of the dominant American power."[45] American racial beliefs coincided with those common in the larger world, in which the dominant empires competed to rule ever more of the globe and carry out their responsibilities, a sense the British poet Rudyard Kipling invoked in his 1898 poem "The White Man's Burden." The burden Kipling referred to was conquering the Philippines, in order to uplift the "half devil and half child" inhabitants.[46] More, American imperialism was simply a continuation of the drive that had filled an empty continent—or so many Americans thought. As Halstead put it, "Washington crossed the Allegheny and held the ground.

Jefferson crossed the Mississippi, and sent Louis and Clark to the Pacific; and crossing the great western ocean now is but the logic of going beyond the great western rivers, prairies and mountains then. We walk in the ways of the fathers when we go conquering and to conquer along the Eastward shores of Asia."[47] In this formulation, the conquest of the Philippines was not only possible but required. This was the feeling that filled the ranks of the American army in 1898.

The soldiers in Manila had expected to go to Cuba but were sent to the Philippines instead. They found it foreign. "All things on the island of Luzon were new and strange," commented a writer for a soldier's newspaper.[48] The Americans longed for the comforts of home, as Halstead wrote: "The novelties of the tropics [soon] lost their flavor. What did a man want with oranges when there were apples? What was a rice swamp compared with a corn field?"[49] Less lyrically but more practically, another soldier told a journalist that "visions of square meals a la America haunt us lovingly and endearingly."[50] The lack of activity also chafed, with one observer complaining of the "humdrum of barrack life and the monotony of what was practically imprisonment in the limits of Manila."[51] More, the Philippines was dangerous. The most serious threat was not combat but disease. American soldiers were susceptible to many of the endemic local diseases, including typhoid fever and smallpox. Within a few months of arrival, the sick rate was about 12 percent of the forces there, a high number.[52] Nor did everyone recover. In the first week of February 1899, for example, eleven American soldiers died of disease.[53]

U.S. soldiers' attitudes toward the Filipinos changed over time. In the beginning, as noted, there was a fair amount of daily interaction between the Filipinos and Americans, both soldiers and civilians.[54] American soldiers talked positively about the Filipinos during this early period, albeit with a strong racial framing. George Telfer, a soldier of the 1st Oregon, insisted that the Filipinos had "as perfect a physique as any race I have seen. They are quick of thought and action."[55]

By the start of 1899, attitudes were becoming more negative, if equally racial. American soldiers often used racially coded language that linked Filipinos with Native Americans and African Americans. The same George Telfer who had lauded the Filipinos in the summer of 1898 started identifying them as "Indians" six months later.[56] Other soldiers described the Filipinos as "niggers."[57] Later, they would identify the Filipino soldiers as "insurrectos" ("insurgents"), a term that both denoted the American belief that the Filipinos were revolting against the legitimate rule of the United States and invoked the obsessive fear of insurrections by the enslaved in pre-Civil War America. The language brought with it all the freighted hostility of American domestic culture, and a similar sense of menace.

More Filipinos understood this than might be guessed. The Spanish had propagandized American racial behavior to the Filipinos, convincing them, as one American tourist traveling through Luzon found, that the United States had "mercilessly and finally exterminated the race of Indians that was native to our soil and that we went to war in 1861 to suppress an insurrection of negro slaves, whom we also ended by exterminating."[58] How far down into the ranks of the Philippine Army that knowledge spread is unknown, but it is clear that many understood what the word "nigger" meant. In addition, the Filipinos formed their own views of the Americans. Repeated encounters over the months had convinced some that the U.S. soldiers were passive. Charles Mabry, a soldier in the Utah Artillery, thought the Filipinos were encouraged by the "apparently submissive attitude of the Americans" and had started to think that U.S. soldiers were "cowards."[59]

The different ethnic groups that made up the Philippine Army had little sense of themselves as part of a single, larger nation, and little trust in one another.[60] The Spanish had never enforced a common language, so the groups spoke a range of different dialects, and, to put it politely, got along with each other not at all well. The Tagalogs made up the majority of the officer corps, which caused further friction with the other Filipinos.

On the economic side, the nineteenth century had remade the Philippine economy into an agricultural one, and the settlement and clearing of the interior land resembled nothing so much as what had taken place on the American frontier, an interesting echo of the experience of the western U.S. soldiers. One historian has noted that in the Philippines there were "pioneers and wagon trains, cattle ranching and rustling, cowboys and bandits, railroad building."[61] The resulting setup was somewhat feudal, with large landowners controlling their communities and demanding the loyalty of their workers. Such patron/client relationships extended beyond simple employment into political and cultural activity.

These ethnic and economic connections served as the basis for the Philippine Army. Much as the United States government relied on the states to put together fighting forces quickly, Aguinaldo and the Filipino leadership relied on local leaders to create the units that filled the army. Each individual leader gathered the men dependent on him economically or politically and became their commanding officer. The units were named after their location of origin.[62] This approach built an army quickly, though the loyalties of the soldiers were almost exclusively to their commanding officer rather than to anyone higher up. Such focused loyalties meant that they were reluctant to obey anyone else. One battalion of Filipino soldiers from Kawit, for example, refused to obey the orders of army commander General Antonio Luna.[63] After years of fighting the Spanish, many of the Filipino soldiers and officers had ample combat experience, but little of it was systematized into doctrine and then translated into training. Because the Spanish had spread their forces thinly, most Filipino combat had been at the company level (hundreds of soldiers, rather than thousands) and with a substantial numerical advantage. The battle they were about to fight would be different.

How many Filipino soldiers were in that force is unclear. The American estimate of the time was 40,000. But the United States tended to see every Filipino as a soldier, folding in laborers and other non-military attendants.[64] A later calculation suggested 15,000.[65] The actual number may have been below even that. Aguinaldo himself had planned for around 25,000 men for the entire archipelago. More than half of those were being used for occupation duty elsewhere, meaning that the Filipino force in the Manila area probably numbered between 10,000 and 11,000 men. This was slightly fewer than the Americans.[66]

Despite that smaller force size, Aguinaldo could not control his army as efficiently as Otis did his because of the command structure. The basic unit of the Philippine Army was the company, consisting of 110 men. The largest was the battalion, consisting of six companies, about 660 men. There were no standardized units above that, nothing like the brigades or divisions of the U.S. Army. Aguinaldo thus had to handle fifteen to twenty different battalion commanders directly, an unwieldy process at best. Because the fighting with the Spanish had mostly been at the company or battalion level, Aguinaldo and his officers had little experience in handling the whole force in battle.

The weapons the Filipino soldiers carried were surprisingly advanced. The Spanish had armed some of their native militia with the same 1893 Mauser that had shown such superiority against the American forces in Cuba. One American observer noted that the "Mauser rifles of the insurgents made hardly any flame in the night, and their presence was known only by the sharp cracks and the whistling of bullets overhead."[67]

As the Filipino resistance against the Spanish expanded, they captured a mélange of weapons. In one takeover of a small town in northern Luzon, a Filipino general reported that he had acquired "378 arms, including Mausers, Remingtons, revolvers and sabers, two cannon of small caliber, ammunition 2,600 Mauser, 17,000 Remington, 100 carbine, and 50 revolver."[68] But the Filipinos had few ways to make more rifles and ammunition—no "Fabrica de Municiónes de Guerra," as Aguinaldo complained.[69] They tried to buy more abroad, but the attempts failed. Some foreign nations would have been willing but were reluctant to annoy the Americans. The Filipino representative in Japan said that trying to buy arms there was like being with "a girl who loves one and wants to say 'yes' but who does not dare to throw herself into our arms for fear of consequences."[70] This was especially critical for ammunition because the limited amounts available meant that the Filipino soldiers could not train that often.

The Philippine Army's artillery was a random assortment of guns captured from the Spanish. They were old and of indifferent quality, and the Filipinos had little experience using them. There seem to have been ten to fifteen pieces in the Manila area, the number roughly comparable to what the American forces had.[71] The largest was an old bronze siege gun north of Manila that fired a solid shot of substantial proportions. None of them could compare to the guns of the American fleet.

Filipino logistics were reasonably effective. Trinidad Perez Tecson, one of the highest-ranking women in Aguinaldo's forces, was the commissariat in charge of food supply for the army, and she managed things efficiently.[72] In addition, the Philippine Republic controlled Central Luzon and its lush agricultural zone, and kept the soldiers well supplied with rice. Finally, the Filipinos managed to equip their men with fairly standardized clothing. If not quite a uniform, it was still more regular than the garb worn by the American units (see Figure 4.1).

Being equipped with such weapons was not the same as knowing how to use them. At every level, the Philippine Army displayed a high degree of ignorance in handling their rifles and artillery, which crippled their fighting effectiveness. At the top, Filipino officers seem to have had an unrealistic idea of the rifles' range. General Luna, responsible for much of the organization and training of the army, thought that the troops should open volley fire at 2,000 meters (roughly a mile) and individual fire at 800 meters. Both of those distances were optimistic even for well-trained armies, and wildly so for the Filipinos.[73] Filipino commanders did not like risking their

MALOLOS—INSURGENT TROOPS AWAITING THE ARRIVAL OF AGUINALDO, SEPTEMBER 13, 1898

Figure 4.1 Insurgent troops waiting to greet Emilio Aguinaldo. (Photo from Marrion Wilcox, ed., *Harper's History of the War in the Philippines* [New York: Harper & Bros., 1900])

artillery and often, as Sexton noted, took them "out of action at a critical time ... to avoid the possibility of capture."[74]

At the bottom, a large number of Filipino soldiers were terrible marksmen. They fired their rifles too soon, without aiming, often without even looking. The result was that they simply could not hit their targets. The campaigns in the rest of the Philippines in 1898 were full of examples where the attacking Filipinos had been unable to inflict much damage on the defending Spaniards. At the siege of the Spanish garrison at Tayabas, in Batangas province, a reported 15,000 Filipinos besieged 443 Spaniards, fired a reported 500,000 rounds at them in the process of several failed assaults, and eventually had to starve them out. Similarly, at Baler, in eastern Luzon, a small group of Spaniards, besieged in a church, held out for ten months—long after Spain had formally surrendered the Philippines to the Americans.[75]

While the Filipinos were bad shots, there is something else to consider. They were there out of loyalty to their patron, and that meant that firing a rifle was not just about hitting a target but also about the public demonstration of effort to that patron. The act of shooting was important; less so was what they hit. The Filipinos had to be seen to be doing their duty, and firing was a good way to do it. Hitting the target, even seeing the target, was not a requirement.[76] In their own way, they were as public and performative as the American soldiers. It is too simplistic to say that the Filipinos didn't know how to use their weapons and more accurate to say that they had a different sense of what use meant.[77]

Their victory against the Spanish and the shortage of ammunition encouraged the Philippine Army to ignore their own defects. During the phony peace of 1898–1899, the Filipino forces neglected drill and training, enough that Aguinaldo wrote to the entire army in October 1898, scolding them and setting out a new daily schedule of drills. The observations of numerous American officers suggest that his order was widely ignored.[78]

The lack of drilling was not the only problem. Filipino troop dispositions were dangerously vulnerable to attack. South of Manila, the units were set up with the San Juan River to their back, meaning they would have to cross it to retreat; that left them terribly exposed to a chasing force. To encircle the Americans fully, Aguinaldo had essentially put the entire force in the front lines. This meant no reserves to contain an American breakthrough.[79] Finally, the Filipinos stored most of their ammunition up front. This gave them easy access to the bullets, but it also meant that the ammunition was vulnerable to capture or loss.

Still, all these points should not be overestimated. The Philippine Army was highly experienced, relatively well supplied, and effectively armed. It had been fighting for years. If it had defects of training, fighting ability, and organization, so too did the Americans.

The Battlefield

In 1899 Manila was surrounded by walls, built by the Spanish in the late sixteenth century. Though impressive-looking, they had only been patchily updated in the centuries since. They were no match for modern gunpowder weapons, a significant factor in the eagerness of the Spanish to surrender. The American and Filipino forces faced each other in ragged lines outside the walled city (see Map 4.1). Roads ran through those suburbs. The main one was a north-south road that ran along the coast north to the town of Caloocan. A railway paralleled the Caloocan road, the only major train connection with the rest of Luzon. Cutting through both lines farther along were the Pasig and San Juan Rivers. The San Juan River, east of Manila, ran roughly north-south. The Pasig River ran east-west past the walled city and intersected the San Juan. Both rivers were navigable for sizable boats, with the Pasig having a depth of up to eighteen feet. The San Juan could be forded by troops at a number of points, but the Pasig could not, splitting the land into two separate fighting areas.[80] On the other side of the rivers from the city, under the control of the Filipinos, was Manila's water reservoir. The water pipes running from the reservoir into the city came into the American lines near where the 1st Nebraska was positioned, making that a potential flash point.

The suburbs were not the modern type—bedroom communities whose residents mostly worked in the central city. Instead, they were small farming towns and villages. North of the city, the land was reasonably open, sloping upward from the American line to the Filipino. With the exception of some dense woods, the land was passable, open to troop movements and offensive operations. The land also allowed for the development of contiguous defensive lines, centered on the major features of the area—the Chinese cemetery, the La Loma cemetery, and the La Loma church, as well as the old Spanish blockhouses. The Filipinos took advantage of the open land to build substantial entrenchments.[81]

South of the city, the land was cut by crop fields, irrigation ditches, and rice paddies, centered around small settlements of houses. What had not been converted to crops or houses remained forested, with small meandering creeks and streams. This was difficult terrain for military operations. The broken-up nature of the land prevented large units of men from moving quickly or cohesively, a hindrance for offensive actions. The few places where movement was possible were easy to see and thus to defend, leading one such road to be nicknamed "Bloody Lane" by the Spanish.[82] This also made setting up a connected defensive line difficult if not impossible. The Spanish had built fortified blockhouses to command this terrain, rather than trenches. Blockhouse 14, for example, covered Bloody Lane. The Americans and Filipinos adopted similar practices. The strong points in their lines were supplemented by regular patrolling of the land between them. Meanwhile, the rest of the units stayed in camps close behind.[83]

The western Manila suburbs, both north and south of the walled city, were dominated by Manila Bay itself. The massive saltwater bay, one of the best natural harbors in Asia, supported a large economic system based on fishing and shipping. In 1898–1899, those waters were controlled by the American fleet, although ships of other empires, particularly the Germans, often entered. To the south, the ruins of the Spanish fleet still poked above water.

The terrain affected both sides. North of the city, the open spaces and rising slope gave the Filipino defenders a substantial advantage. To the south, neither side benefitted from the broken and mixed terrain. East of the city, the awkwardness of the Filipino lines, straddling the two rivers, made for a dangerous tactical situation if they lost ground. West of the city, the dominance of the American navy gave the Americans an advantage all along the coastline. But while the terrain affected the battle, it did not determine the outcome. That was up to the soldiers.

The Battle

The fighting finally started on February 4, 1899, at the most vulnerable spot in the American line: where the 1st Nebraska Regiment's lines ran between the rivers, protecting the water pipes to the reservoir and sticking like a thumb into the Filipino defenses. The Nebraskans knew of their vulnerability, and Otis had ordered them in late January to be aggressive in their patrolling. One key spot was the small village of Santol. Both sides occupied it at various times, and serious confrontations were averted only by frequent negotiations between Colonel Stotsenberg, the 1st Nebraska commander, and his Filipino counterpart (see Figure 4.2).

The phony peace broke down on February 4. Men from the 1st Nebraska Regiment were patrolling Santol when they encountered a Filipino patrol. Private Willie Grayson was in the lead. "I yelled 'halt' . . . and the man moved," he reported. After some more back-and-forth, Grayson "thought the best thing to do was to shoot him. He dropped."[84] The private, though he did not know it then, had fired the first shot of the battle. After some continued firing on both sides, Grayson and his patrol retreated back toward the lines and gathered other soldiers. Grayson's racism is clear in his instructions to his fellow soldiers. "Line up, fellows. The niggers are in here all through these yards."[85] They took shelter behind a water main and then retreated to camp.

The encounter sparked a conflagration. Immediately after Grayson's shooting of the Filipino, the 1st Nebraska came under heavy and sustained rifle fire. The battle that everyone had waited so long for had finally begun.

American Versus Filipino Infantry

Infantry-versus-infantry combat dominated the battle. Ordinary soldiers fought each other individually, in organized groups, and in mass, swirling melees. For both Americans and Filipinos, the experience of the battle was

OUTPOST TROUBLES AT SAN JUAN BRIDGE
General Hale and Colonel Stotsenburg conferring with Colonel San Miguel a few days
before the outbreak of February 4, 1899

Figure 4.2 U.S. officers negotiating with a Filipino colonel. (Photo from
Marrion Wilcox, ed., *Harper's History of the War in the Philippines* [New York:
Harper & Bros., 1900])

confined to their own narrow slice of it, with little idea what was going on
out of eyeshot. In this, Manila reflected something close to the universal
experience of combat, with each soldier dealing with what was immediately in front, to the side, or behind. As with Monongahela and Makuan,
the battle was not a singular experience, but many individual ones. Only
later, in mess tents, hospitals, homes, and other places, would the soldiers get
an idea of how their experiences fitted into the larger picture. Some would
never know.

This was especially true overnight on February 4. No one, either Filipino or American, grasped what was happening. Without direction from their senior officers, both sides tended to fall back on actions that their experience told them might be useful, such as firing or marching to a better position. At the ignition point, the 1st Nebraska gathered itself for action and moved down to the river line to strengthen its defensive positions. Two companies, noted the regiment's history, "advanced to the brush, fired two volleys, and rushed through the timber to the edge of the swamp bordering the river. Here, the boys lay down behind a hedge."[86] Once in position, the Nebraskans spent the rest of the night flat on their stomachs, firing sporadically.

On the other side of the line, confusion also reigned. Many of the higher officers from the Philippine Army were absent. Aguinaldo was in the capital city, Malolos, as were several of his generals, attending a dance—to, as Aguinaldo's physician put it, pay "homage to Terpsichore."[87] Other officers were with their families for the Sabbath.[88] Without their commanders, the Filipino troops had been paying little attention to the front lines.[89]

When the shooting started, the Filipinos across from the Nebraskans reacted with a burst of activity, at least momentarily. An initial wave of firing was followed by "dead silence." Then, after an hour's pause, the Nebraskans heard a "bugle across the river blew three notes." The Filipinos fired a "volley of Mausers," hitting nothing except foliage. The Nebraskans remained quiet, and the Filipinos stopped firing.[90] A group of Filipinos tried to occupy a bridge over the San Juan River but were driven back by fire from the Nebraska troops. After that, the two sides spent the night in a desultory exchange of fire, inflicting few casualties. There was something of a party atmosphere. "The natives were cheerful," one Nebraskan observed. "Their cheers viva, viva, Republica!" carried across the lines.[91] Another observer noted that the Filipinos often added the phrase "Americanos mucho malo!"[92] Neither side suffered many casualties that night—unsurprising, given the darkness.

The firing and confusion spread beyond the 1st Nebraska's front. On the Filipino side, someone fired rockets into the air, a signal to attack the American forces. Who set the rockets off and on what authority remains unclear, and the Filipino soldiers' response was halfhearted. Some Filipino units attacked, but most remained essentially stationary and simply opened up on the Americans. The rapid fire of thousands of rounds echoed the earlier Filipino sieges of the Spanish, such as at Tayabas, and mostly had similar results. Opposite the 10th Pennsylvania, an initial wave of shooting from the Filipinos was taken as firecrackers being let off, until the officer of the day understood what was happening: "Those are not fire-crackers. The ball is opened."[93] Like the Nebraskans, the 10th moved into a defensive line, putting four more companies at the front and throwing out a line of skirmishers. The skirmishers reported several encounters with the Filipinos, but they seem to have been mostly haphazard and spontaneous, quickly broken off and not resumed. During this entire time, the main force of Filipinos kept up their fire, though without managing to hit anyone on the American side. By contrast, because of the darkness, the 10th's main line did not let off a shot during the night.[94] For most of the soldiers on both sides the experience was one of waiting under cover, peering into the night.

The untried American soldiers found the noise of the shooting and the waiting nerve-racking. "It was," Colonel Frederick Funston, commander of the 20th Kansas, noted, "a new world for all but a few of them."[95] As Funston's men marched forward in the dark, they could hear "the spiteful bullets from the enemy's Mausers . . . enlivening the air overhead with their peculiar popping noise."[96] There was little relief in action for Funston's men. They fired a few volleys at the start but, unable to see any targets, soon gave up. Finally Funston had them lie down in the rice and "take it easy." There they stayed, "getting what sleep they could." The Filipinos across from them continued to fire what sounded like "a million cartridges," but no American got hit.[97] Like the 10th Pennsylvania, the 20th Kansas did not suffer many casualties. Lying on the ground behind cover gave "mighty little chance to bullets fired at random through the darkness half a mile away."[98] The fruitless firing did little good for the Filipinos and drew down their already limited ammunition supplies.

Other American units spent more of their time marching, mostly to no purpose. The commander of the 1st California Regiment moved them up to their defensive line at 8:35 p.m., then back to their quarters at 9:15 p.m. He returned them to the line at 9:45, only to move them back to their quarters once more at 12:30 a.m.[99] Finally, at 4:00 a.m., he let them eat breakfast, and then sent them to join the 6th Artillery Battery for the rest of the night. As with the firing, the point of the marching seemed more an instinctive reaction than the execution of a plan.

The central experience of the night of February 4 was that no one had any real sense of what was going on. Lying there in the dark, the Nebraskans, the Pennsylvanians, and the Kansans all knew that something was happening, but not what. The same was true for the Filipinos across from them. The firing and marching afforded both sides a chance to do something, even if with no hope of real effectiveness. The Kansans got some sleep, while the hapless Californians marched back and forth. The one key difference was that the Americans did much less shooting than the Filipinos. The Filipinos had thus done their duty, if wildly and ineffectively. The Americans had not and came into the morning eager for action. They wanted the chance to relieve the useless stress of the night hours and to prove themselves.

First light gave both sides their chance. They could finally see and understand what lay in front of them. "Daylight, although slow in coming, finally dawned upon us, and was never more welcome," as one historian of the California contingent put it.[100] Everyone was exhausted by the overnight vigil, but there was no time to rest.[101] They had a chance now to do their duty. They might have enlisted to fight against the Spanish, one member of the 1st Montana put it later, but at this point fighting the Filipinos was "a matter of self-defense and just vengeance, and to a man they were eager for the call of duty and the orders of their superiors."[102] Thus, as planned, the Americans attacked.[103]

The experience of the attack was not, as popularly imagined, a close-packed line of men charging speedily forward. Rather, this was a rhythmic tactical movement, with stops and starts: "The [advancing] troops would lie down, fire a few volleys, then up and rush ahead ten or twenty rods [roughly 50 to 100 yards], lie down and fire more volleys," noted the official history of the Wyoming Battalion.[104] When they got close, then a full-on charge into the defenders might well happen. As seen with John Bowe's account of his day, attacks were often not so neat: moving forward, lying in the hot sun under fire, dozing, telling jokes, hearing a war cry, rushing forward, and then dozing again. Fear, duty, and napping all intermingled. For some, the stress was too much. Colonel Smith of the 1st Nebraska, the unit's official history sadly noted, "fell from his horse and died of apoplexy [a stroke] at the moment of the charge."[105]

As much as anything, the ground shaped the soldier's experience of moving forward. They clambered through the natural terrain, which included "dense woods and bamboo thickets," as a historian of the Philippines campaign noted.[106] They had to maneuver on and around artificial terrain, such as "stone walls and convents, churches and houses, [and] blazing bamboo huts."[107] It was hard physical work. The terrain, both natural and artificial, shaped the combat as well. The Filipinos had built their defenses using what already existed, and thus much of the fighting happened around a defensive site, such as the old Spanish blockhouses, cemeteries, and churches.

As the American attack advanced, the Filipinos had a choice to make. One option was to stay, try to hold the line, and engage in hand-to-hand combat if necessary. Each soldier had to make his own decision, though one man retreating could often inspire another to go as well. When the 10th Pennsylvania attacked, the Filipinos hit them with a "galling fire" as they advanced. The 10th kept moving forward and finally charged home and "swept" the Filipinos out. But it is clear that not all the Filipinos remained to fight. By the time the men of the 10th arrived, there were "few insurgents" left in the trenches. Many had been killed, but some had chosen to fall back. Many of the remaining defenders chose to surrender rather than fight. Actual hand-to-hand combat was rather rarer than imagined.[108]

Rare but not non-existent—in a number of cases, fighting in the Filipino lines was close and intense. Funston remembered the end of the 20th Kansas's attack: "Over the first line of rifle-pits [we] swept with clubbed rifles, crushing to the earth whoever bore the Filipino colors. . . . It was hand to hand work in indescribable confusion."[109] Writing later, Funston could not or would not even find the words for what happened; he stated simply that this was "the only time in my life that I saw the bayonet actually used."[110] The wounds of such close-range combat were horrific. Bullets fired at close range hardly had time to slow before slamming through bodies. Incompletely burned gunpowder seared scattershot burns on skin. Rifles used as clubs inflicted concussions and internal bleeding, while bayonet stab wounds perforated blood vessels and organs. Most of these wounds were not immediately fatal, leaving the victim to bleed out or die of shock. They did not do so silently, and the wounded intermingled with the dead on the ground. Histories of the battle recount that some trenches were filled with "an unbroken line of killed and wounded" all mixed together.[111] At this range, the experience for everyone was violent and personal. The attackers and defenders resolved into individuals, rather than simply faceless enemies. It was intense and disturbingly intimate.

Most of the encounters were at greater distances, medium to long range, typically several hundred yards. Because the Filipino soldiers frequently retreated before the Americans could close, in many cases neither side came to grips with the other. A witness from the 1st Colorado Regiment described the experience. As the "savage line" of the 1st attacked, "the occupants of the blockhouse never stayed to answer consequences. They fled like sheep."[112] Such a retreat did not come without its own risks. Leaving the defensive cover exposed the fleeing Filipinos to fire from behind, and the "good marksmen from the Rockies brought them down with their terrible Springfield bullets."[113] Unlike close range, fighting at a distance meant that the soldiers never encountered their enemy as individuals. They were no more than targets, "sheep" to be shot down.[114]

In fact, many of the Americans never saw the Filipinos. The defenders started off unseen in their trenches, behind their fortifications, and in their strong points. An officer might appear, directing fire, but the Americans only knew the Filipinos were there from the bullets that flew around them. They could not see the slugs themselves or (because of the smokeless powder) much evidence of them being fired, but they could hear and see their effect on the people and ground around them. Combat became about the bullets and the terrain rather than the people. "They held their fire until the troops were all in sight over the hill and in plain view," noted the official history of the 1st Wyoming, "when they turned loose hundreds of Mausers and Remingtons from the churchyard of San Pedro de Macati, the buildings and kilns, in the village and along the banks of the river. Private Ray F. Weidmer of Company C fell mortally wounded, and Private Harry R. Crumrine of Company F was slightly wounded in the foot, before we could avail ourselves of the natural protection of rice-field levees." The chronicler notes that the Americans "poured volley after volley into their breastworks."[115] Here, for the Americans, there were no individual Filipinos, only a generic "enemy" or "insurgent." They were an invisible presence. When the U.S. forces shot back, they were firing not at the Filipinos but at their breastworks. Only when the Filipinos broke cover did they become visible, but then from behind, not face-to-face.

The contrast between the two experiences—the intensely intimate, close-range, and horrifying violence of the combat in the trenches and the dehumanized, almost invisible enemy of the longer-range engagement—is startling. Because the Americans mostly experienced the fight at long range, they could stay comfortable in their view of the Filipinos as avatars of an inferior race, and not as real people.

Artillery Versus Infantry

Another encounter started during the night of February 4, involving artillery. From the start, both sides used their heavy guns. In the darkness, as for
the individual soldiers, it was hard for the artillery to find targets. "It was
impossible for the Utah guns to accomplish anything," wrote the official
historian of the Utah Volunteer Artillery, "as the location of the infantry
could not be exactly distinguished." So they too had to wait for morning.
"All night the men tugged and toiled to get the pieces in position, that they
might take part in the encounter at dawn."[116] The day did indeed bring
the guns into play, with both American and Filipino forces opening up on
the other.

A fundamental part of the experience of being shelled was that both
sides could see and hear the rounds coming. The muzzle velocity of almost
all the shells was low enough that they were visible in flight. Their targets
could both see and hear them on the way. When the 20th Kansas was
moving up, the Filipinos fired on them with their large siege gun, whose
shell, Colonel Funston recalled, made a "sound like a young cyclone."[117]
Hearing this, "the front half of the regiment all but prostrated itself."[118]
Bravado soon kicked in for the 20th, and as the projectiles arrived, the
soldiers "began to call out derisively, 'low ball' or 'high ball' according to
the merit of each shot."[119]

The effect of being shelled varied for each army. American infantry units
tended to be on the move and were thus less vulnerable; the Filipino shells
passed overhead. No American unit seems to have been hit by a significant number of Filipino shells, though the noise and explosions were still
intimidating. By contrast, the Filipinos experienced something much different. The Americans used their artillery to "soften up" the Filipino defensive lines before an attack started.[120] The Filipinos were pinned to their
fortifications, which made easy targets and did not offer much protection
against the heavy guns. For example, the carefully positioned guns from
the Utah Volunteer Artillery (see Figure 4.5) led off an assault by the 1st
Colorado Regiment on the church and blockhouse that served as the centerpiece of the Filipino line. Several "well-directed shells sent the Filipinos
flying from the blockhouse and a few more accurately trained shots
annihilated the little church."[121]

The illustration presents the view of the strongest Spanish blockhouse outside of Manila in Luzon The men in the trenches are U. S. Third Artillery acting as infantry.

Figure 4.3 The 3rd U.S. Artillery on the firing line in front of a blockhouse. (Photo from Marrion Wilcox, ed., *Harper's History of the War in the Philippines* [New York: Harper & Bros., 1900])

This created an untenable tactical situation for the Filipino defenders. If they remained in their strong points, they were targets for the artillery. But if they retreated, the American infantry could pick them off once they were out from cover. This is, in fact, exactly what happened to the defenders the Coloradans were attacking. When the artillery forced the Filipinos from their cover, "they fell many deep before the blasting volleys of the invincible Coloradans."[122] The Filipinos quickly realized the problem and began vacating their defensive positions as soon as they saw artillery pieces being brought into position.[123]

When it did hit, the artillery inflicted horrific wounds. At one point on the 1st Nebraska's line, the fighting was channeled by the bridge between the two sides. Two Filipino assaults across the bridge, made with "frenzied courage," were "torn to pieces by the shrieking shells and the deadly bullets."[124] Though this type of damage has tended to be identified with World War I, it has a long history before that conflict. Solid shot, slower than rifle bullets but enormously heavier, would demolish anyone it hit.[125] Explosive shells gave off a shock wave that concussed and crushed people, along with a wave of shrapnel of varying sizes, flying at supersonic speed and shredding those it struck.

Doing the worst damage were the naval guns, which, as noted, were much bigger. The shells, especially the 500-pounders from the USS *Monadnock*, were beyond any previous Filipino experience—the Spanish had nothing like it—and undergoing such shelling was utterly terrifying. Their effects were similar to those of the field artillery rounds, but on a much larger scale. The explosive overpressure from a direct hit could knock down a stone building and even at some distance burst eardrums, collapse lungs, and concuss heads.[126] The shrapnel crushed and shredded people.[127]

For all their power, it's not clear how accurate the naval guns actually were. The American ships, without forward spotters, were firing essentially blind. When the Kansans mistakenly came under fire from the USS *Concord* at one point after capturing part of the enemy's lines, none of the ship's shells hit close enough to inflict any casualties. Similarly, naval guns aiming at a Filipino artillery piece came nowhere near enough to hit it, though the crew abandoned it anyway.[128] The effect of the naval guns was perhaps as much about intimidation as actual effect.

The artillerymen often paid for their efforts. They pushed their guns right up to or forward of their infantry and tended to stand upright, making them the most visible and vulnerable targets on the field. The same guns from Utah that did such damage to the Filipinos in front of the 1st Nebraska lines suffered for their work: "Every time one of the cannon roared over the hill, she raised a vicious hail of bullets from the enemy." Soon "Corporal John G. Young received a fatal wound in the lungs. Almost immediately after Private Wilhelm I. Goodman fell dead with a bullet through his brain."[129]

Offense Versus Defense

As we have seen, combat experience in the Battle of Manila was shaped by being on offense or defense. It is worth examining this in detail, as it was a group experience different from the infantry-versus-infantry encounter. When the American soldiers attacked on the morning of February 5, most of the Filipino soldiers held their ground at first. Here the critical moment came for the Americans when they had to calculate whether their attack could break into the line of the defenders. For the Filipinos, the calculation

was whether their defense could stop them. These were close to simultaneous moments, from opposite ends of the battlefield.

The American commanders had deliberately chosen to put their men
on the offensive. They could have remained on the defensive, relying on
their own lines and interior position to ward off a Filipino assault. Instead,
from the moment the darkness cleared, American officers advocated for an
offensive. They had planned for it, and this was the opportunity. General
MacArthur strongly urged Otis in that direction. There was no longer any
chance for a peaceful resolution, he felt. The men were wound up and ready
to move after a night of being under fire, and the Filipino soldiers wouldn't
withstand a vigorous attack. Otis did not disagree. Both believed the enemy
was inferior in every sense. The exact balance between their observations
of the previous month and their racial attitudes in shaping the plan is unclear, but it is hard to imagine either of these Civil War veterans mounting
a major frontal assault against a defended position, even against ill-trained
troops, if they had not perceived the Filipinos as racially inferior.

Otis ordered a general assault by all the American units. North of the
city, MacArthur launched his forces forward at eight o'clock that morning,
starting on the right of his line, with the 1st Nebraska, the 1st South Dakota,
and the 1st Colorado. Success there covered the right flank of the rest of
the units, which attacked a little bit later. As we have seen, frontal assault
did not mean a full-out sprint from one line toward the other. The distance
was too great, and the men would have arrived exhausted, if they arrived
at all. Instead, the assaults started forward slowly, laying down a suppressing
fire from both rifle and artillery. As the Americans got closer, they reached
the moment of decision: they could stop, go to ground, and stay there; they
could retreat; or they could move forward. Within a certain distance, the
artillery could no longer fire for fear of friendly casualties, and the attack
had to move as quickly as possible.[130] Almost all of MacArthur's forces that
morning came to the moment of decision and pressed forward. Officers
and men both believed that they could successfully break the Filipino lines.

On the Filipino side of the field, confusion reigned. Many officers were
still absent, and many units had been scattered by overnight movements.
Aguinaldo had sent out a reassuring order that morning, but it was short on
specifics.[131] For the most part, the majority of Filipino units decided on their
own to remain "strictly on the defensive" during the day.[132] The American
attack was not what they were used to, as one Filipino officer recounted.
When they had fought the Spanish, the officer said, "we would fire and

they would fire, and after a while we would stop and they would stop. [The] Americans jumped up and ran at us."[133]

When the Americans attacked, it was up to the officers and soldiers at the knife end of the assault to decide what to do. Absent orders, Filipino soldiers fell back on their cultural understanding of their responsibilities. They owed service to their patrons, but they did not owe the sacrifice of their lives, either by attacking or by staying in a defensive position that was about to be overrun. When the moment of crisis came, the Filipinos largely decided that they could not hold the line against the United States and retreated.

Why did the Americans feel their attacks would be successful? Why did the Filipino soldiers tend to agree? At that time, a frontal assault on a well-defended line should have been near suicidal, as had been seen in the Civil War, in the Russo-Japanese War a few years later, and, most obviously, as would be seen in World War I. In fact, at about the same time as the Battle of Manila, the British Army was in combat against the Boers, German-Dutch settlers in South Africa, and discovered that mounting frontal assaults against defended positions got their soldiers slaughtered.[134]

The answer to the question lies in accuracy, or its lack. As we have already seen, the Filipinos were terrible riflemen. Sabotaged by their lack of training and shortage of ammunition, the Filipinos could not hit a target beyond a range of about a hundred yards, most especially not Americans moving quickly across a field. As Funston recalled, they were "simply splattering the whole country with bullets, the great majority of them going far over our heads."[135] The Filipino tendency to shoot high made it safer to be on the front lines, with the bullets whistling overhead, than in the rear areas, where the bullets finally plunged to earth. This started to become clear during the nighttime, when not one Nebraskan was hurt, but their camp, far behind the lines, was cut to pieces, with Filipino bullets doing "sad work punching holes in the tents and smashing the furniture and crockery." To avoid death and wounding, the only remaining people in the camp, the Chinese cooks, created an "impregnable position" by barricading themselves with "sacks of flour, potatoes and commissary supplies."[136] The inaccuracy continued during the daytime, something the Americans noted. "As long as they aim at us," one American officer said, "we're all right."[137] Because they could not hit the Americans, they could not hurt them, and the American soldiers soon discovered that they had little to fear as they attacked. George Osborne, of the 1st Tennessee, said that because of this inaccuracy, he was "not all uneasy about being shot."[138]

The Filipino inability to hammer the American frontal assaults meant that the advantage that defenders had with their long-range, modern weapons disappeared. American soldiers should have been cut to pieces long before they reached the defenders. Instead, the attacking units arrived almost intact. The American officers quickly learned the lesson that, as Sexton put it, "regardless of the protection of entrenchments or redoubts, the insurgents either would not or could not stand up before the attacks of American troops."[139] The first frontal assault of February 5 had been a gamble. The follow-up attacks were cold calculation based, as Funston said, on "the experience [we] obtained."[140]

As a result, the American soldiers could cross almost to the Filipino lines and take their attack in without suffering heavy casualties. The Filipino defenders usually retreated when U.S. forces got within a few hundred yards of them. This pattern occurred over and over again on February 5. The Americans would mount a frontal assault and the Filipinos would fall back, getting cut to pieces as they did. Whatever defensive position the survivors ended up at would then be assaulted by the Americans. This was the central tactical trap for the Philippine Army in the battle. They could not hold the line against American attacks, and they could not even inflict substantial casualties in trade. Meanwhile, they were sustaining heavy losses. There was no escaping the trap, and it doomed any chance the Philippine Army had that day.

It is worth taking a look at the course of the day to see the pattern. As noted, MacArthur started a general offensive first thing in the morning. The 20th Kansas, the 3rd United States Artillery (acting as infantry), and the 10th Pennsylvania attacked straight north out of the American lines, with Manila behind them and the Filipinos in front. The rail line and the road northward made this a particularly important area. If the Filipinos could hold those two communication arteries, they could block the Americans from the interior of Luzon. The Filipino defensive position there was a solid one, at the top of a long sweeping hill, upon which rested the Chinese cemetery and, behind it, the La Loma church and cemetery, all of them fortified. The Spanish blockhouses in the area offered the Filipinos another set of hard points (see Figures 4.3 and 4.4).

The 20th Kansas, up against Manila Bay on their left, faced a thick forest occupied by Filipinos to their front. Their initial move forward was checked by heavy fire, and Funston pulled his men back into line and had them direct volleys into the woods (see Figure 4.4). That, along with shelling from

In this view may be seen a strong blockhouse in course of erection, and in the foreground a line of Twentieth Kansas Volunteers skirmishing just before they made their magnificent charge.

Figure 4.4 The 20th Kansas fires on the Filipino lines during the battle. (F. Tennyson Neely, *Fighting in the Philippines* [London: F. Tennyson Neely, 1899])

the ships offshore, dislodged the defenders, and the 20th pushed through the forest and occupied the first line of defensive trenches. To their right, the 3rd Artillery, the 1st Montana, and the 10th Pennsylvania assaulted the area of the Chinese cemetery and La Loma church. Colonel Alexander Hawkins of the Pennsylvania Regiment, in overall command of the attack, sent the 1st Montana forward into the Chinese cemetery and had the 3rd Artillery and 10th Pennsylvania move to their left and right to flank and attack the La Loma church. They were helped by units of the 1st South Dakota, who, having successfully managed their own assault, joined the attack at La Loma. The plan worked. The Filipinos kept up a heavy but inaccurate fire until the Americans had closed to about two hundred yards away, and then they made a "precipitate retreat," pulling back to another line farther north.[141] After the church's capture, the 10th attacked and captured the second Filipino defensive line in the La Loma cemetery, pushing the Filipinos back even farther. None of the American units experienced many casualties.

All across MacArthur's line, when the first attack launched, the Filipino defenders retreated immediately, breaking away from their prepared fortifications. One observer said that the defenders in front of them "scurried

THE UTAH BATTERY AT WORK

Figure 4.5 The Utah Battery at work. (F. Tennyson Neely, *Fighting in the Philippines* [London: F. Tennyson Neely, 1899])

into the surrounding hill like rabbits."[142] Another said—revealingly—that the "Indians were stampeded" by the attack.[143]

South of the Pasig River, the situation was mostly similar, but on a smaller scale. North of the river, the Americans had mounted regimental-sized assaults, but the terrain south of the river forced them to operate in company-sized units. As outlined before, the Filipino defenses south of the river were anchored on Manila Bay and then went straight east to Blockhouse 14. After that the line turned sharply northeast, skirted in front of the San Juan River, and finally ended on the Pasig River. American forces were arrayed inside that long and angled line, and the main southern road leading out of Manila bisected both armies as it headed out just past Blockhouse 14. For the most part, the two armies were a fair distance apart, but at the confluence of the Pasig and San Juan, they were within a few dozen yards of each other.

Major General Thomas Anderson, commanding the 1st Division south of the river, originally planned an assault by the right side of his line between Manila Bay and the blockhouse. Capturing that part of the Filipino line, and especially the blockhouse, would secure the flank of a more substantial advance on the left side of his line and, he hoped, enable him to push the Filipinos back across the San Juan River. He instructed Brigadier General Samuel Ovenshine, commanding the forces there, to attack with the 1st North Dakota, and then, once they had broken in, to pivot to their left and roll up the defenders leading to the blockhouse. At the same time, the 14th U.S. Infantry would attack the blockhouse itself. Once the flank was secure, Anderson thought, he would push forward the left side of his line.

The attack happened in exactly the reverse order: Anderson's left wing assaulted first, and then his right. It's not entirely clear why Ovenshine did not do as Anderson had ordered, but the 1st North Dakota and the 14th U.S. Infantry did not get moving until midmorning. Hours before they moved, the 1st Idaho and 1st Washington assaulted General del Pilar's Filipino units on the far left of Anderson's command. They attacked, noted Sexton, "with shouts that resembled everything from a cowboy's 'yipee' to an old Civil War rebel yell."[144] Again the Filipinos did not hold, and the combined attack quickly broke into the defenses despite point-blank fire from several Filipino artillery pieces. It was the same pattern seen elsewhere: as soon as the United States got close, as the official historian of the 1st Washington wrote, the Filipino soldiers started "leaving their redoubts and their entrenchments . . . and going in all directions."[145]

Even when the Filipinos had an especially strong defensive position, they could not hold. The 14th U.S. Infantry attacked down Bloody Lane against defenses centered around Blockhouse 14, the formidable hinge of the Filipino line. The U.S. attack initially stalled, but the defensive success did not last. A renewed attack on the blockhouse by U.S. forces, including a daring foray by seven American soldiers into the structure itself, carried the position, cracking the defenses wide open.[146]

A similar situation occurred near Blockhouse 11. The Filipino defenders there had built fortifications on top of a mound in the middle of a bare field flanked by two creeks. The only way to attack was from the front, and the Filipino defenders were pouring "a very hot fire" into the attacking Americans.[147] The Americans nonetheless charged over Concordia Creek, through rice fields, and up the steep sides of a knoll. Despite what seemed a suicidal attack, the Filipinos simply could not hold the hill and were overrun by the Americans. There were dozens of dead in the trenches, and many more were wounded or taken prisoner.[148] The losses of the 1st Washington during this attack are not recorded, but for the entire day, they had only nine killed and forty-six wounded.

In all of these cases, the Filipinos failed to inflict meaningful casualties on the American forces. Neither the 14th U.S. Infantry nor the 1st Washington suffered significant losses in their attacks. Nowhere along the line, either north or south of the river, were American casualties heavy. Civil War veteran that he was, MacArthur must have been pleasantly surprised by the relative lack of wounded and dead. "If the Insurgents had known how to shoot," MacArthur conceded later, "the losses to the American Army would have terrified the nation."[149]

Once the defensive lines broke, the Filipinos found themselves falling back with the Americans close behind. Without the protection of their fortifications, often unable to shoot back, and taking heavy fire, they found that their fate depended on the topography through which they were retreating. For example, southeast of Manila, del Pilar's troops found retreat blocked by the San Juan River. Their only chance of escape was to swim the river, but as they did so, the pursuing Americans lined up on the river-bank and slaughtered them mercilessly. William Luhn, an officer with the 1st Washington, wrote, chillingly, "Big game hunting, which the western volunteers had often found a practical necessity while at home, turned into pot shooting of Insurgents attempting to cross the river. The marksmanship of the western volunteers was so accurate that not a single one was seen to reach the opposite bank."[150] Estimates are that about 700 Filipinos were killed in the retreat, and Major General Anderson reported several days later that Filipino bodies "have been floating down the stream ever since."[151]

In other cases, the path of retreat offered a succession of natural defensive positions. For example, south of the river, Filipino units repeatedly used the omnipresent irrigation dikes (for the rice paddies) to fall back a few yards, turn, and shoot at the U.S. attackers, a textbook case of retreating under fire.[152] South of the rice fields, urban spaces provided useful fall-back positions. The 1st California and 1st Wyoming, south of the Pasig, attacked into the towns of Santa Ana and San Pedro de Macati, and found that they had to work their way over walls and around buildings against Filipino resistance centered on several strong points. Albert Southwick, a soldier with the California and Wyoming forces, wrote that "the nigs were so well hidden and using smokeless powder, it was almost impossible to find any of them."[153] The Americans slowed from a rush to a careful advance, filling "the trees and bushes full of lead" and shooting into houses.[154] Some American soldiers burned the houses, despite the women and children inside.[155] The defenders managed to slow the U.S. assault enough that the rest of the Filipino units retreated to safety past the monastery of Guadalupe, a mile south, the only time the Filipinos held.

The overwhelming success and rapid exploitation meant that multiple American units advanced much farther than anyone expected, and the results could be somewhat chaotic. The 20th Kansas was so scattered by its success that Funston had to resort to impromptu measures to continue: "The men were so mixed up that it was hopeless to get a company or platoon intact, so I gathered about a dozen of the officers and men nearest me, and we carried it with a rush."[156] By the end of the day, American units were scattered widely, to the point that Otis did not know where many of his forces were. Most reported in quickly, but the location of the 1st California Regiment remained a mystery for a few hours. Scattered or not, the Americans had won a resounding victory, inflicting heavy casualties on the Philippine Army, suffering relatively few of their own, and breaking the siege of Manila.

At the end of the day, the Americans believed that they had learned another lesson. Otis and MacArthur and Anderson's initial frontal assaults came at least partly because of their racism, and the success of those attacks confirmed that assumption for them. It is telling that in the one place where the Filipinos managed even a hint of success in the defense, in Santa Ana and San Pedro de Macati, General Anderson blamed the American soldiers, who he thought did not "advance with the energy of the rest of the line."[157] For Anderson, it could not be a Filipino success; it had to be an American failure. The corollary to this racial analysis was that if the Filipinos were incompetent because of their race, they could never be anything else. The "American mode of conducting warfare," Otis wrote after the battle, was simply superior.[158] This racist belief would come back to haunt them later when the Filipinos showed themselves adept at insurgent warfare.

The Wounded and the Dead

During the battle and after, both sides had to deal with the wounded and the dead. Bullets carried enormous kinetic energy. They plowed through most obstacles—vegetation, walls, human flesh. No one hit by such a bullet, an American officer commented, "mistook it for a mosquito bite."[159] They shattered bone, tore flesh, and ripped blood vessels, and then often exited from the other side, leaving both entry and exit wounds. An American officer described a Filipino hit by a Springfield round that essentially blew "the man's head off." It looked "as if he had been struck by a shell."[160]

Death could be instantaneous, as it was for Private Charles Pratt of the 1st Kansas Regiment, who was shot through the head and "sank down without a sound." For some time his body lay there, "a gruesome spectacle for those who had occasion to pass near."[161] For most casualties, however, the immediate threat was blood loss and shock. Santiago Barcelona, a Filipino surgeon, described a wounded officer who looked "very pale" from "profuse hemorrhage."[162] The first important thing to do was to stop the bleeding, something well understood at the time. Shock, which could easily be fatal, was known, but how to treat it effectively was not.[163] The bullet would also likely carry fragments of clothing and equipment into the wound with it, introducing a host of germs and setting the stage for infection. Antibiotics were still in the future, but the germ theory was established, and so the medical services knew to clean the wounds as best they could. Nonetheless, infection was not uncommon and often fatal.

The key for the wounded soldier, as always, was to get medical treatment as soon as possible. On the American side, there was a fairly well-organized system of medical care. Every soldier carried a first-aid pack that could be used to help a comrade—an item, one surgeon remembered, that "they were taught to regard . . . as their most precious possession, after their rifle."[164] Each regiment had three surgeons attached to it, a head surgeon and two assistants, along with a number of hospital corpsmen. The doctors were largely civilian, often without "the slightest knowledge of medico-military matters," as one army doctor ruefully noticed.[165] The civilian doctors were quickly shocked out of any complacency. One of them wrote, "We had an idea that we were fully competent to deal with the necessities of the occasion, but soon we found our ignorance was sublime."[166]

During the fighting, the United States set up field hospitals as close behind the front lines as was possible. Originally the stretcher-bearers were Americans, but the medical commanders decided that being white was a disadvantage in the "hot, humid, tropical climate," and they were replaced with "Chinese coolies."[167] Each regiment also had horse-drawn ambulance wagons, and they moved the wounded as well. An injured American soldier collected by the stretcher-bearers and taken to a field hospital immediately behind the line would have his wound cleaned and bound there, and then be loaded on an ambulance to be taken back to the nearest permanent facility. Depending on how severe the wound was, he might be moved into Manila for treatment and recuperation, and even sent back to the United States. On the day of the battle itself, because the Americans were the attackers, their wounded usually remained within the U.S. area of control. The medical system treated those wounded effectively, helped by the relatively low numbers of casualties.

The Filipinos also had a medical system, with bearers at the front to carry the wounded out, treatment centers near the lines to treat them, and then hospitals farther back where they could recuperate. Their doctors were civilians as well, but many of them had served throughout the revolt against Spain and thus had extensive combat medicine experience. Filipino care was effective enough that at least one soldier shot through the lungs with a Springfield bullet survived.[168] The overall effort was crippled, however, by the rapid collapse of their defensive lines. Though they were able to evacuate some of their wounded, many of those stricken fell in areas that came under U.S. control and could not be rescued by their own medical services.[169] "Our hospitals," General Otis reported to Washington afterward, "are filled with [Filipino] wounded."[170] The Americans generally seem to have treated wounded Filipinos well.[171] Rudyard Kipling would have been proud.

There were wounds other than physical. Post-traumatic stress disorder, as the condition is known now, was recognized during the Philippine-American War, though it was then identified as an extreme form of "nostalgia" or "homesickness."[172] It seems to have become much more of an issue later in the war, when the grinding insurgency wore down soldiers on both sides. The psychological impact probably hit the Filipinos hardest, dealing as they were with such a humiliating defeat in their own land. Aguinaldo ordered the disarming of a number of units who were demoralized enough that they could no longer fight.

The dead carried none of the urgency of the wounded, but they still had to be handled. The Americans, for the most part, remained in control of their dead soldiers. Fatalities were transported to the hospital by the same system that took the wounded. After that, they were the responsibility of the head chaplain of the American forces. He would organize a coffin for the body and set up a funeral, with a chaplain giving the service and the playing of "Taps" over the coffin. Regimental comrades were usually in attendance. For the most part, the American dead were buried in graveyards in the Philippines rather than being sent home. The exceptions to this were officers, who were sometimes returned home for burial. Because the Americans had suffered a relatively low number of fatalities and the fighting took place in or near Manila, the system for handling the bodies did not get overwhelmed. Most of the dead were buried quickly and effectively. Later in the war, because American units had gone deep into the jungle, handling dead bodies sometimes became difficult, especially in the warm seasons, when decay rapidly became an issue.

On the Filipino side, as with the wounded, substantial numbers of dead soldiers ended up under American control. Their bodies had to be dealt with before they decayed, risking an outbreak of disease. As was common in almost every modern war in which Americans were involved, photos of the dead Filipinos became a cottage industry.[173] They were sometimes taken as souvenirs, with an American soldier posing beside the dead bodies, as they might next to the results of a big-game hunt (see Figure 4.6). Many such photos were taken by reporters and sent back to the United States for publication, evidence of the "wonderful execution," as photographer Frank

After the battle of Santa Ana, February 5, 1899

Figure 4.6 American soldiers standing over dead Filipinos. (F. Tennyson Neely, *Fighting in the Philippines* [London: F. Tennyson Neely, 1899])

Neely put it, done by the Americans.[174] There is little evidence of the taking of another kind of souvenir, the body parts of the dead, as would happen in World War II.[175]

The Americans put most of the Filipino dead in mass graves, often in the trenches in which they had been killed. It was simpler and faster. Leonard F. Adams, a soldier in the 1st Washington, wrote of burying the Filipinos ("dead niggers"): "We would rake them up in a pile, dig a hole, and dump them in, throw a little dirt over them, and go ahead."[176] The American attitude seemed to be that the remains were a problem to be solved, not individuals to be consecrated.

The Legacy: A Guerrilla War

Not one Filipino defensive line, north or south of the river, remained intact by the end of February 5. The American forces had triumphed with relatively few casualties, less than a hundred dead, and only a few hundred wounded. "The dusky fellows," Earl Pearsall of the 1st Nebraska wrote, "don't care for any more of this warfare with the Americano."[177] The individual soldiers replayed the battle afterward. "They were a happy lot," Funston said of his soldiers, "having gone not without credit through their first engagement, and spent a good deal of the time, when they should have been sleeping, in exchanging experiences."[178]

The defeat did not destroy the Philippine Army, however. Some of the units, especially those of del Pilar's command west of the city, suffered heavily, with numerous soldiers killed, wounded, or captured. Del Pilar admitted that he had experienced a "complete setback.[179] But many of the units had retreated before the American attacks got to grips with them, and so had suffered much less. The Americans estimated that the Filipinos lost 4,000 casualties, including 700 dead, but as the historian Brian Linn puts it, that was "total guesswork."[180] The Filipinos reported 1,050 killed and wounded, a more reliable estimate, but probably too low, given how many fell within American lines.[181] With roughly 12,000 troops at Manila, the casualty rate was as high as 10 percent, high but not catastrophic. In addition to the casualties, the loss of supplies was critical. American units captured large caches of ammunition, compromising a Filipino force already short of bullets and with little chance of sustained resupply.[182]

Despite the problems, Aguinaldo still had an army at the end of the day, and that army set out about gathering itself north of Manila near Caloocan. There they built new defensive lines with "feverish haste," in Funston's account.[183] On February 7, 1899, Aguinaldo issued a decree calling on his officers "to encourage the troops who are cast down by the small advantages gained by the enemy. The old revolutionary leaders are called on; troops completely demoralized are to be disarmed."[184] Two weeks later, he established universal conscription.[185] The Filipinos might have lost a battle, but they had not yet lost the war.

The battle broke the Filipino encirclement of Manila, though American officers reported a number of minor engagements overnight on February 5.[186] Aguinaldo was determined to reestablish a threat to Manila, and he began planning an assault on the capital city. Before he could mount the attack, American forces under MacArthur attacked Caloocan on February 10 and pushed the Filipinos out of the city and northward toward Malolos. There Otis called a halt to the advance because he wanted to reorganize the American forces, still scattered after the unexpected start of the war. Aguinaldo and General Luna, his main military commander, used the pause to attack Manila again, bypassing American forces in Caloocan and mounting an assault against Tondo and Santa Cruz, two northern suburbs of the city. Luna infiltrated his men through the scattered American units north of the city, and on February 22 they started fires in the suburbs and then went on the offensive. They had some initial success and managed to inflict substantial property damage, but the Filipino units were simply not well enough organized to follow up effectively. Moreover, Luna had put his own men into a vise between the American units still in Manila proper and MacArthur's men in Caloocan. The Americans quickly caught the Filipinos in the pincer. Worse, the two suburbs were directly on the coast, and so American ships contributed their fire support, pounding the Filipinos. The resulting defeat was the last time that the Filipinos mounted a serious assault on Manila. After February 1899, American control of the capital city would never be seriously threatened.

The first legacy of the Battle of Manila was that it officially started the war between the United States and the Philippine Republic. The phony peace had been broken and now full-scale war was at hand. At home, the news of the battle helped McKinley gain Senate ratification of the Treaty of Paris (by only one vote). The Philippines were legally American land, at least by the imperial rules of the day. The American public's reaction to the news of the war was mixed. There was not the wild outpouring of excitement that there had been at the start of the Spanish-American War, but Americans were still cheered by news of the triumph.

It might be better to say that the battle started the first Philippine-American war. The conflict that raged after Manila was a resolutely symmetrical one, fought by armies on battlefields, with front lines and rear areas, ranging across the archipelago, but mostly concentrated in the central Luzon plain, and using massed firepower. The *second* Philippine-American war was a guerrilla war that began in late 1899 and took place throughout the Philippines, with almost nothing resembling battlefields or front lines. The shift from one war to another emerged from the lessons of Manila. The lesson the Americans had learned there—that the Filipinos would not stand up to a concerted attack—was one that they never had to unlearn during that initial campaign. The combat that followed Manila was usually a repeat of the first battle, where Filipino units repeatedly cracked under sustained assault from American troops and were unable to inflict meaningful casualties. They fired inaccurately at medium to long ranges, and when the distance closed they proved unwilling to hold their positions against the oncoming U.S. soldiers. The scenes at the Chinese cemetery, the La Loma church, the blockhouses, Bloody Lane, and the San Juan River repeated themselves again and again. Even when a Filipino unit did hold, they often found themselves alone as the rest of their force crumbled. This was an unsustainable tactical equation. The Filipinos could not hold their ground and they were taking much heavier losses than the Americans.

The constant defeats caused fractures in the delicate alliances that held together Aguinaldo's forces. The Tagalog dominance of Filipino society and culture rankled other groups, and many of them began to think about switching sides. On February 12, for example, the local Macabebe ethnic group sent messengers to Otis, offering to join forces and bring 3,000 armed men with them, an omen of things to come. Aguinaldo was saved then by Otis's rigid refusal of the offer. Not all American commanders turned out to be quite as hidebound as Otis, however, and many began actively recruiting the Filipinos to the U.S. side.

By the fall of 1899, Aguinaldo himself was only a few steps ahead of the pursuing Americans, and he realized that he had to change his methods. He made the decision sitting on a mountaintop where he had found refuge with a group of headhunters (whose skills, he was worried, they might be thinking about applying to him). He sent out orders for the Philippine Army to organize into "flying columns and guerrilla bands," and disperse

into the highlands and jungle regions.[187] There they would turn to guerrilla tactics, perhaps unconsciously inheriting the mantle of his former
Spanish overlords and their resistance to Napoleon. This meant focusing
on ambushing the U.S. units and attacking soft targets such as supply
convoys and railroad lines. It meant avoiding open confrontations. The tactical combat resembled Manila in many ways—the experience of infantry
versus infantry at the ground level—but the Filipinos avoided prolonged
engagements. They attacked, then melted away before the Americans could
bring to bear their heavy artillery and go in with an assault. These tactics
let them escape the unsustainable tactical situation that had crushed them
at Manila and afterward.

Aguinaldo found the strategy distasteful, for he believed that he was
conceding sovereignty to the Americans and jeopardizing the nascent
Philippine Republic. But he saw no other choice. What started then, and
lasted much longer than the first war, was the second Philippine-American
war: an asymmetrical insurgency that relied on small units and hearts-and-
minds tactics on both sides. The Americans did not at first understand what
had happened. They had taken the same lessons from the initial fighting that
Aguinaldo had. But they also remained persuaded that the Filipinos were
an inferior race, simply incapable of fighting effectively, no matter what
strategies or tactics they used. Race trumped all. "The Filipinos," MacArthur
resolutely intoned, "are not a warlike or ferocious people."[188]

As a result, when Aguinaldo shifted his approach, the Americans thought
that the Filipinos had simply given up and that the war was over. In a telegram to Washington early in 1900, General Otis wrote that "the war in the
Philippines is already over . . . there will be no more real fighting."[189] He
chose that moment to go back to the United States, leaving the seemingly
peaceful Philippines to the overall command of Arthur MacArthur. It took
many months of insurgent attacks to overcome U.S. dismissiveness and for
MacArthur and the rest of the U.S. military to realize that this asymmetric
war was also "real fighting." Before that comprehension hit, the Filipinos
had built the insurgency across almost all the islands of the archipelago. The
Americans found that the things that had won them Manila—the massive
frontal assaults, the heavy artillery, and the supporting naval gunfire—did
not work against an enemy that attacked and then refused to stand and keep
fighting. Aguinaldo might not be able to win a battle, but he could potentially win a war. Arthur MacArthur wrote the next year that the asymmetric
fighting had "strained the soldiers of the army to the full limit of their en-
durance."[190] The situation was bad enough, and widely enough known, that

MacArthur's son Douglas was heckled at the Army–Navy baseball game (he played for West Point) with the chant "MacArthur! MacArthur! . . . Who is the boss of this show? Is it you or Emilio Aguinaldo?"[191]

Ultimately, the new insurgent war did not end more successfully for the Filipinos. The Americans soon realized that the new form of war they were facing was actually deeply familiar, resembling nothing so much as the experience of fighting Native Americans in the west of the United States. American familiarity with the frontier came in handy, and supplied both experience and tactics. MacArthur had brought with him the understanding of asymmetric war he had gained in the Department of the Dakotas fighting Native Americans. His subordinates brought similar experience. As a result, the United States crushed the main Filipino insurgency fairly quickly. The second war ended on July 4, 1902, not with any particular triumph, but when the violence had died down to a level that the United States could declare victory. By then, Aguinaldo had been captured, convinced to switch sides, and sent on a speaking tour of the United States. Whether he got to attend an Army–Navy baseball game is not recorded.

Postwar, both lessons of Manila seemed to hold. The United States saw itself as superior to non-Western nations for both military and racial reasons, and believed that superiority inherent and unchanging. The way to fight was symmetrical wars, and America's only real rivals were other imperial powers. The result, at the dawning of a new century, was a growing desire to revamp the army away from the frontier-facing model of the nineteenth century and turn it into a technologically advanced force that would be ready for big wars. Asymmetrical war was the wrong kind of conflict, unworthy of an up-to-date American army (it was not "real fighting," to repeat Otis's words). But that was deceiving, as we shall see. Asymmetrical war would come back to bedevil the United States.

If Americans learned those lessons, correct or not, so too did other powers. Non-Western nations and movements saw in Manila and in other similar battles the danger of fighting Western powers on the open battlefield. Whether in China, Southeast Asia, India, or Africa, non-Westernized forces found that such battles were simply impossible to win. The path to resisting imperial conquest, to fighting intercultural war, was not a symmetrical one but rather was based on variations of the asymmetrical strategy that Aguinaldo tried. There were a number of strategists who realized that fact. Their names—Mao Zedong, Che Guevera, and even Mohandas K. Gandhi—are better known than Aguinaldo's, but they were working from the same script.

5

Interlude II

Fighting "Small" Wars

For the American military, the lessons of the protracted guerrilla war in the Philippines were rapidly overshadowed by the massive mobilization required for participation in World War I. Modernized by secretary of war Elihu Root, in a process that mostly ignored the unwelcome history of fighting guerrillas in the Pacific, not to mention the legacy of an entire century of war against Native Americans, the new Army seemingly validated the institutional emphasis on large-scale conventional combat. Henceforth, planning and energy focused for the most part on procurement, doctrine, and training for future wars against enemies similar to the Germans. There were key exceptions, to which we will return shortly, but this emphasis persisted despite the interwar American military experience of so-called small wars in northern Russia, in Siberia, and all over the Caribbean and Central America. Instead, over the next five decades the American military experience in the world wars and the Cold War created a kind of tunnel vision of expectations.

To be fair, there was good reason for such a keen focus. Real or projected enemies such as Germany, Japan, and the Soviet Union wielded mass industrial armies or even, eventually, threatened nuclear annihilation. The symmetry of the confrontation seemed to demand a strategy of overwhelming one's opponent with force and firepower, whether it was more troops, bigger guns, faster airplanes, increased mega-tonnage, or greater precision in targeting. It was this scaling up that suggested to John Keegan the likely end of battle when he wrote *The Face of Battle* in the mid-1970s. After all, how much can the human mind and body endure? In a perverse inversion of logic, however, the combination of the nuclear deterrent and the creation of new insurgent strategic frameworks that relied not on firepower but on attacking national will more indirectly restored a space for battle rather than remotely delivered devastation. American soldiers have continued to trade blows at a personal level, and increasingly frequently they have done so across cultural boundaries, in Vietnam, Iraq, Somalia, Colombia, the Philippines, Iraq again, Africa, and continuing even now, in Afghanistan and beyond.

★ ★ ★

In a number of ways, the Army's deployment to war in Cuba and the Philippines in 1898 was a fiasco. Public revulsion at the War Department's incompetence, mismanagement, and logistical failures, and the devastating illnesses and deaths among the troops in Cuba, prompted a political crisis that led Elihu Root to implement reforms. The secretary of war created a general staff, founded the Army War College, and systematized officer training to a degree long advocated by some within the officer corps.[1] In addition, the ensuing 1903 Dick Act (also known as the Efficiency in Militia Act) broke down the old reliance on state volunteer regiments and created a tighter relationship between the National Guard—the repository of citizen soldiers who could be called up by the president in a national emergency—and the regular Army, which would now provide standardized training and arms to the Guard.[2]

One key result of these reforms was the 1905 *Field Service Regulations* (*FSR*), a manual designed to make drill and tactics uniform across the Army while also setting out principles for combined arms operations and organizing the employment of units above regimental size. Although there had been official and semi-official drill manuals in earlier eras, this was arguably the first formal American institutional publication of what we now call "doctrine."[3] Despite the contemporary American engagement in stability operations in the Philippines, the 1905 *FSR* said virtually nothing about irregular or guerrilla warfare, becoming the first of many times that American doctrinal writers concluded that success in such operations constituted a "lesser included" mission. An army that could master complex, industrial, mass armies could surely handle guerrillas.[4]

Forgetting the Philippines was almost a deliberate process—a turning away from the other face of battle. It was also a byproduct of the modernization process. The Army's accumulated experience in the nineteenth century as a constabulary force on the American frontier, including its institutional proficiency at fighting Indians, had been transmitted informally from one generation of officers to the next. By custom and necessity, the long-service regular officer corps in the so-called Old Army had been both tiny and intimate. Experience was transmitted more or less easily among its members, and many of them were deeply experienced. As David Silbey has pointed out elsewhere, "The lack of a formalized retirement system and the drastic contraction of the army post-Civil War meant that officers spent decades not only fighting the same war, but fighting it in the same rank with the same responsibilities." Arthur MacArthur, for example, so critical to the operations in the Philippines, as we've seen, spent twenty-three years as a captain after the Civil War.[5] The Root reforms aimed, like the many reforms in civilian industries associated with the Progressive Era, to institutionalize such knowledge and to make parts (or people) interchangeable. Systems of formal knowledge supplanted those of informal knowledge; officers now rotated through various positions more frequently, and they gained breadth while sacrificing depth.

Root's Army, again according to Silbey, "was optimized to be large, easily expandable, and able to handle heavy casualties without breaking down. It would not prove to be as effective at counterinsurgency, however."[6] That ineffectiveness was in some ways a consequence of how new systems of formal doctrine ignored the problems of guerrilla warfare and of constabulary operations. In the immediate aftermath of the Philippines War, for example, the War Department ordered J. Franklin Bell, who had commanded the counterinsurgency operations in Batangas, a province in Luzon, in 1902, to write up a summary of his methods. Instead he turned to teaching modern conventional war, and it was under his direction that the Army published the 1905 *FSR*, which, out of its roughly two hundred pages, specifically discussed unconventional operations on only four, all of which involved legalistic definitions of what a partisan, a guerrilla, or a "war rebel" was.[7] There was no discussion of strategy or technique for such operations.[8]

In Andrew Birtle's analysis of U.S. Army counterinsurgency doctrine across the twentieth century, he found some courses at Fort Leavenworth's "School of the Line," some articles in the Army's professional journals during the first two decades of the century, and a slight increase in interest during the 1920s and 1930s, followed by declining interest. In part this reflected the Army's increasing desire to focus on large-scale combat operations and a corresponding unwillingness to shoulder any other kind of mission, including constabulary or anti-guerrilla operations. Informally after 1915, and formally after 1927 and until World War II, the United States Marine Corps assumed that role, eventually publishing *The Small Wars Manual* in 1935. In the 1920s and 1930s, so-called minor warfare occupied a small part of the various revisions of the *FSR* and an equally small part of the instructional regime at the Infantry School at Fort Benning. World War II naturally brought a sharp decline in interest, and counterguerrilla warfare "disappeared from the curriculums of wartime service schools," as it did from most Army doctrine in the 1930s and 1940s. Birtle concludes that the Army "emerged from World War II with virtually no written doctrine or corporate expertise on the conduct of counterguerrilla and pacification campaigns."[9]

There are a number of ironies here. First, there is no inherent equivalence between an enemy from a different cultural sphere and a "guerrilla." World War II would decisively prove that point. In occupied Europe the Allies fought alongside resistance organizations with which they felt cultural affinities, while simultaneously fighting a conventional war against Japan. American insistence on equating otherness with guerrilla tactics persisted, despite the history of unconventional warfare in the American Revolution and American Civil War. One lecturer at the Infantry School in the early 1930s argued that "in small wars the psychological factor is preeminent" because "all savage people respect power and are quick to detect weakness."[10]

American soldiers had simply come to expect non-European cultures to fight as guerrillas, and guerillas' inherent tactical need to avoid symmetrical challenge seemingly confirmed their inferiority in the soldiers' minds. This assumption that a guerrilla would be culturally alien (and vice versa) to them suggested strategic responses rooted in the old model of the "ladder of civilizational development" and presumptions of the "white man's burden." The guerrillas resisted because they did not yet understand the benefits of civilization, American strategists argued, and if we improved their infrastructure and provided medical care, all backed by unyielding violence when necessary, they would eventually make peace.

A second irony is that the long period of institutional and doctrinal disinterest in "small wars" coincided with a surge of exactly such conflicts—briefly interrupted by World War II—in the form of assorted Cold War proxy conflicts and wars of decolonization. After the Philippines War, the new American empire began to flex its muscles. U.S. Army or Marine forces were sent to intervene or as constabularies to govern the Philippines and suppress the Moro insurgency there (1902–1913). They also were asked to deal with the Boxer Rebellion and follow-on missions in China (1899–1901, 1912–1938); the second Cuban intervention (1906–1909); Cuba (1912); Haiti (1915–1934); Dominican Republic (1916–1924); Russia (1918–1919); Siberia (1918–1920); Mexico (1914, 1916–1917); Honduras (1903, 1907, 1911, 1912, 1919, 1924, and 1925); Panama (1918–1920, 1921); Nicaragua (1912–1925, 1926–1933); and ultimately the occupation of Germany from 1918 to 1923. The Marines bore most of this burden, and their experience was what led to the composition of the *Small Wars* manual, but the imprint of these experiences on the military as a whole was slight, overwhelmed by the stupendous mobilizations and industrial requirements for fighting World Wars I and II. Early Cold War interventions, other than in Korea, were often covert and managed by the new CIA rather than by the military. That long lack of attention and corresponding lack of doctrine or training would haunt the Army as it began to deal with the Maoist-inspired insurgencies from the 1950s through the 1980s.

And that leads us to the final irony. In some ways American successes in the Philippines may have persuaded the U.S. Army at the beginning of the century that an enemy with modern rifles could be overcome by rapid attacks in the open. As Chapter 4 pointed out, "Filipino units repeatedly cracked under sustained assault from American troops and were unable to inflict meaningful casualties." This reinforced American racial prejudices about non-Western enemies, and also led the Filipinos to shift to a guerrilla war. Veterans of that war convinced themselves of the efficacy of the offensive, even in the face of entrenched forces with modern rifles. As one officer put it, "The experience obtained in our attacks . . . convinced me that by sweeping the ground that we were advancing over with a storm of bullets we could so demoralize the enemy that his fire would be badly directed."[11] This set of beliefs likely contributed to the Army's insistence on so-called open warfare tactics when it arrived in France in 1917.[12] Senior American officers clung stubbornly to the notion that American men would fight better than their European counterparts. Fortunately, most officers on the ground adjusted to the conditions they found.[13]

Officers up and down the ranks, however, agreed that the experience of World War I demanded wholly new approaches to national mobilization and to emergent technologies. Both put enormous demands on the American military, focusing its attention ever more on the problem of large-scale conventional combat, primarily as imagined against other Western-style states. When the United States committed to the war in 1917 the active Army numbered 133,000 men, with 185,000 more in the National Guard. Early planning calculations suggested the American Expeditionary Force would need 1 million men; that number was later adjusted to 5 million. The scale of the mobilization challenge was enormous, and the Allies were reeling, especially after Russia made a separate peace with Germany in March 1918. A solution was to implement a draft, which further spurred volunteerism. Ultimately 4.8 million served, of whom 2.8 million had been drafted.[14]

Immediately after the war, the "National Army" was demobilized, and the strength of the Regular Army was set by Congress in 1920 at 130,000.[15] This established a pattern for much of the rest of the twentieth century. American forces in World War II, Korea, and Vietnam would combine a draft with draft-induced voluntarism to man their wartime organizations. As in 1865, 1899, and 1919, the cessation of hostilities was followed by rapid demobilization. U.S. forces in World War II went from 12 million at the time of Japan's surrender in August 1945 to 1.5 million by 1946.[16] That smaller number still vastly exceeded previous American peacetime forces, even on a scale relative to population, but reflected a strong preference to return to a small military force. The post-Korea demobilization was not as sharp, as the emergent Cold War confrontation required maintaining a larger defense establishment. The draft had been renewed already in 1948, and it remained the primary form of mobilization through the end of the U.S. presence in Vietnam in 1973.

World War I also saw the beginning of far greater emphasis on industrial and technological capacity as a key determinant of success in conventional interstate warfare. Other than artillery and machine guns, most of those technologies were only previewed in World War I, including tanks, aircraft, bombing, motorized transport, and chemical weapons. Having matured between the wars, all but the last would prove central to ground combat in World War II (naval combat is beyond our scope here). The pressure of global war accelerated development of a long list of other militarily crucial technologies, including radar, wireless radio communication, medical capabilities in a number of areas, rockets, missiles, and ultimately atomic weapons.

World War II also featured the United States in a cataclysmic war with the Japanese Empire, a largely conventional confrontation between two vastly different cultures using similar technologies and strategies. The experience of intercultural combat in that war has been amply studied. Certain aspects of it support our overall claim that soldiers' experience of combat was materially altered by its intercultural qualities, and that cultural differences altered the outcome of battles, strategies, and soldiers' lives after the war was over.

Historian John Dower led the way in demonstrating the power of mutual American and Japanese racism to affect both sides' behavior. Both nations wielded industrially equipped militaries, and both viewed the other as culturally inferior. That belief only intensified with the outbreak of war, perhaps more noticeably in the United States, where racial prejudice was heightened by the sense of having been treacherously attacked. As Dower has shown, racism and vengeance combined with the extreme challenges of fighting in the jungles and tropics of the central and southern Pacific to produce brutality on both sides. Prisoners were relatively rare there compared to operations in western Europe, and the taking of body parts as souvenirs—to include mailing such body parts home to family members—was not unheard of. Veterans of fighting in the Pacific were sometimes thought of by new recruits as having "gone Asiatic," meaning that they had lost their moral compass.[17] They fought differently. There was no such equivalent adjective for veterans in Germany going "Germanic." In the demanding confines of combat in the Pacific, American soldiers increasingly imagined what they did as "processing." This semantic shift, as discussed by historian Craig Cameron, had real implications for the American experience of combat. Soldiers were no longer "fighting," they were merely "processing the enemy."[18]

After World War II, the Cold War confrontation with the Soviets ultimately posed a seemingly insoluble problem: how to build conventional and nuclear forces to deter a general war, while also managing and winning the many smaller conflicts directly or indirectly inspired by the worldwide Communist movement—most of which erupted in culturally different zones of the world. American forces fighting in those conflicts would also struggle with their assumptions of cultural supremacy. Backed by vast military and technological superiority, such assumptions were a powerful drug and led to strategic miscalculations, such as about the willingness of the North Koreans to invade the South in 1950, and the willingness of the Chinese to intervene later that same year. It also led to an increasing belief that technology, especially airpower, could solve nearly any problem, and at less cost.[19] Eventually American doctrinal and cultural unpreparedness for guerrilla war combined in a particularly toxic brew with assumptions about Vietnam being, as Lyndon Johnson put it, a "piddling, piss-ant little country" to frustrate the American intervention there.[20]

The military had nonetheless improved its preparedness for unconventional war. An early manual came out in 1951, and John F. Kennedy's demand that the military be able to handle limited as well as all-out wars pushed the Army to acknowledge a wider spectrum of possible missions.[21] It was clear to most observers that by the Kennedy administration, if not before, both superpowers' possession of nuclear weapons was putting a cap on military escalation. Future wars would have to be contained, limited to the lower end of the spectrum of conflict, to include unconventional and guerrilla wars—both fighting them and supporting them. FM 100-5 *Operations*, published in 1962, broke new ground in the Army's official approach to the use of special forces and the conduct of unconventional war, and there were some in the senior ranks of the Army who were thinking hard about the Communist insurgencies emerging around the world and what the U.S. military role would be. In the early 1960s there was growing cross-fertilization between military and civilian agencies. General Maxwell Taylor told West Point cadets in 1962 that a "wholly different kind of force" would be needed for such wars.[22] Despite this seeming openness to new ideas and new methods, the senior Army leadership remained decidedly conventional in its preferences.[23]

The war in Vietnam was a key landmark in the American experience of intercultural combat. In some ways, the intervention there was among the most contradictory in the American history of such conflicts, and those contradictions are one reason that we have not dedicated an entire chapter to it (the other reason is that it already has been subjected to an enormous volume of analysis). Unlike America's earlier intercultural fights, and unlike those the United States is fighting now, the military in the Vietnam War was supported by the draft, and it was constrained in its use of violence (at least doctrinally) by international agreements as well as by the ongoing nuclear standoff with the Soviet Union. Whatever strategy or policy the United States adopted in Vietnam, it could not trigger that larger war. Perhaps most confounding of all was the regional political situation, one in which an independent North Vietnam was supporting the insurgency in the South and directly intervening with its own regular troops, shielding its movements through Laos and Cambodia. Many senior military officers involved in advising Presidents Kennedy and Johnson agreed that it was a difficult strategic situation. Ultimately, the puzzle proved too complex to solve.[24]

Part of the strategic failure resulted from policymakers consistently (some would say stubbornly) viewing the problem in Vietnam exclusively through the lens of stopping the spread of Communism. American involvement began as it supported France's effort to retain colonial control there. When the Viet Minh revolutionaries defeated the French at Dien Bien Phu in 1954, the United States maneuvered during the treaty negotiations to create a divided Vietnam, nominally to be united soon thereafter by elections. The election was never held, and the United States chose to remain firm in preserving South Vietnam as a separate, non-Communist state. The American vision for reforming the country clashed with that of South Vietnam's president, Ngo Dinh Diem, and the resultant lack of real progress allowed the Communists to make significant gains in the countryside.[25] The United States gradually increased its military aid, and the number of its in-country advisors, until finally intervening in 1965 with conventional ground combat troops and an escalating campaign of bombing the North.

Early ground combat missions were aimed at establishing secure areas in the South, in order to prevent air bases and other facilities from being overrun. To expand those security zones, U.S. forces launched large-scale conventional force missions, intended to find and kill enclaves of guerrillas. Meanwhile, U.S. forces supported the South Vietnamese government's efforts to pacify and control the countryside. The traditional historical narrative of Vietnam emphasizes the period from 1965 to 1968 as one focused primarily on so-called search-and-destroy methods, often accompanied by massive amounts of firepower, indiscriminately employed, resulting in deforestation, civilian deaths, and ultimately the alienation of the population. After the Communists' Tet Offensive in early 1968, according to this narrative, a chastened American command structure turned more decisively to the pacification mission, only to be undermined by Richard Nixon's determination to withdraw U.S. troops amid growing dissatisfaction in the United States.

The debate over America's strategy (and tactics) continues to rage. There have been schools of revisionists, neo-revisionists, and more. Some argue that the war effort had always included a strong pacification component. Others argue that the search-and-destroy missions had been succeeding and that the combined Communist war effort (meaning the insurgents in the South and their supporters in the North) had been on the verge of breaking, especially after the Tet Offensive, which all agree was a military disaster for the North but a propaganda bonanza.[26]

Although disagreements about the potential outcomes and the actual strategies abound, there is agreement about two things. First, combat, when it occurred, was intense, savage, disorienting, and usually asymmetrical. The Americans possessed an overwhelming advantage in firepower; the Communists (both the South's guerrillas and the North's regular forces) usually chose the time and place for engagements, including determining when any given combat would end. Vietnam presented a challenging variety of topography: rice paddies, jungles, mountainous highlands, extensive marshy river deltas, and more. It also presented American soldiers with a variety of combat experiences: patrols in pursuit of guerrillas, clearing underground bases, defending firebases from attack, helicopter assaults into presumed enemy positions, and even wide-open almost-conventional combat when in contact with the regular troops from North Vietnam. The technology for such combats was not far removed from that used in World War II. Helicopters and jet aircraft had changed time and space calculations, but much of the equipment for men on the ground exchanging fire remained very similar.

What made the experience of combat in Vietnam different was the environment, the set of assumptions that Americans made about their enemies, and the diverging meanings each side imputed to the outcomes of their engagements. The Vietnamese knew they could not match the firepower of the Americans, and so they didn't tie their fate to the outcome of any individual encounter. They sought, following Mao Zedong's prescription for revolutionary war, to protract the war and ultimately undermine the will of the enemy to continue. American forces would have to be attacked in a conventional manner, but that would come only after a protracted phase of guerrilla war. The exact timing of such a conventional attack was a matter of some debate within North Vietnam; it was tried in 1964, 1968, and 1972, and it was ultimately successful in 1975.[27] Most of the time, however, this strategic goal of protraction meant they attacked only when they chose to. Guerrilla forces would fade into the background of the civilian environment and emerge when they saw opportunity or advantage. No single engagement, even one initially perceived as advantageous, was considered decisive. American soldiers, on the other hand, were accustomed to seeing every combat as potentially decisive, at least in terms of controlling terrain. American forces could dominate terrain, but typically they then moved on and their control evaporated, sucking the meaning from whatever sacrifices they had just made.

Or so it seemed. Tactically, American soldiers learned a number of lessons about fighting guerrillas, and they did seemingly "win" nearly all of those encounters (the myth holds that the Americans won *all* of them). Strategically, the military leadership did inch toward a better understanding of the demands of pacification in an insurgency—although whether achieving a positive outcome was ever possible is a debate without end. But this leads us to the second piece of common ground among historians: after the war, the military quite deliberately began to forget all that it had learned.[28]

There were good reasons for forgetting. The war and the domestic social unrest that accompanied it nearly broke the Army, leaving it beset by indiscipline, drug use, the departure of experienced non-commissioned officers, a careerist officer corps interested only in "punching their tickets" for promotion, a loss of faith in the senior leadership, the struggle to find recruits for the new all-volunteer force, and the fissure that emerged between the public and those in uniform. Institutionally, the Army had to do something, and one of the things it chose to do was to concentrate on the mission that it understood, one that involved the greatest existential threat to the United States: a Soviet invasion of western Europe.

From the mid-1970s until the end of the Cold War (and beyond), the Army focused its doctrine, training, and equipment purchases almost entirely on that challenge. The lessons of counterinsurgency and guerrilla warfare were essentially expunged from the manuals and from the service schools. The first post-Vietnam FM100-5 *Operations*, published in

1976, quite literally removed the chapters on unconventional warfare, military operations against irregular forces, situations short of war, Cold War operations, and stability operations, all of which had been in the 1962 and 1968 versions.[29] As for the schools, in 1971 the Army dropped stability operations training from basic combat courses and the next year discontinued jungle and counterguerrilla warfare training from advanced individual training for enlisted men. In 1974 West Point ended its mandatory counterinsurgency course, as did the Infantry School for its new lieutenants. The Command and General Staff College (for majors) went from forty hours of instruction in low-intensity conflict in 1977 to eight in 1979. More than merely turning away from Vietnam, the officer corps also began to interpret their defeat as the fault of a weak-willed public and politicians, and this provided an excuse to ignore the deeper lessons of the war.[30]

Instead, the new all-volunteer Army focused on fighting and winning a hypothetical conventional war against the Soviet Union, and it started by rewriting its operational doctrine, buying and incorporating new technologies, and reasserting old notions of professional expertise for its officer and non-commissioned officer corps.[31] A fresh infusion to the defense budget begun under President Jimmy Carter (in response to the Soviet invasion of Afghanistan) and expanded under Ronald Reagan energized the strategy, ultimately producing, under George H. W. Bush, the seemingly spectacular success of ground forces slashing through the Iraqi army during Operation Desert Storm in 1991.[32]

There were a number of ironies to this, setting the stage for the American experience of combat in Afghanistan in the 2000s, the subject of Chapter 6. First, the doctrine produced in the late 1970s and early 1980s, ultimately known as "AirLand Battle," essentially reimagined the campaigns of World War II—although compressed in time, conducted across longer distances, and taking advantage of technologies that allowed for precision shooting well beyond the line of close combat. It even looked specifically at German operational models and thinking about delegating tactical control down to the lowest level (the so-called *auftragstaktik*). The doctrine completely ignored what the Army was then calling "low-intensity combat" or "contingency operations." The 1986 FM 100-5 *Operations* manual devoted three pages to the latter and none to the former.[33] To be fair, there were many doctrinal manuals on specific subjects, including a 1972 FM 31-23 *Stability Operations* and a 1990 FM 100-20 *Military Operations in Low Intensity Conflict*, but it was the FM 100-5, the Army's core document, that set the priorities for training and procurement. The irony is that the 1991 victory against Iraq came precisely at the end of the Cold War, revitalizing the military's reputation with the public, though now also putting it in an environment that encouraged using the military in new and more expansive ways—much like those Marine operations in the early twentieth century. They were no longer strictly imperial missions to secure territories or control trade, but instead were humanitarian or peacekeeping operations, in places such as Haiti (1994–1996), Somalia (1991–1993), Liberia (1990–1991), Bosnia-Herzegovina (1994–2005), Macedonia (1993–1994), Albania (1999), Kosovo (1999–present), and more.[34]

The second irony is that the Army's new battlefield dominance might be irrelevant to future operations. Potential enemies looked at the 1991 Gulf War and determined that facing the United States in a conventional operation was hopeless for at least the near future. Some, notably North Korea, sought protection through nuclear deterrence. Others, especially non-state enemies, looked to terrorism as the best weapon. That weapon looked even stronger after the "Black Hawk Down" incident in Somalia in 1993, when eighteen American soldiers were killed and dragged through the streets, an episode followed by a swift American withdrawal from the country. Enemies such as al-Qaeda concluded that the United States public had no stomach for a protracted conflict. They didn't need overwhelming force to win; they only needed the spectacle of casualties, even if on a small scale.[35]

The military officially acknowledged the existence of "military operations other than war," or MOOTW.[36] Creating a new term gave it doctrinal validity, but, as political scientist Rosa Brooks points out, it highlighted that "there were the 'large-scale combat operations usually associated with war,' . . . and there was some other stuff the military was forced to do from time to time."[37] The officer corps' resentment of such missions was clear. This resentment was heightened by the Army's fear that growing reliance on airpower and other long-range precision weapons, coupled with special operations forces (what was called the "revolution in military affairs"), might reduce or even eliminate the need (and therefore the budget) for a traditional army.

One thing at least was clear about the post–Cold War world: if the Army wanted to be relevant, it was going to have to be more deployable and more mobile. The chance for a months-long buildup in a place like Saudi Arabia—a country with modern ports, airports, and in-country military bases waiting to be occupied—was unlikely to be repeated. There were also voices in the Army that saw the opportunities presented by digital information and networking, and by the late 1990s they were successfully pushing for a lighter, more deployable Army, newly capable of using digital communication networks to track friendly and enemy forces in real time and to more effectively transmit target information to other services—primarily for airpower.[38] This effort at "Transformation," however, was still conducted under the aegis of the old AirLand Battle doctrine, only now there was the imperative to get to new places on the globe quickly, and generally the Army simply hoped that conventional combat with a peer competitor was unlikely. The 2001 edition of *Operations* (now FM 3-0, replacing 100-5) included a chapter outlining various kinds of "stability operations," putting them on the same level as offensive and defensive operations—despite some widespread misgivings.[39]

Since the Root reforms in 1903, there has been persistent emphasis within the American military on winning decisively in large-scale combat operations against "near-peer" foes. Whether right or wrong, the doctrines used by military leaders in the 1990s were logical; they were also narrowly focused.[40] Officers' cultural inclinations were arguably even more narrowly focused than the formal doctrine. As a result, American soldiers once again found themselves unprepared for an enemy they did not expect.

The third irony of the 1991–2001 period emerges only in retrospect. The terrorist attacks on September 11, 2001, redefined what the U.S. military would be doing for the next two decades, and with it the experience of combat. The Army was almost entirely unprepared for the unfolding of events in Afghanistan in the fall of 2001, and while it adapted quickly, the Central Intelligence Agency took the initial lead in the fight against the Taliban.[41] In 2003, the invasion of Iraq pitted the Army and Marines again against a state-based foe, and the Transformed Army, heavily supported by complete control of the air, made quick work of a conventional enemy. What followed, however, continues to haunt the policies of the United States and the soldiers who carry it out.

Chapter 6 takes us deeper into that experience in Afghanistan, nearly a decade after the first U.S. combat troops arrived there in 2001. The enemy was by then no longer unexpected. By 2010 they were recognizable, but they were also still driven by beliefs that remained alien to Americans, and they had adopted a way of asymmetrical warfare that was all its own. The combination produced yet another face of battle.

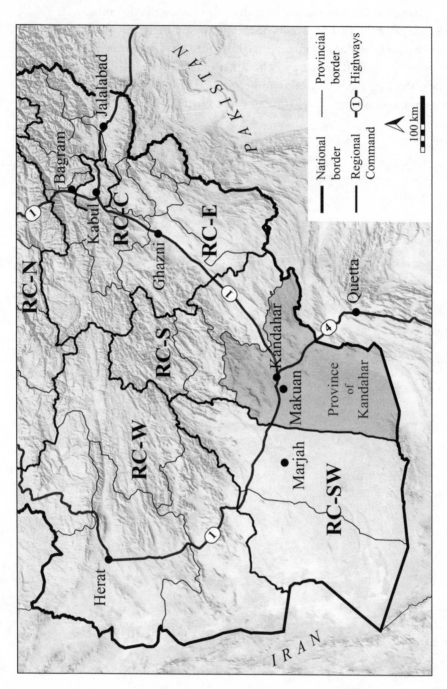

Map 6.1 Kandahar Province and RC-South. (Map by Matilde Grimaldi)

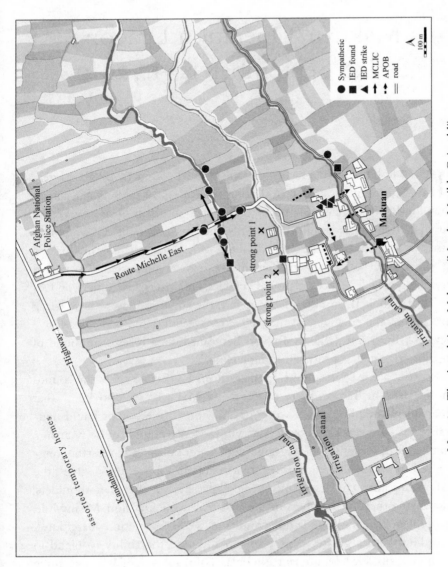

Map 6.2 The Attack into Makuan. (Map by Matilde Grimaldi)

6

Makuan/Operation Dragon Strike, September 15–17, 2010

The Muslim call to prayer and the muffled sound of digging interrupted the night's stillness, alerting the American soldiers of Captain Brandon Prisock's Bravo Company that Taliban insurgents were awake and busy planting mines around them. After the day-long fight on September 15, 2010, for control of the Afghan village of Makuan, strategically located in the district of Zhari in Kandahar province, supported by tracked breaching vehicles, trucks, armored vehicles, bulldozers, helicopters, and A-10 Thunderbolt II ground-attack aircraft, the Americans were now being matched by the enemy's two most effective weapons: improvised explosive devices (IEDs) and darkness. To Staff Sergeant Joshua Reese, the sound of digging triggered "a really sickening feeling."[1]

Prisock, a 2004 West Point graduate from Louisiana, knew the sounds meant that the Taliban were reoccupying Makuan. He also knew that their dilapidated Soviet-era weapons and homemade bombs could neutralize his company's firepower. Carrying seventy pounds of body armor, combat gear, ammunition magazines, and water bottles, and wearing long-sleeved uniforms in temperatures that regularly topped 105 degrees, the Americans also wore "screaming eagle" patches on their left shoulders, identifying them as members of the 101st Airborne Division. Meanwhile, the Taliban fought in simple robes and sandals—and sometimes barefoot—affording them a greater degree of mobility and the ability to blend in with civilians. First Lieutenant Nicholas Williams, one of Prisock's three rifle platoon leaders, summed up his feelings upon entering the alien world of Makuan: "We were strangers in a strange land fighting someone on their home turf. . . . The call to prayer was a constant reminder that this wasn't our world."[2]

The battle for Makuan, which lasted for three days in mid-September 2010, was the opening thrust of Operation Dragon Strike, at the time the largest single U.S. Army operation of the war. After trading blows with the Taliban for nearly nine years, U.S. commanders intended for Dragon Strike to deliver a knockout punch. The operation involved more than 8,000 American and Afghan National Army (ANA) soldiers fighting for control of Zhari district.[3]

The idea was to crush the will of the Taliban. Zhari, where Mullah Omar had founded the Taliban in 1994, occupied a strategic position on the western doorstep of Kandahar City, Afghanistan's second-largest population center, with just under a million people. Yet since the start of the war in 2001, the American-led coalition had not made securing Zhari a priority. The 2008 election of President Barack Obama, however, altered the strategic calculus. Describing Afghanistan as a "war of necessity," the new president deployed 21,000 additional troops into theater in March 2009 and announced plans to send another 30,000 nine months later. The Pentagon envisioned that this new "surge"—as it was called—would retake swaths of southern Afghanistan long dominated by the Taliban, providing an opportunity to prepare the ANA, which was scheduled to take the lead on the battlefield in the fall of 2011. Commanders selected the 101st Airborne's 2nd Brigade, some 5,000 soldiers, to carry out Dragon Strike, along with 3,000 ANA soldiers. Prisock's Bravo Company, which consisted of 230 men, was given the campaign's first mission: clearing insurgents from Makuan, a small village of some twenty acres, consisting of dirt streets and walled adobe compounds.[4]

Opposing Prisock and his men were an unknown number of Taliban fighters, both veterans and new recruits plucked from western Pakistan's radical madrassas. The Zhari-based Taliban had benefitted from years of largely undisputed control of the district, where they erected IED assembly points, ammunition caches, food stockpiles, bunkers, tunnels, and makeshift medical facilities throughout the villages and densely cultivated agricultural fields.

The Taliban welcomed the forthcoming offensive. "We are not scared of NATO, or of the Americans," Taliban commander Mullawi Mohammadi boasted. "Whoever comes, we will kill them." The Taliban's Makuan fighters were eager to pit their pressure-plate, trip-wire, and remote-control IED tactics against Bravo Company, despite its military superiority. As darkness settled in on the night of September 15, the Taliban worked on their next move. Even as his soldiers heard the sound of digging in the distance, Prisock, who had only commanded the company for ten days, prepared to counter it.[5]

The Campaign

Brandon Prisock was in his second year as a West Point cadet when terrorists slammed jetliners into the World Trade Center and the Pentagon in September 2001. Prisock was born in November 1978 in Zachary, Louisiana, and his family traced its military service back to the American War of Independence. His great-grandfather had attended West Point, one grandfather served in World War II and another in Korea, and his father had dropped out of college and volunteered to fight in Vietnam. Young Brandon initially fell in love with baseball rather than soldiering. But when Mississippi State University failed to follow through on a scholarship offer in 1997, he enlisted in the U.S. Army. Three years later the Army selected him through a special program to attend the U.S. Military Academy at West Point, and in 2004 he was commissioned a second lieutenant of infantry.[6]

Prisock's journey to Makuan commenced with President George W. Bush's speech on September 20, 2001, nine days after the 9/11 terrorist attacks. Bush declared that the United States was engaged in a war to defeat "the global terror network." He identified an enemy defined by their weakness—"terrorists," who resort to indiscriminate attacks on vulnerable populations because they lack the military capability to attack a state in any other way. The war, the president continued, "will not be like the war against Iraq a decade ago, with a decisive liberation of territory and a swift conclusion. It will not look like the air war above Kosovo two years ago, where no ground troops were used and not a single American was lost in combat." Those serving under arms "should not expect one battle, but a lengthy campaign, unlike any other we have ever seen. It may include dramatic strikes, visible on TV, and covert operations, secret even in success." Despite the speech's prescience, it took years for Americans to recognize just how challenging this asymmetrical and intercultural contest would be, both in terms of achieving a strategic success and in the experiences of the men and women on the ground who, like Prisock, would fight it.[7]

In the immediate aftermath of 9/11, however, the enemy seemed at least territorially contained. The al Qaeda terrorist network that had carried out the attack was based in Afghanistan, and the ruling Taliban regime protected them. Having never imagined the Taliban or al Qaeda as a prime adversary, the U.S. military had no plans for conventional ground operations in Afghanistan. Previous terror attacks had been treated as criminal acts pursued by law enforcement (as after the World Trade Center truck bombing in 1993) or had spurred retaliatory missile strikes (Operation Infinite Reach after the bombing of the U.S. embassies in Kenya and Tanzania in 1998).

Forced to improvise a plan rapidly, and fearful of duplicating the Soviet Union's decade-long fight in Afghanistan (1979–1989), U.S. Army General Tommy Franks's Central Command (CENTCOM) favored small special operations forces (SOF) detachments, airpower, and anti-Taliban militias. Franks anticipated that SOF-directed surgical air strikes would rout al Qaeda and their Taliban defenders, paving the way for the creation of a new Afghan government and a rapid military exit. Getting bogged down was not an option, nor was anything reminiscent of the Soviet quagmire.[8]

Initially, the plan followed the script. On the evening of October 7, President Bush authorized the commencement of attacks. The strikes, conducted by Air Force B-2 stealth bombers from Missouri, Navy fighter jets, and Tomahawk cruise missiles, obliterated early-warning radars, surface-to-air missile sites, airfields, and command-and-control installations. During the air campaign's second week, AC-130 gunships and Kuwait-based F-15E Strike Eagles attacked Taliban and al Qaeda formations, such as they were.[9]

After the air onslaught had softened Taliban and al Qaeda positions, modified Chinook helicopters known as CH-47s carried the first SOF personnel into northern Afghanistan. On the night of October 19–20, the Americans linked up with anti-Taliban Northern Alliance forces. Within three weeks, the synchronization of overwhelming SOF-directed air strikes and Northern Alliance ground offensives led to the fall of Mazar-e-Sharif, the first town liberated from the Taliban. By the end of November, the offensive had also driven the Taliban from the key northern cities of Taloqan and Konduz. On November 14, Northern Alliance forces captured the capital, Kabul.

Having routed the Taliban and al Qaeda in northern Afghanistan, the U.S. military turned its attention to the south. Following a series of pitched battles, Kandahar City, the de facto Taliban capital, fell on December 7. Less than two months into the conflict, the SOF-directed air campaign had reached its zenith, leading to the deaths of more than 10,000 Taliban and al Qaeda fighters, the capture of thousands of prisoners, and the collapse of Taliban rule in strategic cities and across six of the country's thirty-four provinces.[10]

Yet the U.S. military had failed to destroy al Qaeda and the Taliban. Why? In retrospect, two reasons stand out. First, conducting military operations in a landlocked country the size of Texas, with porous and rugged borders, proved daunting, even for the world's mightiest military power. This geography was made more challenging by the destruction of many of Afghanistan's airfields and much of its infrastructure during the Soviet-Afghan War. Second, CENTCOM's decision to rely on precision firepower and local ground forces limited the U.S. conventional forces to a mere 10,000 soldiers, most of whom were based just to the north of Kabul at Bagram Airfield and in small outposts around Kandahar. Given Afghanistan's size, this meant they were widely scattered. The small number of U.S. troops restricted commanders' ability to pursue and overwhelm fleeing al Qaeda and Taliban remnants. In December 2001, enemy combatants consolidated in a sanctuary at Tora Bora, nestled in the country's rugged northeast, near the border with Pakistan and forty-five miles southwest of Jalalabad. This concentration seemed to present U.S. commanders with the possibility of a decisive battle, one they pursued despite the limited troop numbers. For twelve days, American SOF hammered al Qaeda with air strikes as local militias fought to overrun their positions. Intertribal feuds among the militiamen, as well as the absence of U.S. conventional ground forces, allowed senior al Qaeda leaders, perhaps even Osama bin Laden himself, to escape the noose and bolt into Pakistan.

Another opportunity presented itself in March 2002, at the Shahi Kowt valley in Paktika province, where American conventional forces experienced their first large-scale combat during Operation Anaconda. During three weeks of intermittent fighting, approximately 2,000 soldiers from the 10th Mountain Division, 101st Airborne Division, and SOF detachments conducted search-and-destroy operations against a large collection of enemy combatants. The Americans killed between 200 and 800 fighters, temporarily demolishing the ability of al Qaeda and the Taliban to mount major operations. Victorious or not, the Americans encountered setbacks in the Shahi Kowt, and multiple intelligence failures, the enemy's doggedness, unrealistic expectations, and the failure to use artillery effectively foreshadowed future tactical and operational difficulties.[11]

Nevertheless, by the end of March 2002, the U.S. military assumed that al Qaeda and the Taliban were defeated and that the war was all but over.

For the Taliban, however, this was only the opening phase of a protracted, violent struggle, one to be measured in years rather than operations. Its commanders returned en masse to western Pakistan, where they regrouped, recruited replacements, and waited. The United States maintained a token force of 7,000 soldiers to deal with lingering resistance, to spearhead re-construction projects, and to provide security for a loya jirga, a gathering where political leaders from across the country would select an interim president, which was scheduled for June. In support of military operations, the Combined Joint Civil-Military Operations Task Force dug wells and rebuilt bridges, medical facilities, roads, and schools. At the loya jirga, held on June 11, 2,000, Afghans chose Hamid Karzai as interim president under a new Afghan Transitional Authority.[12]

Having vanquished al Qaeda and the Taliban and devised a road map for Afghan self-rule, the United States appeared to have achieved its stra-tegic aims. Yet of course the Taliban was reconstituting itself inside of Pakistan's tribal regions. The Bush administration's growing obsession with Iraq afforded them valuable breathing space. Beginning in the fall of 2002, the U.S. military began to divert manpower, equipment, logistics support, and intelligence assets to the Iraq buildup. Some have suggested that the U.S. military had more than enough assets to handle both conflicts. The truth is more complicated. U.S. military command structures at the the-ater level typically have two planning staffs, one for ongoing operations and one for future operations. In this case, both Iraq and Afghanistan fell within CENTCOM's authority, and the rapid shift of attention to Iraq de-prived the effort in Afghanistan of planning capabilities at a critical junc-ture. Seizing the opportunity, the Taliban methodically moved ammunition, weapons, mortars, and other supplies back into Afghanistan.

As the spring 2003 fighting season dawned, the Taliban leadership, still in Pakistan, orchestrated military attacks across southern Afghanistan's Pashtun heartland, including Zhari district, and began converting villages such as Makuan into fortresses. Comprising 40 percent of Afghanistan's 30 million inhabitants, the Pashtuns constitute the country's dominant ethnic group. They filled the Taliban's ranks. By the end of 2003, the insurgent group controlled more than 80 percent of Zabul province, where the U.S. mili-tary maintained only a small footprint, and much of three other southern provinces. The Taliban also unleashed a campaign of violence and coercion. In the spring of 2003, they executed a Salvadoran International Red Cross worker and burned his corpse, killed two U.S. SOF soldiers in Helmand province, and executed an Italian tourist in Zabul. In the summer months, the Taliban staged at least one attack every other day across three restive southern provinces. The United Nations suspended travel to Afghanistan, and aid organizations abandoned Helmand and Kandahar provinces. Preoccupied with the race to Baghdad, the Bush administration showed little appetite for curtailing the spiraling violence in the south. During a May visit to Kabul, secretary of defense Donald H. Rumsfeld announced the end of major combat operations for the 8,000 soldiers stationed in theater. It was the opportune moment, he asserted, to transition from combat to reconstruction and peacekeeping.

Declaring the end of "major combat operations" was more than a matter of rhetoric. Military planning procedures at the time divided conflicts into phases, with key tasks designated for and a relative force size corresponding to each phase. Rumsfeld's announcement meant that he had allowed, or perhaps even authorized, CENTCOM to begin drawing down the force in Afghanistan—without fully considering what force levels would actually be appropriate for a stabilization operation in a country that lacked infrastructure and was under attack from forces across its border.[13]

In fact, as regards the latter, Lieutenant General David Barno, the top U.S. military officer in Afghanistan, officially adopted a counterinsurgency (COIN) strategy in the fall of 2003—a strategy that in many ways does not neatly fit into the U.S. military "phasing" paradigm, since its manpower requirements might actually exceed those of active combat operations. Identifying the Afghan people's hearts and minds as the ultimate aim, Barno emphasized humanitarian assistance, reconstruction, and population protection. But he lacked the forces to carry out the mission. Many, including undersecretary of defense Dov S. Zakheim, the Pentagon's chief financial officer at the time, later sharply criticized the Bush administration's failure to build upon the initial military success. The administration, he said, had taken its eye off the ball and not only allowed the Taliban and al-Qaeda to regroup but turned Afghanistan into "world's largest producer of illicit drugs."[14]

This proved an understatement. The meager number of troops responsible for implementing Barno's COIN strategy symbolized the widening gulf between what the United States hoped to achieve in Afghanistan and the resources, especially manpower, that it was willing to commit. In strategic planning parlance, the commitment of American *means* was insufficient to support the *ways* (a COIN strategy) or the desired *ends* (a stable, democratic, and multi-ethnic Afghanistan). According to Field Manual 3-24, *Counterinsurgency*—written after 2003 and not yet available to CENTCOM force planners—successful COIN campaigns typically required a ratio of 20 to 25 counterinsurgents for every 1,000 inhabitants. COIN operations in Afghanistan would therefore have required a minimum force of 600,000. Barno commanded 14,000 U.S. troops. Infantry battalions consisting of 800 soldiers patrolled areas the size of New England states, and the mission increasingly relied on civil-military provincial reconstruction teams (PRTs), each consisting of a few dozen soldiers who dispensed reconstruction assistance. In the summer of 2004, a dozen PRTs operated throughout Afghanistan, with the majority located in the troubled Pashtun south. A year later, in July 2005, the number had ballooned to twenty-two, with thirteen controlled by the U.S. military and nine directed by the North Atlantic Treaty Organization (NATO). Yet even the PRTs remained under constant siege. Almost from the beginning, theater-level planners complained that their requests for just 500 to 600 more combat soldiers to serve as security elements for the teams went unanswered. The bulk of U.S. Army infantry battalions were committed to Iraq.[15]

Prisock's winding road to Makuan ultimately reflected the decisions that commanders and policymakers made in these crucial years about overall strategy and force structure. In the meantime, however, he was just beginning his military career. Weeks after graduating from West Point, he married his girlfriend, Kara, and reported to Fort Benning, Georgia, for the Infantry Basic Officer Leader Course. Soon thereafter, the Army moved them to the West Coast, where he commanded a platoon of Strykers with the 2nd Infantry Division at Fort Lewis, Washington. Developed in the early 2000s, Strykers were eight-wheeled infantry-carrying armored vehicles that transported up to nine soldiers. Prisock deployed with his brigade in late 2006 to Mosul, Iraq, and the following year took part in Arrowhead Ripper, a complex and bloody series of operations that drove al Qaeda militants from Baqubah, northeast of Baghdad. After the deployment, Prisock and his family (he and Kara had two young children) reported back to Fort Benning, where he commanded a basic training company and completed the Army's elite Ranger school, earning the highly coveted Ranger tab.[16]

Meanwhile, back in Afghanistan, the Taliban's campaign of terror intensified. Increasingly turning to IED attacks, targeted assassinations, and suicide bombings, it turned 2006 a bloody stalemate. During the year, the group launched almost 1,300 IED attacks—compared to 530 the previous year. They also carried out 141 suicide bombings that were responsible for 1,166 casualties (there had been only six such attacks in 2004), murdered 85 teachers and students, and burned down nearly 200 schools. Between May 2006 and May 2007, the Taliban assassinated 406 Afghan policemen. Astonishingly, in the midst of this violence Rumsfeld withdrew 3,000 soldiers from the south, decreasing the overall U.S. commitment to 16,000.

Perhaps even more effective than the violence were the ways the Taliban intimidated local tribal elders and government officials with so-called night letters, threats delivered to homes and mosques, warning potential government collaborators of payback and physical violence—a threat often made good on. Not unreasonably, Afghans saw the night letter deliverers as permanent and NATO security patrols as temporary. Small wonder that the coalition consistently struggled to secure the support of the rural population, a central tenet of any COIN strategy.[17]

In 2006, the Taliban massed thousands of heavily armed and trained fighters in Zhari and neighboring Panjwai district. In a prelude to Makuan, NATO launched Operation Medusa that summer. The operation was intended to clear the Taliban from Kandahar City's western hinterland, including the so-called Green Zone, the densely vegetated strip of irrigated terrain sandwiched between Highway 1 to the north and the Arghandab River to the south. Despite assorted frustrations and even some tragic friendly fire, a coalition task force spearheaded by the Canadian 1st Battalion of the Royal Canadian Regiment, could finally claim victory. By mid-September, Afghan troops aligned with NATO dislodged the remaining fighters from the Zhari village of Pashmul in grisly hand-to-hand combat. Estimates of Taliban casualties ranged as high as 1,500, including hundreds of Pakistan-based reinforcements killed by air strikes.[18]

Despite the success, NATO's post-Medusa intelligence summaries carried ominous warnings about the insurgency's resilience and strength in Zhari. The Taliban had expended 400,000 ammunition rounds, 2,000 rocket-propelled grenades (RPGs), and 1,000 mortar rounds during the fight, and Canadian soldiers later discovered 1 million rounds of unspent ammunition, suicide bomber training facilities, and a surgical hospital. Meanwhile, in other regions of the mountainous country, isolated American outposts were increasingly outgunned and reliant on airpower. From June to December 2006, NATO conducted 2,100 air strikes in Afghanistan (Iraq witnessed only 88 in the same period despite its descent into a bloody civil war). Yet air superiority remains a poor surrogate for boots on the ground. NATO and

American forces in Afghanistan now amounted to 40,000 troops, still short of the new COIN manual's recommended ratio. Stretched thin by the sectarian upheaval in Iraq, the U.S. military and its allies had become bogged down and lacked a clear path to "victory."[19]

After Medusa, the Taliban, although pummeled, replenished their losses, adapted, and exercised patience. Touting itself as Afghanistan's government in exile, the group would henceforth eschew large-scale confrontations and decisive battles. Rather, Taliban commanders favored slowly eroding American and NATO's political will, while also continuing to establish themselves in rural communities as the real authority and as arbiters of local justice. As one analyst observed, the Taliban began to favor "small groups of fighters rather than large formations . . . living with locals in family compounds and mosques." From those locations, Taliban fighters could store weapons, conceal themselves, attack coalition soldiers, and "then melt back into the population."[20]

The resort to guerrilla tactics should not have surprised an American army that had struggled against exactly those techniques, and exactly that blend of political and military functions, in its long war in Vietnam. Like the Vietnamese, the Taliban, unable to match American firepower, attacked their opponents' will. Murray Brewster, a Canadian war correspondent who visited Zhari and Panjwai following Medusa, wrote about the Taliban's tactics. As he put it: "There would be no more standing, fighting and dying before coalition guns for a long time. Instead they would battle almost exclusively by remote control and pressure plate [IEDs], exacting a slow, steady bleed of dead and wounded."[21]

After a relatively quiet 2007, war returned with a vengeance to Zhari. By the end of 2008, at least 1,200 fighters had established positions south of Highway 1 in the region's densely cultivated agricultural terrain. The positions, including the stronghold of Makuan, were defended from ground attack by reinforcing layers of IEDs that resembled minefields. From these positions, the insurgents used RPGs and 82 mm recoilless rifles to attack military vehicles and harass commerce on Highway 1, the "ring road" that connects Afghanistan's major cities and enters Kandahar City from the west. Increasingly focused on force protection, Canadian forces in the area lost the initiative. Zhari became an insurgent hotbed with IED assembly points, ammunition caches, concrete bunkers, and tunnels scattered throughout the villages and agricultural fields. Mullawi Mohammadi, the Taliban commander quoted in the introduction to this chapter, boasted in May 2010 that his fighters were "safe and comfortable in our many hidden places," a likely reference to the insurgency's sophisticated defenses that were built up and reinforced in this period.[22]

To establish their legitimacy, the Taliban erected shadow governing institutions. Exploiting the corruption and dysfunction of the Afghan judicial system, they instituted sharia courts to adjudicate disputes, issue warrants and subpoenas, and dispense justice. In 2008 alone, Taliban courts in Zhari ordered twenty-seven executions. Insurgent leaders also collected zakat taxes from farmers and formed a committee to investigate complaints of abuse and corruption against heavy-handed commanders. Violence underwrote the Taliban's political clout. Local commanders selectively executed tribal elders allied with the provincial or national governments. By one estimate, from 2001 to July 2010 the Taliban assassinated more than five hundred elders in Kandahar province. In just one month, December 2006, the Taliban executed twenty-six men in a Panjwai district village who were accused of cooperating with NATO. The headless corpses were publicly displayed as a warning to future collaborators. NATO's failure to prioritize operations in Zhari between 2007 and 2009, when the district was often patrolled by no more than a battalion of soldiers, set the conditions for the coalition's major 2010 offensive.[23]

Dragon Strike was a reflection of the shifting U.S. strategy in Afghanistan following President Obama's election. After his January 2009 inauguration, he initiated a review of Afghan military strategy and oversaw the deployment of an additional 21,000 soldiers and Marines two months later. In an August speech, Obama made erasing the Taliban's gains in Zhari and across the south his top foreign policy priority: "This is not a war of choice. . . . If left unchecked, the Taliban insurgency will mean an even larger safe haven from which al Qaeda would plot to kill more Americans." Early in December 2009, while speaking at the U.S. Military Academy, Obama formally announced the deployment of 30,000 additional troops to Afghanistan as part of a military buildup aimed at retaking Helmand and Kandahar provinces from the unholy alliance of Taliban insurgents and weak governance.[24]

In the modern U.S. military, however, one does not just "add" troops; almost every soldier carries with them a complex command and supply structure and an array of logistical constraints. Where the Taliban's recruitment of 1,000 men may translate into 1,000 new fighters, the structure of the American military meant that adding 1,000 troops involved first integrating them into existing structures in order to manage and sustain them.

In this case, the surge required activating a new corps-level headquarters, the International Security Assistance Force (ISAF) Joint Command (in October 2009), and deploying (in March 2010) a second sustainment brigade to theater for the first time. This proved expensive. In 2009, planners calculated that every additional 1,000 troops would cost $1 billion; delivering a single gallon of fuel to troops in country cost roughly $400.[25]

As the 2010 spring fighting season dawned, the Afghan war entered its ninth year, with no end in sight. To break the insurgency's stranglehold around Kandahar City, the theater commander, General Stanley McChrystal, identified the clearance of Zhari district as a primary military aim, assigning the mission of Dragon Strike to Colonel Arthur "Art" A. Kandarian's 2nd Brigade Combat Team from the 101st Airborne Division. Dragon Strike constituted the vanguard of the entire 2010 Afghan surge and morphed into one of the war's single largest operations. Brandon Prisock, who arrived at the 2nd Brigade's 1st Battalion, 502nd Infantry Regiment (1-502 IN) in late 2009, would command its initial operation.[26]

The Forces

The Battle of Makuan would witness a collision of three vastly different tactical cultures. The U.S. military, the ANA, and the Taliban offered dramatic contrasts in motivation, training, weapons, esprit de corps, technology, tactics, professionalism, and cohesion. Their clash reflected a kaleidoscopic degree of asymmetry that exceeded any seen in American military conflict since the conclusion of the Vietnam War.

In 1973, following the end of the Vietnam ground war, Congress abolished the draft and authorized an all-volunteer force. Its size, at the time, was 2.25 million. In September 2010, the size of the active-duty force was 1.46 million. Accounting for reservists and national guardsmen, however, the overall troop strength of the total U.S. military in September 2010 tallied 2.32 million, or 0.75 percent of the U.S. population. Since the inauguration of the all-volunteer force, a declining proportion of Americans claimed military experience and, by 1999, it was less than 6 percent. A decade following the 9/11 attacks, a total of 4 million Americans were on active duty, compared to the 8.7 million Americans who served in Vietnam (1964 to 1973). And its personnel were older: the average age of U.S. military personnel jumped from twenty during Vietnam to twenty-eight and a half in

2011. Despite the widening civil-military gap, those serving celebrated their volunteer status. In one 2011 survey, 82 percent of veterans opposed the reinstatement of a draft.[27]

Dragon Strike tested the durability of the post-9/11 Army and revealed much about its composition and character. In 2010, 1.13 million men and women served in the Army, which consisted of two components: active and reserve (the latter including both the National Guard and Army Reserve). During the decade following 9/11, and specifically between 2003 and 2010, waging two wars simultaneously demanded the ongoing deployment of 200,000 uniformed personnel, straining both components and requiring the Army to grow from 480,000 active-duty personnel in September 2001 to 562,000 in September 2010. In 2004, to meet these requirements, the Army began expanding the number of moral waivers issued for recruits with criminal (including felony) convictions. In that year, 12 percent of recruits required waivers. In 2006, the Army approved waivers for 8,219 enlistees; the following year, the number climbed to 10,258. Struggling to fulfill expanding recruitment quotas as the popularity of the Iraq and Afghan wars plunged, the Army boosted its maximum recruitment bonus from $6,000 in 2003 to $40,000 in 2008. The continuous cycle of deployments likewise strained the reserve component. By early 2007, when the Iraq surge commenced, nearly 420,000 guardsmen and reservists, almost 80 percent of the reserve component's combined strength, had been deployed to Iraq or Afghanistan. One out of five of those part-time soldiers had deployed more than once. In total, between October 2001 and August 2011, 2.3 million Americans deployed to Iraq and/or Afghanistan, many of them on multiple occasions. The plummeting proportion of Americans going to war led one scholar to deplore a "new American practice of *war without the people*."[28]

In any case, the 2010 Army was one of the most diverse in American history. In that year, women accounted for 15.5 percent of the active and reserve components. For the active component overall, whites held 72 percent of all officer commissions and constituted 62 percent of the force. African Americans and Hispanics, respectively the next-largest demographic groups, accounted for 19 percent of the active-duty commissions and one out of every three enlisted personnel. Within the active-duty Army, 88 percent of enlisted personnel had earned a high school degree or GED. Across the U.S. military, uniformed personnel cited a multitude of motivations for joining the all-volunteer force, including educational and economic opportunities. In one 2011 survey, which consisted only of veterans who had served since

2004, 75 percent cited educational benefits as an important reason for their service; 57 percent said they hoped to acquire skills for later civilian employment. The absence of employment chances outside the military was a primary motivating factor, playing a role in the enlistment of one out of four recruits after 2003. Remaining consistent with results from previous decades, 65 percent of enlisted personnel hoped to "see more of the world." Finally, in the same 2011 survey, six out of ten cited the 9/11 terrorist attacks as a principal justification for entering military life. After experiencing the crucible of war, these veterans judged themselves more patriotic than fellow citizens.[29]

While they possessed their own unique stories and backgrounds, those leading Bravo Company into Makuan in the early fall of 2010 revealed two common qualities: they hailed from families with a tradition of military service, and they were galvanized by 9/11. Prisock's executive officer, Captain Luke Rella, had received his commission from Officer Candidate School at Fort Benning, Georgia, in June 2007. As the company executive officer, Rella served as Prisock's second-in-command, coordinating mission planning, logistical support, and the forwarding of tactical reports to the battalion headquarters. A New Hampshire native, he married his high school sweetheart the day of his commissioning. As he put it, "My patriotism mixed well with my desire to experience war, fight, and lead." Rella's two grandfathers had served in the Army and Navy during the Korean War (1950–1953), and he never forgot his intense rage when the World Trade Center towers were destroyed during his senior year of high school. Having served as a rifle platoon leader in Iraq in 2008, Rella's deployment to Zhari was his second.[30]

Prisock's rifle platoon leaders were on their first deployments. First Lieutenant Williams, twenty-four, was a graduate of ROTC at Virginia Tech University. Williams also vividly recalled seeing the Twin Towers fall in high school and adopted a "I'll fight them there so it never happens here again" mentality. Second Lieutenant Taylor Murphy had always wanted to experience military life. As a child, he loved hearing his father reminisce about his time in combat as a company commander in Vietnam. "I always wanted to be in the military. I was drawn to the adventure and physical challenge. I enjoy the mindset surrounding a military operation and mission," he said. A 2009 West Point graduate, Murphy was on his first combat deployment at Makuan. He kept a copy of the September 12, 2001, *New York Times* as a reminder of why he serves.[31]

Bravo Company's officers expressed pride in serving in the storied 101st Airborne Division, nicknamed the "Screaming Eagles." Many had watched the 2001 HBO miniseries *Band of Brothers,* which dramatized the division's exploits (specifically those of the 506th Parachute Infantry Regiment) in Europe during World War II. More recently, however, the actions of a few criminals had sullied Bravo Company's reputation. During a 2006 deployment to Iraq, several soldiers from the company made international headlines after gang-raping and murdering a fourteen-year-old Iraqi girl and then executing her family. Two soldiers from the 2006 tour remained in the company in 2010, and Prisock leveraged their guilt and shame to enforce strict discipline and cultivate togetherness in Zhari. "The decline in standards and unacceptable behavior was a contributing, if not proximate, cause of the [2006] criminal acts that stained the organization," he stated. "This unwillingness to falter and allow any further disgrace held the organization together tightly!"[32]

The Taliban could not hope to match the U.S. Army in firepower, numbers, or training. With a senior leadership of between 200 and 1,000, the group had approximately 36,000 fighters under arms across Afghanistan and Pakistan when Bravo Company arrived in Afghanistan. In the south, the Taliban's inferiority led to its strategy of avoiding pitched battles where NATO could bring the full weight of its combined arms arsenal. Taliban commanders perfected tactics using small-arms fire to lure coalition soldiers into pressure-plate IED traps, creating a steady drip of casualties that dissolved NATO's political will.[33]

Interviews with Taliban fighters, though rare, suggest a mixture of motivations for fighting. By early 2010, those in Afghanistan sought to retaliate against NATO, whose air strikes, nighttime SOF raids, and abusive interrogation practices swelled the insurgency's ranks. In Kandahar province, insurgents accused coalition soldiers of committing indiscriminate violence, including assassinating innocents, sexually assaulting Muslim women, defiling the Quran, burning crops, and using dogs as torture instruments. They also increasingly interpreted the American presence as a permanent occupation that imperiled Islamic norms, cultures, and traditions. As one Taliban fighter put it, "At the moment our country is invaded, there is no true sharia. Can we accept these [conditions] for money? How then can I call myself a Muslim or an Afghan?" Furthermore, pervasive corruption and dysfunction within the Afghan national government and its security forces drove disaffected young Pashtuns into the insurgency.[34]

Their training and operational effectiveness remained inconsistent. Taliban fighters were notoriously poor marksmen. Accurate shooting demands breathing discipline, trigger control, sight adjustment, proper posture, and regular practice. The Taliban's decentralized structure, as well as the increasing targeting of its fighters by American unmanned aerial vehicles, rendered routine practice impossible to implement. A proclivity for discharging their AK-47 assault rifles on automatic mode increased their inaccuracy, leading them to consistently fire above intended targets. Accuracy was further diminished by the medley of ammunition and broken-down weaponry. Kalashnikovs seized during raids in 2010 lacked key components or had sustained significant damage; likewise, captured Taliban ammunition caches included cartridges manufactured on different continents over several decades. Many cartridges seized in Helmand province during the Marine Corps' early 2010 Marjah offensive were filthy or corroded, suggesting that the insurgency had difficulty supplying its fighters. All of these factors reduced their effective firing range to less than 150 yards.[35]

To neutralize U.S. firepower and exploit its tactics and techniques, the Taliban used small-arms fire to lure Americans into lethal IED traps. Captain Thomas Grace, a company commander in 2010 with the 1st Battalion, 3rd Marines, in neighboring Helmand province, described this tactic and the "dilemma" it posed: "From day one, at the sound of the sonic pop of the round, Marines are taught to seek immediate cover and identify the source/location of the fire. Cover is almost always available in Afghanistan in the form or dirt berms, dry/filled canals, and buildings. Marines tend to gravitate toward the aforementioned terrain features. So what the insurgents would do was booby-trap those areas with I.E.D.s. Whether they were pressure plates or pressure release, they were primed to detonate as Marines dove for cover." Increasing reliance on IEDs shifted production techniques. Between 2003 and 2006, the Taliban primarily used military ordnance to construct IEDs. In 2007, the group moved to fertilizer-based bombs. Ammonium nitrate, imported into Afghanistan from Pakistan, China, and India, was easy to acquire and transport, becoming the base explosive element in 85 percent of IEDs at the time of the battle of Makuan. In total, IEDs inflicted 60 percent of American and coalition combat deaths between 2003 and 2014.[36] By the time of Dragon Strike, the proliferation of IEDs in Afghanistan had climbed to a new high: 2,677 in 2007, 3,867 in 2008, and 8,159 in 2009. In addition, the average size of IEDs tripled, from roughly twenty-two pounds in 2008 to sixty-six pounds in 2010.[37]

IEDs killed and maimed with industrial efficiency. Prior to the invasions of Afghanistan and Iraq, the U.S. military had had little experience with explosive blast injuries since the Vietnam War. With the increasing size, scale, and sophistication of IED, by 2010 they emerged as one of the primary characteristics of the Afghan war. Injuries associated with IED explosions spanned a wide spectrum, ranging from concussions to amputations to nonvisible internal injuries, such as ruptured organs or pulmonary hemorrhages, capable of hastening death days later despite the lack of external wounds. Injury patterns associated with IED blasts, according to the Centers for Disease Control and Prevention (CDC), depend on a combination of factors: the quantity and chemistry of the detonated materials, the physical environment, the delivery method, the distance between the explosion and victim, and the presence of protective barriers between the "blast wave" (the overpressure impulse radiating from the detonation) and the victim, such as walls, vehicles, or body armor. The CDC has identified four blast injury categories: primary, secondary, tertiary, and quaternary. The primary category relates to injuries stemming from the body's absorption of the blast wave, including "blast lung," perforated eye globes, ruptured eardrums, abdominal perforations and hemorrhages, ruptured spleens and livers, acute renal failure, concussions, and traumatic brain injury. The secondary category refers to the broad range of injuries resulting from the impact of explosive fragments and debris projectiles on the body. Tertiary injuries occur when the blast wind launches bodies off the ground, often resulting in compound fractures, amputations, and open and closed brain injuries. Finally, quaternary injuries refer to all other explosion-related injuries not classified as primary, secondary, or tertiary, particularly burns and crush injuries. Combat medics at Makuan would treat all four categories of blast injuries.[38]

The U.S. military proved initially ill-prepared for the IED threat and resulting level of asymmetrical combat. One key lesson from earlier conflicts, however, whether "insurgencies," "proxy wars," or imperial wars for territory as in the Philippines or within continental North America, was the indispensability of winning the allegiance of local allies. This lesson, at least, was not forgotten. In modern doctrine, virtually the whole point of a COIN strategy is to train indigenous military, paramilitary, or police forces to take over combat responsibilities. As part of President Obama's plan to begin withdrawing the additional surge forces in late 2011, U.S. strategy transformed "partnership" into a prerequisite for war termination. It was in this context that more than 3,000 soldiers from the newly minted ANA's

3rd Brigade, 205th Corps, joined Kandarian's team to create Combined Task Force (CTF) Strike. This kind of partnership paired U.S. and ANA units to conduct combined combat operations—*shohna ba shohna,* "shoulder to shoulder." Senior U.S. military planners anticipated that the coupling of trained American mentors with green ANA soldiers would forge Afghan units into self-sustaining combat organizations capable of taking over the fight against the Taliban in late 2011, facilitating a drawdown of forces and eventual exit.[39]

At Makuan, Prisock's soldiers conducted their assault alongside ANA allies. But the *shohna ba shohna* approach added to the jarring cultural dislocations felt by Bravo Company soldiers, who were combatting a "foreign" enemy while simultaneously fighting alongside a "foreign" ally. Almost a decade after its creation by President Hamid Karzai, the ANA in 2010 was still very much a work in progress. In December 2002, Karzai established the ANA as a volunteer force of 70,000 Afghans drawn from the country's array of social and ethnic groups. Divided between infantry units, an air corps, and a new Ministry of Defense, the ANA was constructed from scratch. In the summer of 2002, the U.S. military had opened the Kabul Military Training Center to provide basic training for recruits, emphasizing physical fitness, small-unit tactics, weapons instruction, marksmanship, and fire and ma-neuver. A year later, to promote the recruitment of a tribally diverse force, the coalition established National Army Volunteer Centers in all thirty-four provinces. Yet identifying suitable recruits proved difficult due to a paucity of national health, criminal, and financial records. The Afghan government struggled to recruit Pashtun soldiers from Helmand and Kandahar prov-inces, crippling efforts to build relationships between the ANA and those villages, including Makuan, most likely to support the Taliban. Despite these challenges, 7,000 Afghan soldiers had been trained by July 2003.[40] Over the course of the decade, the U.S. military steadily expanded the ANA. By July 2010, it encompassed 134,000 soldiers divided into six "corps," each assigned to one of ISAF's six regional commands. The growing size of the ANA masked its leadership crisis and operational capabilities. By the close of the year, the ANA had 18,191 officers and 37,336 non-commissioned officers on its books (compared to operational requirements of 22,646 and 49,000, re-spectively). Increased quantity did not equate to increased quality. Ordinary Afghan soldiers in 2010 still lacked basic skills. According to one estimate, 86 percent of recruits were illiterate and therefore could not read or write operations orders, interpret a map, record serial numbers from weapons and equipment, coordinate artillery fire missions, or study doctrine and tactical manuals. This stunted the growth of specialized branches, including logistics, finance, signals, and human resources.[41]

The American and Afghan soldiers who would fight at Makuan were also subjected to shifting strategies and shifting commanders. Counterinsurgencies inevitably struggle with the paradox of fighting to secure and support the population while simultaneously destroying the insurgents who threaten the population. Eliminating active enemies tends to be a rather violent undertaking, often undermining any collective sense of security or support. Soldiers on the ground and under fire often found it difficult to discern their commander's relative emphasis on one mission versus the other—that is, to decide who was the enemy and who was not. The initial plans for stabilizing the area around Kandahar, as formulated by Regional Command–South (RC-South) commander British Major General Nick P. Carter under General McChrystal's overall ISAF command, received a dramatic shift of emphasis in early July when U.S. Army General David H. Petraeus, the architect of U.S. COIN doctrine, took over ISAF. Petraeus immediately doubled the number of SOF raids aimed at decapitating the Taliban's leadership. He increased the number of manned and unmanned air strikes and eased his predecessor's allegedly restrictive rules of engagement—rules that had required soldiers to go through several layers of authority to secure permission to kill an insurgent, or that required soldiers to assess an insurgent's "hostile intent," even if he possessed a weapon.[42] In the first three months of Petraeus's command, U.S. aircraft dropped 1,600 pieces of ordnance (an assortment of bombs, missiles, and so on), nearly half the number dropped the entire previous year. Impatient with a supposedly soft approach that they worried was perpetuating the conflict, senior leaders in Washington extolled the Army for finally "tak[ing] off the gloves" by intensifying the scale and tempo of operations.[43]

Petraeus also unshackled CTF Strike. On July 9, just four days after taking command, he met with Carter, Kandarian, and their staffs at Forward Operating Base (FOB) Wilson. Petraeus made clear that eliminating Taliban forces in Zhari constituted the war's main effort, and he encouraged Kandarian to wield the stick rather than the carrot. Explained Major Clint Cox, CTF Strike operations officer, "Operation Dragon Strike was born from this change in mission."[44] Prior to Petraeus's visit, CTF Strike anticipated more of a hearts-and-minds approach. Kandarian's original mission statement emphasized "securing" the population in order to in-crease the Afghan government's "provincial capability and promote eco-nomic growth."[45] After receiving Petraeus's guidance, Kandarian rewrote the mission statement. It now stated that CTF Strike would attack into southern Zhari and "destroy" the Taliban's command-and-control nodes, their IED stockpiles, and their "will." It was a new war, and one that seemed to promise more of what the U.S. military was accustomed to.[46]

Dragon Strike now resembled a more conventional operation. It aimed to seize insurgent sanctuaries and support bases, capture or kill high-value targets, and eliminate the insurgency's "accelerants": IED components, explosives caches, weapons, money, and propaganda materials. The goal was to restore commerce on Highway 1 and revive life and commerce in and around Kandahar City's agricultural hinterland. To do all this, however, com-plicated the order of battle. Clearing the IED obstacle fields would require bomb-detecting dogs, advanced Vallon handheld mine detectors, bulldozers, additional combat engineer support, and M58 mine-clearing line charges (MICLICs), all of them part of a Cold War–era weapons system designed to explosively breach conventional minefields.[47]

The nature of the operational environment reflects the experience of combat. Tactically and strategically, context is everything, especially in an asymmetrical and intercultural fight. Combat formations in today's U.S. Army, for example, shift rapidly as assets are attached or detached. This means that faces around a soldier change, as do the voices on the radio. Meanwhile, the struggle to identify clear strategic objectives against an enemy whose long-term perspective is fundamentally so different and alien and even in-decipherable to Americans means that U.S. commanders frequently change their minds. The nature of the U.S. military's officer assignment system combines with the vagaries of U.S. domestic politics to rotate commanders in and out of country on a constant basis. Stability and continuity suffer, as do the soldier's understanding of the mission and the expectations for their behavior in combat. After Braddock was killed at Monongahela in 1755, the British Army ran through a series of replacements before landing on Sir Jeffrey Amherst, who remained in command from 1758 to 1763. In the American war in the Philippines, Major General Elwell Otis commanded U.S. forces there from the spring of 1898 to May 1900. His successor, Brigadier General Arthur MacArthur Jr., remained in command until the end of the war in 1902—short tenures, yet long enough. In contrast, by 2010 there had nearly been more commanders than years of war in Afghanistan (precise numbers are elusive because of the complex and fluid relationship between NATO, ISAF, and United States Forces–Afghanistan).

Eventually, however, context became action, and by September 1, Colonel Art Kandarian's four maneuver battalions were in position along Highway 1 and prepared to attack. Located twenty-four kilometers west of Kandahar City, Makuan represented one of Kandarian's early objectives. The village served as a critical Taliban IED factory, a consolidation position for ambushes, and a staging area for insurgents moving in and out of Kandahar City. Due to the frequency of ambushes originating from Makuan, soldiers referred to the stretch of Highway 1 to its north as "RPG Alley." On June 13, just two weeks after CTF Strike assumed its mission, Makuan-based insurgents unleashed a torrent of 82 mm recoilless rifle rounds and RPGs at an American convoy returning to FOB Wilson. The attack damaged several vehicles and seriously wounded nine soldiers, including Prisock's battalion commander and the brigade command sergeant major.[48]

Prisock's Bravo Company received the task of seizing Makuan. His command consisted of three rifle platoons: Second Lieutenant Charles Ragland's 1st Platoon, Second Lieutenant Murphy's 2nd Platoon, and First Lieutenant Williams's 3rd Platoon. Each consisted of three separate infantry rifle squads and a headquarters with three permanently assigned members (the platoon leader, platoon sergeant, and radiotelephone operator). A mortar section with two 60 mm mortars supported the air assault company. Following a decade of war, Bravo Company, mirroring many U.S. Army light infantry companies, included a mix of experienced, battle-hardened noncommissioned officers and younger soldiers experiencing combat for the first time. As with all of CTF Strike's operations, Bravo Company would be partnered with ANA soldiers.[49]

D-Day for the Makuan assault was September 12. Lieutenant Colonel Johnny Davis, the 1–502 IN commander, planned to insert Bravo Company, a platoon of U.S. Army Rangers, and partnered ANA units to the south of Makuan via helicopter. This kind of "vertical envelopment" would bypass the IED obstacles defending the village's northern approaches. After being inserted, the soldiers would move north toward the objective and clear it, destroying IEDs and explosives caches. As the attack unfolded, Davis's HHC (the separate company within a battalion that contains the assorted headquarters elements, called the Headquarters and Headquarters Company or HHC) would take up a blocking position along Highway 1, where, according to the plan, surprised insurgents would retreat and be captured or killed. Prior to every mission, Bravo Company's soldiers rated its difficulty based on the number of tourniquets they packed. Williams judged the Makuan mission a "five- or six-tourniquet mission," meaning he expected the worst.[50]

Just before September 12, the mission abruptly changed. Reflecting the high operational tempo and overlapping and independent command structures, RC-South at the last moment committed the Rangers to a different mission, depriving Bravo Company of AC-130 gunship support, critical intelligence and surveillance assets, and responsive close air support. Without these enablers, Davis deemed the helicopter insertion plan too risky. Instead, he settled on a deliberate, methodical breach into the village from the north, beginning on September 15. Many soldiers fretted that the new plan squandered the element of surprise and would directly lead them into the insurgency's IED minefields and prepared firing positions. "We're definitely tipping our hand [to the enemy] at that point," Williams observed.[51]

Williams's apprehension reflected a new reality. In 2010, the U.S. Army's operational concept defined an offensive "decisive operation" as a "sudden, shattering action . . . that capitalizes on speed, surprise, and shock." Yet the density of IEDs south of Highway 1, the battlefield terrain's limits on how far soldiers could see to shoot, and that same terrain's tendency to force the troops' movements into narrow paths obviated American superiority in firepower and maneuverability. An assortment of well-armed, dug-in Taliban fighters awaited Prisock's forces. During the summer of 2010, the Taliban, recognizing Zhari's symbolic and tactical significance, surged weapons, communications equipment, and fighters into the district. In Senjaray, Zhari's largest village, the number of insurgents spiked from a couple of dozen to several hundred. Mohammed Niyaz Serhadi, the Zhari governor, estimated that the government controlled less than 10 percent of his district. In the summer, Green Zone–based attacks on logistics convoys and other Highway 1 traffic spiked to as many as five per day. Mortar attacks against American combat outposts and forward operating bases became routine. By September, most Green Zone villages, including Makuan, were no-go areas for coalition soldiers.[52]

The Taliban's forces in Zhari comprised a collection of small, loosely organized groups that benefitted from local autonomy. The *delgai* represented the Taliban's basic tactical operating group in Kandahar province. Consisting of five to twenty fighters, each *delgai* operated within a specific geographic space under a commander who recruited and trained his own fighters. Using a combination of charisma, kinship bonds, and informal relationships established through the crucible of armed conflict (*andiwal* networks), the commander attracted his own fighters. As a consequence, very few foreigners (with the exception of Pakistani Pashtuns) were active in the Zhari insurgency. The fighters themselves had access to a varying supply of 82 mm recoilless rifles, RPGs, 82 mm mortars, and assault rifles and machine guns of mixed quality.[53]

Taliban regional commanders exercised a varying degree of control over the *delgai* units. They translated the strategic vision of the Taliban's Pakistan-based leadership into concrete tactical actions. In general, each regional commander directed up to ten *delgai* units and circulated throughout the battlefield to coordinate attacks and observe battlefield dynamics. Mobility protected them from SOF-directed raids. According to one estimate, Zhari boasted thirty *delgai* commanders and twelve regional commanders. The density of fighters enabled the loosely affiliated insurgency to maintain a near-siege of Highway 1, where they erected checkpoints to extort exorbitant tolls. By the time Prisock's soldiers attacked, 40 percent of the IED strikes on Highway 1 for the *entire* country occurred on the thirty-three kilometer stretch of road between Kandahar City and Howz-e-Madad in western Zhari.[54]

Tactically, the Taliban appropriated techniques, infrastructure, and staging areas from the Soviet-Afghan War, when the mujahedeen had built trenches, bunkers, underground shelters, ammunition caches, and ambush positions throughout the Green Zone. From Makuan, Ashoqueh, and other villages south of the highway, they had coordinated ambushes on Soviet convoys from reinforced firing positions before withdrawing into bunkers deeper in the Green Zone. Mulla Malang, a mujahedeen commander, recalled his fighters' control of Highway 1, when they set up "road blocks, conduct[ed] ambushes, mine[d] long stretches of the road and demolish[ed] bridges, underpasses and viaducts using unexploded aerial bombs."[55] By 2010, the Zhari insurgents had established a similar series of prepared attack positions and bunkers two hundred meters south of the highway. Deeper in the Green Zone, they supported the forward positions with rear staging areas replete with interconnected bunkers, trenches, and tunnel systems. To protect their positions from a northern ground assault, the Taliban buried a series of IEDs that resembled a Cold War minefield just off the highway. They were ready for the attack.[56]

The Battlefield

The Zhari Green Zone became one of the most challenging battlefields faced by the twenty-first century U.S. military. Indeed, the terrain itself proved to be Prisock and his men's primary opponent. Earlier that spring, the men from Davis's 1–502 IN were the first CTF Strike soldiers on the ground in Zhari and had patrolled the dense foliage to keep pressure on the Taliban while the other units trained with their ANA partners. The thick and tangled growth enabled small numbers of insurgents to outmaneuver and outgun American platoons that boasted vastly superior firepower, technology, and training.

The Green Zone was an amalgam of dense pomegranate orchards, towering marijuana fields, irrigation canals surrounded with canopies of trees, and scattered corn and wheat fields. An endless maze of *qalats*—multi-story adobe huts encircled by hardened mud walls—punctuated the verdant landscape. Most befuddling in the terrain surrounding Makuan were the endless earthen "grape rows." Although technically "vineyards," the term does not do credit to how much of an obstacle they were. Bereft of wood-cutting tools, Zhari grape farmers built thousands of rows of the hardened embankments, eight to ten feet in height, to elevate their vines. Colonel Kandarian's soldiers compared the grape rows to the Normandy hedgerows that had encumbered the soldiers of the 101st Airborne Division's 502nd Parachute Infantry Regiment—the unit from which CTF traced its lineage—in the summer of 1944. Conditioned to think of agricultural landscapes as manicured and checkerboarded monoculture fields, the Americans didn't know what to make of the random, almost haphazard placement of stone walls, nor of the unkempt fields and orchards that seemed to blend into one another, creating a terrain that funneled movement in only one or two directions. The perceived disorder of Zhari's agroecology seemed to them to mirror that of Afghan political institutions (see Figure 6.1).[57]

At times the U.S. soldiers felt more at war with nature than with the Taliban. First Lieutenant Daniel Plumb, a Bravo Company platoon leader prior to Makuan, called the terrain an "overgrown labyrinth." The son of a retired U.S. Air Force colonel and a 2008 graduate of the U.S. Military Academy, Plumb joked that an overhead view of his platoon patrolling the grape rows would resemble a Pac-Man video game. Captain Daniel Luckett, the executive officer of 1–502 IN's HHC, described them as "a snarl of

Figure 6.1 Bravo Company soldiers patrol in Zhari district's "grape rows." (Photo credit Brandon Prisock)

disorienting mounds of earth which hid enemy combatants and canalized routes of travel [at] vulnerable choke points." Since the Taliban's preferred tactic was to bury pressure-plate IEDs at choke points, the Americans were forced to crawl methodically up and over every mound rather than walk on the fixed paths at the base of the rows. The resulting physical exhaustion and mental fatigue constricted the pace of operations and dramatically reduced opportunities to kill insurgents.[58]

Luke Rella marveled at how the grape rows, which were separated by narrow irrigation waterways, created their "own climate bubble" intensifying the heat of the summer. Each morning, soldiers observed a thick haze rising from the rows. The humidity triggered extreme perspiration on men already loaded down with seventy pounds of combat gear, and the moisture often ruined night vision goggles, radios, and IED frequency jammers. Soaking wet combat uniforms frequently tore at the crotch; as a result, soldiers often patrolled "commando," with their undergarments and genitals exposed to the elements.[59]

Combined with the restrictive terrain, the presence of IEDs mentally distressed the Americans and ANA. The term "improvised explosive device" fails to capture the complex nature of the Taliban's tactics. Hastily assembled with household supplies, basic tools, and fertilizer, IEDs were indeed simple devices, but their employment proved quite sophisticated. Lieutenant Murphy compared their use to trapping principles he had learned growing up in Minnesota. "Find the trails that are heavily used and set your trap/ IED along them," he explained. Americans quickly learned to shun well-traveled footpaths (i.e., choke points), avoided patrolling the same route twice, and often chose to slog through the irrigation canals, where it was impossible to bury IEDs. "If you are wet, you are alive" became the soldiers' motto. According to Murphy, another "particularly nasty insurgent tactic" involved planting IEDs at locations where U.S. troops were likely to seek cover and concealment. As mentioned, insurgents often massed small-arms fire on patrols in the open, hoping to draw them into pressure-plate IEDs hidden near tree groves, mud walls, *qalats*, or other structures. To counter this tactic, the Americans abandoned the time-honored infantry tactic of seeking cover while returning fire. Rather, Murphy and other platoon leaders ordered their platoons to establish fire superiority in the open.[60]

Zhari's odors were just as unsettling for the Americans. The district's absence of running water and sanitary systems generated an olfactory nightmare. The stench of feces, according to Plumb, who was on his first combat tour, overwhelmed his soldiers' senses. In addition to sewage, the smell of sweat-soaked uniforms caked with Zhari's finely textured "moon dust" soil was unpleasant. At the coalition's combat outposts, the burning of plastic water bottles and other synthetics added a toxic element to the pungent array. Conversely, a few soldiers, including Sergeant Nick Christensen, grew to admire the scent of grapevines and other sprouting vegetation, which other soldiers likened to freshly mowed American suburban lawns. Zhari's heat and humidity also provided a perfect incubator for marijuana to spread beyond the fields where it was cultivated and to sprout up promiscuously in mud wall cracks, foot paths, and every other space devoid of vegetation.[61]

If the terrain seemed alien, so too did the Taliban's way of war. As the assault on Makuan approached, few factors intensified the enmity more than the contestation of cultural norms about how and when to accept, wage, and conclude battle. Overmatched by American firepower, air support, and ability to command and control the chaos of combat, as we've seen, the insurgents avoided pitched firefights and denied the Americans an opportunity to pursue and kill them by abandoning their weapons after brief exchanges of fire and entering mosques or public gatherings of civilians. The insurgents moved into and exited the field of battle on their own terms. According to Sergeant Christensen, the fluidity of insurgents between combat and civilian spaces violated his concept of combat: "They are cowards, to the fullest extent. Someone who fires any kind of weapon at you, throws it down, and picks up an inanimate object that deems him a nonhostile target" fought as if "there are no rules."[62]

The battlespace's obstructed fields of fire and limited visibility enabled the Taliban to mass small-arms fire onto American patrols from a distance, with little fear of accurate or sustained return fire. On many occasions, the Americans struggled to pinpoint the origins of fire.

Concealed by the dense agricultural vegetation and endless maze of *qalats*, walls, and grape rows, the Taliban's assaults slowed combat to a crawl. Americans were fearful of inflicting civilian casualties and damaging private property, which meant they had to spend a disproportionate amount of time identifying the precise origin of hostile fire. As Plumb put it, "Your first thought on contact was always 'Where the *#! are they shooting at me from!?'" Outside the grape row labyrinth, the constant IED threat forced infantrymen to fix their field of vision on their feet rather than the horizon. The physical and psychological tolls of patrolling daily in an overgrown minefield drained stamina. Explained Christensen: "We're moving further than most people have walked in two years. It's real and people get killed on both sides. . . . It's very demanding. It's easy to do for a week, it's easy to do for a month, but it's very difficult to do for a whole year!"[63]

The realization that the insurgents had copied the mujahedeen's playbook and enjoyed a home turf advantage proved unsettling. In Lieutenant Williams's judgment, these factors conspired with the coalition's burdensome rules of engagement, the COIN mission, and the local Pashtuns' affinity for the Taliban to afford insurgents an "absolute advantage." "We rarely saw them first, almost never got the first shot," recalled an exasperated Williams. As September 15 drew nearer, he worried about what the combat in Makuan would look like. "I will never forget the shock/realization that my infantry rifle platoon, with its full complement of equipment, was being pinned down by a couple of shitheads with thirty-year-old AK-47s, a PKM [a light machine gun], and a recoilless rifle."[64]

Williams's observation raises questions about whether conflicts involving sharp moral and cultural asymmetries can ultimately be resolved on the battlefield. If the belligerents applied such different definitions of victory, defeat, combatant, and the boundaries of battle, how could any amount of lethal force set conditions for an end state acceptable to both parties? If the Taliban were not bound to timelines and at any point could reconstitute themselves from within a cross-border sanctuary, little would result from Americans killing them or destroying their weapons caches. There seemed no connection between tactical actions and strategic outcomes. All this loomed large over Prisock and Bravo Company as the sun peeked over Makuan on the morning of September 15.

MICLICs Versus IEDs

At daybreak, Prisock rehearsed the final plans with his platoon leaders and welcomed a platoon of U.S. Marine Corps assault breacher vehicles (ABVs) into his command. Though revised, the plan of attack remained simple and straightforward (see Map 6.2). Based on intelligence and surveillance, the battalion staff expected that the Taliban's defense of Makuan would mirror the mujahedeen's tactics. Captain Marvin "Trae" Morgan III, the battalion assistant operations officer, anticipated that the Taliban would use prepared firing positions from deep inside the Green Zone to slow the American movement through mutually reinforcing IED minefields south of Highway 1. Once the Americans had been lured into any number of IED traps, the insurgents would discard their weapons and melt into the civilian population before air support arrived.

To mitigate the risks to Prisock's task force and break the Taliban's defense of Makuan, Lieutenant Colonel Davis selected a narrow, dusty path that went into the objective area. The battalion designated the path as "Route Michelle East," and Prisock assumed it too would be littered with IEDs. The plan would thus begin with a breaching operation led by combat engineers under protective fire from other troops. It required combining not only various types of troops but also different services. Davis's battalion lacked sufficient engineers, so he had requested additional support and the platoon of ABVs. Once the task force had explosively breached into Makuan, infantry soldiers would establish patrol bases and then conduct a compound-by-compound search for insurgents, IEDs, and homemade explosives. With the Taliban ejected from Makuan, commerce would return to Highway 1, and terrorized farmers who had sought refuge in Kandahar

City would return to their agricultural fields in Zhari. As was often the case, American planning envisioned a clear end state in which the synchronization of combat power seamlessly translated into killing enemy fighters and seizing key terrain.[65]

The opening of Dragon Strike invited intense media attention. Western media outlets spun a narrative that a decisive victory in Zhari, the Taliban's birthplace and spiritual heartland, would hasten the war's termination. CBS News reporter Mandy Clark described the forthcoming campaign as "a much-anticipated offensive to kick the Taliban out of its hometown" and "crucial to President Obama's Afghanistan strategy." In a breaking news segment, ABC News dramatized Dragon Strike's scale and strategic importance: "It's a massive U.S. offensive in southern Afghanistan," the news anchor reported. "Eight thousand American troops, along with Afghan and international forces, are moving to take control of territory that the Taliban has controlled for years." The *New York Times*, while also portraying the operation as "crucial" to President Obama's overall strategy, pointed out that driving the Taliban from the agricultural districts encircling Kandahar City would be bloody, lengthy, and costly. During a previous weeklong embedment with coalition forces in Kandahar, the paper's reporters "observed that every time soldiers left their bases, they were either shot at or hit with bombs, often hidden or booby-trapped."[66]

Despite the media blitz, most Americans understood little and cared even less about what would happen in Zhari. In a *USA Today*/Gallup poll taken in July 2010, registered voters ranked the war in Afghanistan as sixth in importance for the upcoming midterm elections, behind the economy, healthcare, unemployment, the federal budget deficit, and terrorism. A month later, a record-high 43 percent of Americans told Gallup that the war was a "mistake." After nine years of war, the American public may have had a better grasp of the winnability of the war than the Obama administration.[67]

The ABVs provided the vanguard of Prisock's assault (see Figure 6.2) and attacked the minefields of IEDs, use of which, as noted, was reaching a new high. Indeed, during 2010 IEDs killed 268 American servicemembers, a 178 percent increase over 2009 and as many deaths as in the previous three years combined. During their highly publicized 2010 Marjah offensive, however, the U.S. Marine Corps in neighboring Helmand province pioneered a conventional response to the Taliban's unconventional IED tactics: Cold War–era mine-clearing line charges, or MICLICs, fired from the 72-ton ABVs. MICLICs were 350-foot-long rocket-propelled explosive

Figure 6.2 Marine Corps assault breacher vehicle attacks into Makuan with Bravo Company. (Photo credit Brandon Prisock)

line charges containing 1,800 pounds of C4 explosive—essentially a long rope of explosives fired over a field of mines or IEDs. The line charges were discharged from the turret of an ABV, a tracked armored combat vehicle fitted atop the chassis of an M1A1 Abrams main battle tank. First fielded in Afghanistan in late 2009, the ABV possessed a number of subsystems, including dual line charges, a lane-marking system, a remote control system, a mounted Browning .50 caliber (12.7 mm) machine gun, and a front-mounted steel plow that jutted out from the modified vehicle's bow. When the MICLICs were detonated, the mammoth explosion triggered "sympathetic detonations" of IEDs, creating a mine-free path, twenty-six feet wide and a hundred feet long, for vehicles and dismounted infantrymen. Following the line charge detonation, the ABVs' front-mounted plows "proofed" the breached lane in order to destroy any IEDs or homemade bombs that had managed to survive the explosion.[68]

In addition to the ABV platoon drawn from the U.S. Marine Corps' 3rd Combat Engineer Battalion, Prisock's attack force featured fearsome combat power. In a routine example of how the modern U.S. military pulls components from across branch and service lines for specific missions, Prisock's command ballooned from three platoons to the equivalent of nine. In addition to Bravo Company's three rifle platoons, mortar section, and the Marine ABV platoon, Prisock commanded engineers from the 101st Airborne Division's 1st and 2nd Brigades, an explosive ordnance disposal team, a human intelligence collection team, U.S. Navy Seabees, an advanced trauma life support unit, and U.S. Air Force explosive-sniffing dogs—giving his task force an overall strength of 230 uniformed personnel. The Seabees' D8 bulldozers, as well as several mine-resistant ambush-protected (MRAP) vehicles, rounded out Prisock's command.

In addition, although not under Prisock's command, a six-man team of Air Force special forces pararescue jumpers from the 46th Expeditionary Rescue Squadron (ERQS), 451st Air Expeditionary Wing, stood by at Kandahar Airfield, prepared to provide urgent personnel recovery or combat search-and-rescue support. In the air, a wide assortment of unmanned aircraft—Predators, Ravens, Reapers, and Shadows—gave Prisock battle damage assessment, surveillance, lethal, and target acquisition capabilities. Two M777 155 mm howitzers at FOB Wilson provided artillery support. Beefed up with this assemblage of combat power, Prisock might have appreciated Prussian war theorist Carl von Clausewitz's timeless dictum: "Everything in war is very simple, but the simplest thing is difficult." The Battle of Makuan would be no exception.[69]

At sunrise on September 15, Prisock's men crossed the line of departure and rolled south. At 7:15 a.m. Prisock radioed for the howitzers to rain down smoke rounds to obscure the initial breaching route. In short order, the lead ABV moved into position on Route Michelle East and fired the first MICLIC, which uncoiled and snapped on the dirt. Within seconds, two men armed with AK-47 assault rifles darted from within the maze of grape rows adjacent to Michelle East to investigate the line charge. After a hurried look, they turned toward Prisock's men and charged, firing as they ran. Seconds later, the MICLIC detonated, kicking up a thick pall of dust, fire, and smoke as it shook the earth. The blast all but incinerated the insurgents, hurtling one detached torso some two hundred yards into the air. Disoriented, several other fighters concealed in a tree line south of the detonation fled deeper into the Green Zone as Americans atop an Afghan police station's water tower a few hundred meters away pounded them with

Mark 19 40 mm grenade launchers. The ABVs also let loose with punishing barrages of .50-caliber machine gun fire.[70]

Ten minutes after the first MICLIC exploded, the attack force rolled forward and discharged the next MICLIC; neither set off any sympathetic detonations (see Figure 6.3). After the ABVs had proofed the breach lane, they inched forward and fired a third MICLIC, which landed correctly but failed to detonate. To trigger it, a Marine engineer sprinted forward and attached handheld explosives to the line charge, manually igniting it. This time the explosion set off an IED. Over the next hour, Prisock's attack force methodically fired three more MICLICs while inching south, destroying seven IEDs and enabling the Americans and ANA to reach a bridge spanning an east-west irrigation canal. By 10:00 a.m., after a little over two and a half hours of work, the ABVs had breached a lane just under a kilometer long. Rocked by the titanic explosions, the insurgents retreated to prepared firing positions and ammunition caches on the canal's southern side.[71]

Figure 6.3 Bravo Company detonates MICLICs during its attack into Makuan. (Photo credit Brandon Prisock)

The MICLIC's concussive effects and raw power fit the conventional paradigm of a breaching operation, but Prisock's soldiers had never experienced a MICLIC explosion. Physiologically, Lieutenant Murphy recalled how the "deafening thump of the explosion" caused his chest to tighten and triggered a momentary shortness of breath. Williams marveled that the pressure extending outward from the blast radius produced a "whole-body experience." The explosions particularly awed and excited the younger soldiers. Appropriating a cliché from the 2006 Hollywood box office hit *300*, which glorifies Spartan tenacity at Thermopylae, they mockingly shouted in the direction of the insurgents that "our MICLICs will blot out the sun, and we will fight in the shade!" Long flummoxed by spiraling IED casualties, the U.S. military had finally discovered a means for countering them.[72]

After the initial breaching, Prisock's advance stalled at the bridge. Canals and creeks had been a chief planning concern because they funneled vehicles and soldiers toward bridges, narrow choke points where insurgents buried IEDs. Also, the thick tree growth around the waterways afforded insurgents cover and concealment. At the canal, Prisock observed homemade bombs crammed underneath the stone bridge's opposite side, and several IEDs dangled from tree branches on the canal's far side. It was an ingenious trap. If combat engineers crossed the bridge and attempted to defuse the bombs on its bottom side, they would expose themselves to the tree-borne IEDs, which insurgents could detonate remotely. Complicating matters, Prisock's engineers doubted that they could destroy the entire bridge without first securing the other side, and the IED threat precluded that option. With few good options, Prisock ordered the Marines to fire a MICLIC over the bridge. The resulting explosion detonated IEDs atop the bridge, but it did not incinerate the bombs below or in the nearby trees. Unable to cross the bridge, the stationary soldiers, Marines, and Seabees seemed on the verge of becoming a target of opportunity for the insurgents.[73]

After tense deliberation, Prisock called in an air strike to destroy the bridge. Two hours after his force reached the canal, a pair of A-10 Thunderbolts appeared overhead and dropped two 500-pound bombs, which set off at least nine IED explosions and leveled the bridge. Fearful that the Taliban had also buried IEDs parallel to the canal, Prisock directed the ABVs to fire MICLICs to the east and west on the near side of the canal. After the smoke and dust had cleared, the Navy Seabees sprang into action with their bulldozers, erecting a makeshift earthen bridge wide enough for the military vehicles to cross. Without a culvert, however, the impromptu bridge became a dam, and by 4:00 p.m. the area flooded.[74]

Soldiers Versus Insurgents

Up to this point, Prisock, with his ABVs, control of the skies, and indirect fire support, possessed the initiative. Although no documentary evidence from the insurgents exists, the sequence of events suggests that the Taliban abandoned the battlefield after the MICLICs rendered the IED obstacles to the north of Makuan ineffective, retreating to a series of concealed holes and prepared positions south of the canal, where they reorganized and waited for a chance to strike back. With the Americans and ANA momentarily stalled, the insurgents reengaged. They opened up with 82 mm recoilless rifles, RPGs, and AK-47 assault rifles from the opposite bank. Shattered tree branches and shrapnel rained down on the Americans, snapping Specialist Mark Baidinger's femur and lacerating his arms and back. As Prisock radioed for a medical evacuation, the Americans, concealed within the maze of grape rows, returned fire with their M-4s, M240 machine guns, and 60 mm mortars.

According to Lieutenant Williams, the firefight "snapped us back to reality." At the same time, a handful of ANA soldiers popped up from behind the grape rows and recklessly discharged their weapons from the hip, a harbinger of future events. Nevertheless, the mortar fire quickly drove the insurgents into Makuan. After the firefight, the Seabees finished the bridge, the flood dissipated, and Williams's platoon cleared the last two hundred meters before entering the village.[75]

By dusk, the Americans and ANA had secured two compounds at the northern edge of Makuan and converted them into strong points 1 and 2. Williams's and Murphy's platoons and the company's headquarters element occupied strong point 1, while Ragland's platoon settled into strong point 2 with the ANA. The night was miserable. Exhausted and caked with mud from the canal crossing, few soldiers slept. Adding to their discomfort, they had abandoned their assault packs at the canal, depriving them of cold-weather gear and blankets as the temperature plunged. Makuan resembled a ghost town. There were no signs of adults, children, or livestock. Yet the Muslim call to prayer combined with the eerie sound of men burying IEDs—the moment in time that opened this chapter—attested that the enemy lurked in the darkness. "They were watching us," Specialist Jason Leigh observed. "There was somebody out there."[76]

At 3:00 a.m. on September 16, Prisock ordered the men to begin clearing the village. Ragland's and Murphy's platoons searched compounds suspected of insurgent activity, while Williams's men destroyed tree lines adjacent to irrigation canals and wadis (dry streambeds), leveled insurgent firing positions, and used C4 explosives to blast openings in the mud walls encircling pomegranate orchards. The omnipresent IED threat rendered the compound-by-compound searches slow and methodical. Soldiers used mine detectors, bomb-sniffing dogs, and explosives before entering each structure. The anti-personnel obstacle breaching system (APOBS) emerged as one of the soldiers' favorite weapons. A miniature version of MICLICs, APOBS could be transported in backpacks by two-man teams, enabling engineers to destroy IEDs and homemade bombs on narrow paths. In Makuan, engineers fired seven APOBS, destroying five IEDs. The Americans and Afghans uncovered plenty of evidence that the enemy were alert and active. The discoveries included 82 mm recoilless rifle parts, RPGs, small-arms ammunition, IED components, bedding supplies, fresh fruits and vegetables, and a makeshift medical facility. The Americans and ANA were living among an elusive, faceless enemy who blended into the terrain and preferred to fight from a distance and at night with opportunistic assault rifle fire and buried IEDs. No discernable front lines or rear areas existed.[77]

As the grinding contest between a highly trained and technologically superior military organization and evasive insurgent fighters unfolded, the latter dictated both the speed and rhythm of engagements. Specialist Anthony Bower complained that Zhari insurgents were "ghosts on 'banker's hours,' as they would attack us early in the morning, seemingly sleep in the heart of the day, and then hit us again just before darkness sat in." He explained that in the daytime the insurgents typically cloaked their movements and hostile intent by using children as spotters, dressing as women, and "maneuvering with sheep." The pattern, however, varied inside Makuan. At 3:30 a.m., as Murphy's platoon was providing security for engineers blowing up a tree line, the infantrymen came under attack from recoilless rifle fire. In the darkness, Murphy's soldiers spotted two men sprinting through a pomegranate orchard. After the Americans returned fire, Murphy ordered a mortar fire mission. As the mortar team adjusted their fire, the insurgents responded with a pinpoint hail of recoilless rifle rounds that exploded nearby. Murphy sustained shrapnel wounds to his wrist, but after a combat medic had dressed the injury he refused to leave the fight. He then radioed Prisock about the enemy's accurate recoilless rifle barrage, and Prisock in turn called in AH-64 Apache and OH-58 Kiowa helicopters from the 101st Combat Aviation Brigade. The helicopters made several runs against the insurgents. A-10 Thunderbolts then arrived and made multiple low-altitude passes above the orchard, tearing up the terrain with their 30 mm autocannons. Estimating the number of insurgent casualties proved impossible, but Williams observed a detached torso somersaulting through the night sky after one of the A-10 runs. "Good stuff, fun times," the lieutenant quipped.[78]

After a handful of minor engagements, air strikes, and APOBS detonations, the men returned to the strong points and stole some sleep. The night, however, produced a bewildering assortment of sensory experiences, straining the American and ANA soldiers' capacity to maintain awareness, poise, and respond effectively in the face of violence. Just before sunrise, the insurgents again sprang into action, reoccupying several compounds, digging IED holes, and even attending to their prayers, depriving the American and Afghan soldiers of much-needed rest. Makuan was a village of nighttime ghosts. Staff Sergeant Reese admitted that "it was a really sickening feeling. I personally heard them digging."[79]

At daybreak on the sixteenth, the American platoons and their partners resumed blowing up tree lines, clearing IEDs from footpaths, and targeting compounds pinpointed for insurgent activity. Bravo Company only encountered the enemy twice during the day. In the first instance, a single teenager wielding an AK-47 bolted from an American patrol. In the second, a small number of insurgents directed small-arms fire at Delta Company's MRAP all-terrain vehicles, which were positioned in a blocking formation near the rebuilt bridge. After briefly engaging the insurgents, the Americans radioed for A-10 support, which arrived too late. Neither the American nor Afghan soldiers suffered casualties. Nevertheless, the day's events reinforced the Americans' spiraling frustration. The Bravo Company soldiers saw the insurgents as "cowards" who refused to stand and fight and who manipulated the coalition's rules of engagement to their advantage. The Americans also bemoaned that that the Taliban did not participate in sustained firefights, preferring instead to retreat into common areas where civilians usually gathered. Bower's "ghosts" refused to be seen or killed.[80]

Around 7:30 p.m., Lieutenant Colonel Davis ordered Prisock to complete clearing Makuan before noon the next day, September 17. Davis wanted the mission finished before RC-South pulled Prisock's critical assets—including the ABV platoon, air support, and surveillance assets—and assigned them to another unit. The larger goal of Dragon Strike, of which Makuan was only the opening prelude, depended on simultaneity, a concept defined in U.S. Army doctrine as "the execution of related and mutually supporting tasks at the same time across multiple locations and domains." Colonel Kandarian wanted to disrupt the insurgency's command and control, erode its will to fight, and overwhelm its decision-making process by launching simultaneous offensives across multiple locations in Zhari. Clearing Makuan was taking too long. Having received Davis's orders, Prisock prepared for the most daunting challenge of his young command: finishing the clearance of a village riddled with homemade bombs in the darkness.[81]

The Americans and Their ANA Allies

The concept of partnership with the ANA introduced another dimension into Makuan's asymmetrical context. As Secretary of Defense Robert Gates highlighted at the onset of the 2010 troop buildup, training and professionalizing the ANA by partnering them with seasoned American combat units underpinned the coalition's strategic calculus and ultimately its "exit strategy." Judgments about the partnership's potential pace and effectiveness, however, ultimately depended on one's cultural vantage point and expectations, as Colonel Kandarian acknowledged the following month. Looked at from an American perspective, it was "going slower than I personally would like." Looked at from an Afghan perspective, "they are moving with great speed, or they perceive that they are." Bravo Company's final night in Makuan laid bare the possibility that pairing culturally dissimilar soldiers in the crucible of combat widened their sense of alienation rather than gelling them into cohesive fighting formations.[82]

Prisock's soldiers were partnered with a new *kandak* (battalion equivalent) from the ANA's 205th Corps. Three weeks into 1-502 IN's deployment, Bravo Company received the *kandak* at Kandahar Airfield and facilitated its movement to Zhari. Immediately the Americans diagnosed a number of organizational oddities: the *kandak*'s officers were untrained, it had only a handful of non-commissioned officers, and it lacked any semblance of esprit de corps or unity of purpose. This was not a recipe for success. Initially, the company's partnering routine consisted of keeping ANA units in the background, allowing them to shadow their American counterparts on patrols, and shielding them from casualties. When the ANA engaged in firefights, their performance did not impress. Prisock judged that most of the Afghan soldiers were only "halfhearted in their efforts to pursue/destroy the Taliban." Other Bravo Company soldiers groused that the ANA were more committed to smoking hashish than killing the enemy.[83]

The night's chain of events tested the partners' delicate cohesion. As darkness fell on the evening of September 16, Prisock ordered Williams to depart strong point 1 with fifteen Americans, six Afghans, and Air Force Staff Sergeant Brent Olson and his bomb-sniffing German shepherd, named Blek, and search a series of compounds and grape huts (tall, thick-walled buildings for storing grapes) that intelligence had identified as hotbeds of insurgent activity. After clearing the first compound, Williams's team moved to a two-story grape hut with exterior stairs leading to the second level. An American soldier waved his mine detector over the stairs, finding no metal signature. Olson then directed Blek to walk up the staircase to sniff for IEDs. The dog found nothing. With the staircase cleared, three ANA soldiers ascended it in a compact single-file line. The first two Afghans reached the top of the staircase just as the third triggered an IED buried in the fourth step. The gigantic blast punctuated Makuan's unnerving silence, engulfing the ANA soldiers in a flash of flames and smoke. Temporarily blinded and deafened, Williams struggled to regain his bearings, composure, and vision. "As the blast hit me, [the Afghans] all disappeared in a wall of dust and smoke," he recalled. "The ringing in my ears eventually gave way to the sound of my own voice repeating that nobody move[.] I would move to them." Over the past months, Williams and his platoon had learned the hard way that the enemy often planted multiple IEDs together: "Where there is one IED there is always another." He feared that panicked, concussed soldiers would stumble onto other IEDs nearby.[84]

Once Williams had steadied himself, he checked his soldiers for injuries. Encountering one of his squad leaders, he asked about his condition. "What?!," the staff sergeant yelled. "I CAN'T HEAR." Williams identified his injuries as disorientation and momentary deafness and handed him off to his platoon sergeant and a medic. With his eardrums still ringing and the pungent odor of smoldering flesh assaulting his nostrils, Williams retraced his steps back to the staircase and discovered two wounded Americans. The blast had thrown them onto the ground. As he wiped streams of blood from their faces, Williams observed that their wounds were superficial, from rock shards impaled in their skin. He again alerted a medic and moved the final distance to the staircase.[85]

At the blast site, Williams encountered a macabre, chaotic scene, demonstrating the devastating effectiveness of IEDs. Through his night vision goggles, he spotted a "crumpled heap of charred, bloody ANA uniforms and body armor a few meters from the stairs." At that exact moment, the "crumpled heap"—a wounded ANA soldier—regained consciousness and in a desperate, shrieking tone called out for Allah. Moving closer, Williams discovered that the detonation had severed both of the Afghan's legs above the knees; only eight-inch fragments of his fleshless, jagged femurs remained. Williams dragged him to a casualty collection point inside the compound his men had just searched, but upon entering that compound, he uncovered additional IEDs. He needed to find a new rally point.[86]

As Williams dragged the ANA soldier's scorched torso out of the first compound, the other Afghans' poise and discipline vanished. They staggered toward the lieutenant, wildly pointing their M16s at him and each other. Williams attempted to restore order and assuage their fears, but his Afghan translator, wounded in the blast and frozen from fear or a concussion, had "forgotten every English word he knew." Williams admonished the Afghans in broken Dari to remain calm and still, but they continued to inch forward. When they were within feet of Williams and the grievously wounded Afghan, they triggered another IED. The explosion mangled two more ANA soldiers and knocked the wind out of Williams. Struggling to regain his balance and gasping for air, he moved to the blast site, cut away the Afghans' charred uniforms, and applied tourniquets. He now tallied eleven wounded. Hearing the staccato of automatic weapon fire, Williams braced for the enemy, lurking somewhere in the darkness, to overrun his exposed position.[87]

The three remaining uninjured ANA soldiers with Williams may have attributed the mayhem to American incompetence or, even worse, malfeasance. Shouting in Dari, they pointed the barrels of their M16s at the Americans. Disregarding the threat of additional IEDs, they collected the three wounded Afghans, along with their detached limbs, and sprinted back to the strong point. Once inside, they piled the wounded and severed limbs into disorganized heaps, shocking the Americans there. (Williams would later discover that the Afghans who had remained in the strong point with the Americans after he departed with his party on their clearing mission had tried to leave when they heard the explosions; when Staff Sergeant Reese blocked the doorway, the Afghans shoved the muzzles of their M16s in his face, and he stepped aside. Once outside, they discharged their weapons in every conceivable direction. That was the fire Williams had heard after the explosions and misinterpreted as an imminent ambush.)

Meanwhile, Prisock alerted the battalion headquarters that he had a mass casualty situation on his hands, requiring an urgent medevac. He then ordered Murphy to organize a quick reaction force, proceed to Williams's position, and organize a helicopter landing zone. But before either the reaction force or the medevac helicopters could get to Williams's position, the remaining ANA soldiers abandoned the war zone, never to be seen again.[88]

The Afghan soldiers' behavior that night, along with their perceived lack of discipline, periodic drug use, and treatment of their dead and wounded, fed the Americans' belief that the Taliban were more admirable than their ANA partners. Under the strain of combat, the binary categories of "partner" and "enemy" collapsed into each other. The Americans no longer differentiated friend from foe, ascribing instead an irredeemable cultural otherness to everything Afghan. Upon reflection, Sergeant Christensen likened making partnership work to "herding cats." In his judgment, not only did the ANA "lack discipline, training, motivation, and morale," he concluded that many of them served as "double agents with no loyalty ... to their own country." The battle's jarring intercultural dislocations extended to the Americans' own allies.[89]

Yet the ANA soldiers were not wholly responsible for the breakdown. As Murphy later reflected, "We also did a poor job of fully understanding and respecting their cultural holidays, prayer times, etc." Nevertheless, Makuan illustrated that training indigenous police forces, the bedrock of waging counterinsurgencies and imperial conflicts, rested on the shaky assumption that the shared experience of combat against a common foe would forge cohesion in culturally mixed units with divergent conceptions of soldiering, esprit de corps, and the nature of combat itself.[90] But with cohesion irreparably damaged and the boundaries between partner, ally, and adversary blurred, the conditions became more favorable for a tactical stalemate or defeat, ultimately casting doubt on the feasibility of the coalition's preferred exit strategy.

The Wounded

With the Afghans gone, Murphy's platoon departed strong point 1. Captain Prisock, fire support officer First Lieutenant Eric Yates, and other members of the company headquarters element left a short time later. To avoid the maze of IEDs, Prisock chose a route through a marijuana field before linking up with Murphy on a foot trail adjacent to a mud wall. Murphy reported to Prisock that Sergeant Zac McDonald had scouted a safe route to Williams's vulnerable position. Time was of the essence. The soldiers were jittery, worried that the insurgents were coordinating a new attack.

Shortly after the combined team moved out, Yates stepped on a buried IED. The blast pelted soldiers with scorching shrapnel, lifted others into the air, and mortally wounded Yates, who for a time remained conscious and able to speak. Prisock, who was thrown onto the ground by the blast, likened the experience of surviving an IED to "being punched in the face. The overpressure makes you feel weak and off balance." As the smoke cleared, Murphy initially counted only five combat-effective soldiers, while much of his platoon required various degrees of medical assistance. Sergeant Michael Babinski, one of the medics, rushed to Yates's side and tried to stop the bleeding. Prisock radioed Lieutenant Colonel Davis that he had a second mass casualty, and scurried to prepare three helicopter landing zones. In total, twenty-six Americans and Afghans required medical evacuation for injuries ranging from traumatic brain injury to severed limbs.[91]

Moments after the blast, First Sergeant Nathan Stone observed that Yates's radio was missing. Fearful about the important communication device falling into the Taliban's hands, Prisock rounded up a team of engineers to help retrieve it. After returning to the blast crater, the engineers used Bangalore torpedoes to create breaching lanes in the vicinity to enable them to search for the equipment. Pulsing with adrenaline, Prisock abandoned concern for his safety. "Most soldiers hit that point where you have to give up caring what happens to you to do your job," he explained. "Those that can make this decision are functional in combat. Those that can't make that decision cannot function." After a fruitless hour of searching, Prisock called off the search. Meanwhile, several Americans took turns holding Yates's hand, reassuring him, and praying as they awaited the medevac helicopters.[92]

Once Murphy finally reached Williams, the two lieutenants updated each other. Within minutes, they discovered that Staff Sergeant Jamie Newman was missing. Williams suspected the worst. As he put it, "A missing solider after an IED [detonation] typically only means one thing: the IED was large enough to throw the soldier from the blast site and at that point you [are] just trying to find the body." Sergeant McDonald repeatedly failed to reach Newman on the radio, so a group of soldiers returned to the vicinity of the IED attack that had mortally wounded Yates. A cursory search turned up shards of Newman's uniform, his ID card and ammo pouch, and blood streaks and puddles. They soon spotted Newman's lifeless body in a shallow ditch. They retrieved the staff sergeant, placed him in a body bag, and carried him to strong point 1. Newman would be the last casualty from Bravo Company's hellish night in "that Godforsaken village," as Captain Rella, the company's second-in-command, called it.[93]

As the night of September 16 rolled on, medics rushed to stabilize and triage Prisock's wounded. Sergeant Paul Huston, a company medic, agonized over assessing the severity of IED casualties. "As a medic, I think the hardest thing for me is where to get started, cause a lot of times I'm seeing guys that have been blown to literally pieces and I gotta figure out where to start," he explained. Blocking out the moment's chaos, Huston hustled to take advantage of the "platinum 10," the ten minutes following a battlefield injury in which the minimization of blood loss is critical to a soldier's survival. The multiple mass casualties, which he described as a medic's "ultimate challenge," required him to prioritize who required the most urgent care, including the application of tourniquets, quick blood-clotting substances, and bandages.[94]

The most searing sensory experience for combat medics centered on the sharp odors associated with charred bodies ripped asunder by IEDs. As Huston scrambled to triage the wounded, "the smell of blood and hemorrhage, pulverized tissues and organs, bowels and bladders, human meat cooking in the sun and drying out, the rubber smell of body bags, burnt human tissues, [and] the smell of quick clot doing its job" overwhelmed him. "The toughest part psychologically for me . . . is the smells," he concluded. "You never forget these smells."[95]

When the first medevac chopper landed, the soldiers first loaded Yates's nearly lifeless body. The congested night sky soon buzzed with six additional helicopters circling overhead, including two UH-60 Black Hawks belonging to the Air Force's 46th ERQS. The Air Force pararescuemen generally did not execute medevac missions, but the spiraling number of coalition casualties in southern Afghanistan demanded additional support. Given the mayhem and tense situation on the ground, the 46th ERQS brought a significant amount of firepower along with their medical and search-and-recovery assets. Conducting on average three to five missions per day, the pararescuemen—all of whom were registered paramedics—were inserted via helicopter into Makuan. They carried M4 rifles fitted with M203 grenade launchers, extrication gear (jaws of life, inflatable lift bags, saws, and crash axes), fully packed medical rucksacks, and satellite communication equipment. On the UH-60s, the pararescuemen hauled enough medical equipment to conduct minor surgeries on wounded soldiers during the flight back to Kandahar Airfield.[96]

After landing in an overgrown marijuana field near the designated helicopter landing zone, Captain Nicholas L. Morgans's pararescuemen collected the triaged soldiers and loaded them onto the Black Hawks. In all, the medevac lasted ten minutes. "We were in and out, quick," Morgans recounted. As the Battle of Makuan spiraled past its fateful climax, the irony that the medevac served as the mission's most routine and uneventful phase was lost on none of the soldiers. Once the wounded were flown away, the remaining Americans were evaluated for traumatic brain injury, hearing loss, and concussions—signature non-fatal IED wounds.[97]

At battalion headquarters, Davis and his staff, worried about the IED threat and the loss of Yates's radio, grappled with how to end the battle. The strain of combat had yielded an ambiguous outcome, one in which both sides could claim victory. The Americans had seized a key objective south of Highway 1, but they had been unable to destroy Taliban forces or mold their ANA partners into a combat-worthy organization. On the other hand, the Taliban had inflicted a good number of casualties at a low cost and obliterated the cohesion between the Americans and the Afghans, yet they had failed to defend the strategic village or throw Dragon Strike off course.

After much deliberation, Davis came to a decision after midnight on September 17: they would simply destroy most of the unpopulated village. At sunrise, twenty-three of the U.S. Army's M142 rockets slammed into targets across the village, leveling compounds, *qalats*, mud walls, and irrigation canals. In the words of one American staff sergeant, Makuan became a "parking lot."

The series of explosions roused the men from their well-deserved slumber. "We were jolted back to consciousness by deafening earth shaking explosions [that] caus[ed] pieces of the hard mud wall to crumble and fall onto us as we scrambled to grab our kit and weapons," Williams recalled. Prisock and his platoon leaders, now fully awake, wasted little time reflecting; instead they began to plan the next mission.[98]

The Legacy

As the opening act of Dragon Strike, the Battle of Makuan inaugurated the 2010–2011 campaign for Zhari. General Petraeus had envisioned that the operation would drive the Taliban out of the agricultural districts surrounding Kandahar City while providing a window for the ANA to train with Americans before taking over the battlefield the following autumn. During the three-month offensive, CTF Strike cleared every village in Zhari, Maiwand, and Panjwai districts; it destroyed 390 IEDs, 16,000 pounds of homemade explosives, 50 weapons caches, and 34 bunker complexes; finally, it discovered and confiscated 50 AK-47 assault rifles, 10 RPG launchers, and 21,000 rounds of ammunition while conducting 863 air assault operations (about three per day). CTF Strike soldiers also captured 177 suspected insurgents and 28 high-value targets, including Mullah Mullan, the Taliban's Zhari shadow governor, as well as Mullah Satar, a major IED facilitator. The Americans and Afghan partners seized key Green Zone terrain, including Makuan and Sangesar (the village where Mohammed Omar had formed the Taliban), and restored commerce on Highway 1, which U.S. soldiers had cursed as "RPG Alley" only a few months earlier. The return of civilian traffic to the previously deadly highway represented one of Major General Carter's highest objectives, and he praised the grittiness and combat prowess of CTF Strike: "This is the greatest achievement of my command." Ultimately, 28 CTF Strike soldiers paid the ultimate price, while an additional 222 were wounded in action, many with single or multiple limb amputations. In 2012, the U.S. military awarded CTF Strike the Presidential Unit Citation for "conspicuous gallantry and intrepidity in action" during Dragon Strike, the highest decoration bestowed on uniformed military units.[99]

Tactically, Dragon Strike represented one of the most indisputably lopsided American victories of the grinding, decade-long war, but it also symbolized how conventional firepower and "victory" do not always yield strategic dividends. New York Times correspondent Carlotta Gall observed only a month into the offensive that the coalition had "routed" the Zhari-based Taliban. Failing to anticipate the sheer intensity of the coalition's assault, dozens of Taliban fighters were quickly killed and their sanctuaries destroyed. As one senior member of the coalition in southern Afghanistan crowed, Dragon Strike encompassed "'big army' in the classic sense." The combined scale, ferocity, and tempo of the attack led hundreds of insurgent fighters to flee; many of them returned to Pakistan, where they would again train and wait for an opportune moment to strike back. "We are not there anymore, we are not preparing to fight a big battle, but we are waiting," a Taliban fighter explained to Gall. "We are waiting until this force has been exhausted and has done all they are supposed to do, and later on our fighters will re-enter the area."[100]

By the spring of 2011, glimpses of progress popped up across the restive south. In Zhari and Arghandab districts, attendance at *shuras* (governing councils) had increased, villagers began to disclose the location of home-made bombs and IEDs (sometimes even carrying them to U.S. bases), and locals hurled stones and verbal insults at insurgents. But the transformation proved short-lived. The Taliban regrouped and evolved, as they had done after 2003. In early 2011, an anonymous Taliban commander based in Kandahar conceded that the American campaign in Zhari had battered his forces and "reduced" their morale. But he was undeterred, promising that the Taliban would wait out the American onslaught and ultimately persevere. "It will not be difficult," the commander predicted. "We have a lot of brave fighters. . . . We do not bring in tanks and heavy equipment. What we bring is very light and simple." Small wonder that he judged Dragon Strike as little more than a hollow American victory and a momentary setback in a long-term, existential struggle. As he recognized, the coalition, despite piling up tactical victories, had not translated those military successes into concrete strategic gains that ended the war or thwarted the Taliban's political ambitions.[101]

As the U.S. military rapidly reduced its footprint in Afghanistan and transferred responsibility for conducting the war to the Afghan government in early 2015, the Taliban slowly began to retake broad swaths of Afghanistan, particularly in the south and east. Two years later, after President Donald J. Trump agreed to send up to 4,000 additional troops to Afghanistan to curb the spiraling violence, Mullah Abdul Saeed, a Taliban commander in Logar province, mocked the United States' inability to defeat his forces or hasten the war's termination. "One hundred and fifty thousand Americans couldn't beat us," he boasted, adding that the deployment of several thousand additional Americans "will not change the morale of our mujahideen." Queried

about the terms under which the Taliban would enter into a political settlement ending the war, Saeed responded: "Foreigners must leave, and the
constitution must be changed to sharia."[102]

The coalition's post–Dragon Strike strategy, drawdown, and conduct after
2010–2011 have raised fundamental debates about the overall strategy and
military aims for Afghanistan. By the summer of 2017, the United Nations
Security Council described the war as an "eroding stalemate in which the
Taliban have increased the territory they are able to contest and, in some
areas, have begun to consolidate their hold." In August of the same year,
the Special Inspector General for Afghanistan Reconstruction (SIGAR)
assessed that only 57 percent of the country's 407 districts were under the
Afghan government's "control or influence," while 30 percent of the districts
remained "contested." Furthermore, SIGAR detected an uptick in districts
(13 percent) under insurgent "control or influence." So dire had the situation apparently become that the U.S. military instructed SIGAR not to release information about the number of controlled, influenced, or contested
districts in its January 2018 report, despite the data being unclassified. In
addition to the spiraling violence, the "unsustainable" number of casualties
absorbed by the ANA, rampant government corruption, ineffective governance, and an explosion in opiate production (worth an estimated $3 billion
in 2016) that bankrolled the insurgency suggested that the 2010–2011 Zhari
campaign, despite inflicting heavy temporary losses on the Taliban, had not
brought the Americans any closer to achieving a desired strategic end state
than the destruction of al Qaeda and the 2001–2002 toppling of the Taliban
had.[103]

Ultimately, the most immediate American legacy of the war in Afghanistan
may be the U.S. Army's decision to choose to forget. Mirroring the way the
Army in the 1970s and 1980s expunged everything associated with Vietnam,
the contemporary Army has begun to relegate its inconclusive involvement
in Afghanistan and Iraq to the dustbin of institutional history. In particular,
the Army has transitioned from "unified land operations," a 2011 concept
emphasizing the "three-dimensional" nature of warfare, including simultaneous offensive, defensive, and stability operations, to "large-scale combat
operations" (LSCO). The Army sealed the transition to LSCO in its October
2017 Field Manual 3-0, *Operations*. Three of the updated field manual's eight
chapters focus solely on LSCO tactics and procedures. The word "counterinsurgency" appears but twice in the bulky manual's eight chapters. In its
"overview of Army operations," the manual expounded: "The experiences

of the U.S. Army in Afghanistan and Iraq in the early 21st century are not representative of the most dangerous conflicts the Army could face in the future. While the Army conducted combat operations in both locations, for the most part it focused its efforts on counterinsurgency operations and stability tasks. . . . In the future large-scale combat operations against a peer threat will be much more demanding in terms of operational tempo and lethality."

In the manual's foreword, Lieutenant General Michael Lundy, the commanding general of the Combined Arms Center and the commandant of the Command and General Staff College (CGSC) at Fort Leavenworth, Kansas, singled out Russia, China, Iran, and North Korea as the "major regional powers . . . actively seeking to gain strategic positional advantage." His assessment echoed then Chief of Staff of the Army General Mark A. Milley's declaration the previous October that war against a "high-end enemy" was "almost guaranteed." In support of this anticipated future, the Army University Press published a seven-book series in October 2018, the first one dedicated exclusively to American LSCO since 1914.[104]

This selective amnesia, however well-intentioned in preparing soldiers for potential high-intensity conflicts, betrays the institution's own rich history and normative experience. Since the American Revolution, the country's military encounters have mostly resembled messy, intercultural conflicts with indecisive outcomes rather than LSCO against "high-end" adversaries. Conflicts involving the wholesale mobilization of the nation's human and material resources, such as the Civil War and World War II, have been anomalous affairs. Rather, Americans-in-arms have traditionally acted as a frontier constabulary force and imperial policemen, served as peacekeepers, participated in punitive expeditions or raiding parties, and deployed to support a diverse range of overseas contingencies. If history is any guide, Americans soldiers of the future will find themselves in the crucible of combat in dusty, remote hamlets like Makuan rather than against the "major regional powers" in places of the U.S. military's own choosing.

While the Army has moved on and tried to forget, the memory of Makuan remains sharp with Bravo Company's soldiers, who continue to grapple with combat's complex and contested legacies (see Figure 6.4). Brandon Prisock, still serving as a U.S. Army officer, judged the battle a tactical victory that did little to hasten overall strategic success or war termination. He bemoaned the fact that Americans had lost the political appetite for

Figure 6.4 Bravo Company's officers inside an occupied Makuan compound. (Photo credit Brandon Prisock)

furnishing the appropriate resources to finish the job in Afghanistan, a nod to the Taliban's wait-it-out approach.[105]

For Luke Rella, who left the Army in 2015 and then graduated from law school, the aftermath remains searingly personal. On the night of September 17, Prisock ordered Rella to remain at the strong point; Eric Yates ended up taking his place on the fateful patrol that cost the fire support officer his life. Survivor's guilt haunts him: "This is a problem I face and pray about almost daily. The name of Eric Yates is engraved on a band wrapped around my right wrist. He died in the mass casualty event after I was pulled back from going to the village that night," Rella reflected. "This reminder does not give me the warm and fuzzy of a victory."[106]

Now a field-grade officer and a father, Nicholas Williams recently completed the Army's CGSC at Fort Leavenworth. He remains ambivalent about whether Dragon Strike was worth the sacrifice, especially since the post-2011 drawdown led to the abandonment of the Zhari combat outposts that his men had fought so desperately to seize. "The company had a hard time with understanding the purpose of what we were doing and why," he reflected. Tucked away in Williams's basement is a box full of mementos and objects from Zhari: "I have a 'tough box' full of gear . . . that just smells like Afghanistan. Nine years later, Afghanistan feels like a lifetime ago, a story that happened to someone else, somewhere else, but that box always brings me back."[107]

7

The Other Face of Battle

Preparing for the Wrong War

Nicholas Williams's "tough box" of memories (see Figure 7.1), and especially the impact of its smell, offers us his experience of combat in a way we can all relate to. A specific odor can strike a chord of memory and return us to a past time and place. But it is also beyond one's capacity to describe. We can't hope to articulate Williams's experience of combat in Afghanistan. Not even Williams can do that.

Still, that box in storage offers at least a metaphor for the experiences hauled home from war—the things that were carried. The box is there and it is real, whether it is opened or left untouched. That last choice—leaving it unopened—seems to dominate the military at the moment. Williams remembers. The institution he served prefers not to.

This book's primary purpose has been to explore the experience of combat between culturally disparate enemies—the other face of battle. To explore how soldiers in combat respond to unexpected sights, smells, tactics, and more. It did not set out to make a single specific argument about strategy, guerrilla war, counterinsurgency, or PTSD. What it does show, however, is that combat is defined by more than simply an exchange of bullets determined by angles, reload time, cover, penetration, and so on. There is no universal soldier whose sensory system connects to the brain in the same way in all times and places. Neuroscience increasingly shows us that the brain constantly fills in our perceptions with assumptions based on experience. As one neuroscientist put it, the brain forms "best guesses by combining prior expectations or 'beliefs' about the world, together with incoming sensory data."[1] Going into combat is by definition fraught with unexpected input. Add to that an enemy with a wholly different cultural framework, and the

Figure 7.1 Nicholas Williams's "tough box" of memories. (Photo credit Nicholas Williams)

brain struggles to fill in the gaps with the right assumptions. All combat, after all, is also an experience created by the opposition.

In the end, while not specifically calling for policy change, this book is a sort of tough box of experiences, and it suggests some broader issues relevant to understanding the past and to dealing with the future of the U.S. military.

★ ★ ★

The three battles that make up the narrative of this book are distinct from each other in many ways. (We feel obliged to point out that the fact that their names all begin with "M" is purely coincidental.) At Monongahela a fundamentally conventional army was heavily defeated in open battle by irregulars. At Manila the conventional force triumphed against an enemy that started out alike in terms of equipment and tactics but then morphed by degrees into an asymmetrical insurgent. At Makuan an American conventional force that was quite experienced in its environment and remarkably specialized for its mission could not translate those advantages into a clear success against an insurgent enemy, even if it tried to absorb intercultural differences into its ranks. In the end the village was not won but obliterated.

These three fights were conducted by very different American armies. Worldviews and experiences within those different armies, and within the different Americas from which they originated, varied from each other as widely as they did from those of their respective enemies. Even so, the shared intercultural quality of these battles has generated some themes we can both recap and assess for the future.

Dismissiveness

It has been common over the centuries for American soldiers to under-estimate their enemies. The British Army and the American colonists at Monongahela were exceptional in this regard. Experience had taught them how deadly in combat Indians were in the wilderness, and they knew enough to be afraid. Nevertheless, within the set of assumptions that General Braddock carried was a belief that a sufficiently large force moving along a well-constructed supply route could protect itself from them. Solid, volley-firing formations in a mutually supporting arrangement should have been immune to their attacks. But actual combat overwhelmed logic and preparation. In the aftermath, the British and the colonists ascribed defeat not to the martial superiority of their irregular foes but to the failings of the fallen Braddock and his panic-stricken enlisted soldiers.

At Manila, racist assumptions nearly undermined the confluence of cul-tural and technological factors that led Americans to victory in that battle. Those assumptions did undermine them when the war shifted into a guer-rilla conflict.

The Americans at Makuan, like their counterparts at Monongahela, had enough experience with their enemy to know what to expect. But they couldn't let go of conventional thinking about warfare. They continued to dismiss the Taliban as "cowards" who failed to fight traditionally and who insisted on blending in with civilians. American commanders and soldiers knew enough about Taliban capabilities to prepare extensively—such as with the safety net generated by control of the skies—but, like Braddock, they assumed that sufficient preparation would bring clear success.

The tendency to misjudge the enemy's capabilities in intercultural combat is not a problem unique to Americans. In one sense it is simply a variation of a nearly universal ethnocentrism. China's ruling dynasties long saw themselves as the center of the world and considered all outsiders to be barbarians (an English word that derives from the ancient Greeks' attitude toward non-Greeks). Chinggis Khan believed in the Mongols' universal right to rule. Japan famously based their strategy in 1941 on an assumption of American "softness" and lack of will, and they held to that for almost the duration of the war, structuring their tactics accordingly.[2]

Dependence

This tendency to underestimate the "other" was ironically matched by a dependence on that very same "other." At Monongahela, despite the myth that Braddock ignored his Indian allies, he made a real effort to enlist them. That pattern held for virtually every Anglo-Indian war in American history: Indians fought on both sides, and their services were seen as indispensable.[3] Following the Monongahela disaster, the British Army adapted to North American warfare with a growing reliance upon ranger and light infantry companies as well as thousands of Native warriors drawn primarily from the Iroquois Confederacy and the Cherokees. The key role of Indian Scouts in the plains wars of the late nineteenth century no doubt was one reason behind the eventual creation of the Filipino Scouts and then the Filipino constabulary.[4] The former enhanced tactical operations in the jungle, while the latter made governance possible.[5]

The outcome of the fight at Makuan was profoundly shaped by the alliance with Afghan National Army forces, who proved brittle and unreliable under fire in that instance. Despite this, American strategic goals could not be achieved without them. The ANA and other Afghan state security forces will ultimately determine whether or not U.S. strategic ends in the region are met.

Unfortunately for the indigenous or local forces involved, American dependence on them has historically been transactional and transitory. American forces accommodate themselves to indigenous aid, learn how to use it, and then discard it, despite the protestations of personnel who knew what foreign allies had contributed and who hoped for official recognition and fair treatment. The difficulty that local interpreters from Iraq or Afghanistan have had in getting visas for residence in the United States, despite the ongoing danger to themselves and their families, has been well documented.[6] This tendency to discard former local allies has rarely been more tragic than in the Trump administration's decision to withdraw from northern Syria in October 2019, abandoning the Kurds, longtime allies in the fight against the Islamic State, to a Turkish invasion.

More Is Not Always More

Dependence on local allies, especially those deemed "culturally alien"— however defined, whether racially, ethnically, theologically, or linguistically— is rarely the first choice; it's usually the last resort. The U.S. invasion of Afghanistan in 2001 depended heavily on local factions already opposed to the Taliban. Braddock and his successors, as noted, were fully persuaded of the value of Indian allies. Even so, the distinct and not unreasonable prefer- ence has always been to rely on one's own forces. When the environment proves challenging or shifts, however, the American tendency has been to seek solutions in technological superiority and the assumption that more is more: heavier guns, more rounds per minute, more precise targeting, thicker armor, helicopter insertion, and so on. These are things that can be meas- ured, produced, delivered, and deployed. Very often they can indeed be de- cisive, especially in conventional warfare. In our case studies, however, the record is mixed, and it is worth dwelling briefly on why that might be.

Braddock's original mission in 1755 was to oust the French from Fort Duquesne, and then in a fit of strategic hyperventilating, to march his force from there north to Lake Erie, capture several smaller forts along the way, and ultimately take Fort Niagara—totaling some 629 miles overland. Such a mission really did seem to require a lot of "more": an overwhelming body of troops to protect themselves while building a ten-foot-wide road into a hostile, mountainous countryside; a siege train to batter the modern artil- lery fortress the French were building; an almost inconceivable number of wagons and horses to carry supplies; Royal Navy sailors to assist with artil- lery and to construct boats; and preferably some Indian allies to help provide intelligence and a wide security net around the march route. This expansive list of needs wasn't unjustified—much of it really was necessary to deal with Fort Duquesne. But it was also unrealistic. The strategic calculations fo- cused more on the French, and therefore on European notions of territorial control, than on the geography in which they found themselves and the strategic mobility and tactical expertise of their more likely immediate foe, the Indians.

Furthermore, the primary instruments of this expedition—British regulars recruited largely in Britain and Ireland—were presumed to have what they needed for the mission based solely on their training in conventional operations. It is not that the British officers failed to comprehend the vast challenge of North America (although some did fail), but that they still presumed that operating there was a simply a smaller-scale version of the missions they were used to in Europe and that their troops could handle it. At Monongahela, it was the difference in the nature of combat—the unexpected sounds, sights, and methods of their enemy—that broke their nerve. Having "more" had not sufficed. The outnumbered French and Indians, armed only with muskets, war clubs, and tomahawks, had proven that in the woods of North America less was more.

In the Battle of Manila, the Filipinos initially confronted the U.S. Army in a symmetrical manner in a relatively confined space. Adding "more" therefore seemed to make good sense, and indeed at first may have been decisive. Not least among the American advantages was their use of naval and riverboat artillery support. The coastal location and the focus of strategic attention by both sides on controlling the urban capital made such advantages critical. Furthermore, when the Filipinos initially retreated, American pursuit took advantage of the relatively good road network spreading out from Manila to run them to exhaustion. As the war moved deeper into the countryside, however, and as Aguinaldo's forces shifted to guerrilla tactics, and, perhaps most of all, as the political situation of competing tribes, war chiefs, insurgents, and other local power players became more complicated, simply having "more" became less useful. Ultimately, neither numbers nor qualitative technological advantage played much of a role. The war was eventually (and at great cost) won by small, mobile pursuit forces following the model developed in the wars against the Plains Indians. Ironically, that model had never been folded into formal doctrine and was soon forgotten in favor of building an army for more conventional operations against European foes.

In some ways the false decisiveness of the Battle of Manila paralleled the events in Afghanistan in the fall and winter of 2001–2002. There American advantages in the air and with precision weapons proved decisive in ousting the Taliban from their urban centers.[7] Although American commanders imagined what they were doing as "less"—trying to put as few boots on the ground as possible and thereby avoiding the appearance of replicating the Soviet occupation—they nevertheless were delivering "more" in terms of deploying forces with a vast qualitative technological superiority. As we all know, however, that swift victory proved illusory. Even going in "light" sometimes proved counterproductive.

In early 2002, for example, the plan for Operation Anaconda—an operation designed to prevent al Qaeda from fleeing to refuge in Pakistan—deliberately left behind the usual artillery, and planned to rely almost entirely on air support. Unfortunately, the enemy proved to be more numerous than expected, well fortified on the mountainsides, and equipped with mortars and machine guns. Ultimately, although still lacking any larger artillery, American forces were able to bring up the mortars they had left behind and establish fire superiority.[8] Even so, key al Qaeda leaders, including Osama bin Laden himself, escaped the dragnet, and the Taliban went to ground both locally and in the mountains of Pakistan. American strategic focus then shifted to Iraq. Some key American planning staff officers who normally would have been working on Operation Anaconda were back in the United States already planning for that invasion.[9] Gradually the Taliban reemerged to contest for control of the populace in the countryside and undermine the willingness of the international community to support the nascent Afghan state.

By the time of Operation Dragon Strike and the fight at Makuan in 2010, American strategic attention had returned to Afghanistan, where the need to train up local forces was incontrovertible. Without an effective Afghan National Army to take over the fight, the United States had no other exit strategy except unilateral withdrawal. Meanwhile, the Americans told themselves that the ANA needed time to mature and grow, and while they did, U.S. and NATO forces would do the heavy lifting. It was yet another version of American planning for a "knockout punch." At Makuan every conceivable relevant tactical asset was brought to bear. Even at this micro tactical level, the answer was "more." The result was an unstable situation, allied casualties, and an ambiguous outcome (village obliteration) whose strategic implications were probably counterproductive. American strategic planners in 2010 declared they had "taken the gloves off": they deployed M1 Abrams tanks to Afghanistan, increased airstrikes, and dramatically increased the enemy body count—and they proudly proclaimed progress.[10] In the years since, it has become clear that using "more" had not produced "more." Although the precise security status of Zhari district in

2021 is classified, recent news reports from the area suggest that government control is at best tentative.[11]

The failure of "more" in part reflects the complexity of the strategic and the political challenge when Americans are involved in combat. Let's put this another way. There is a famous problem in mathematics known as the "three-body problem." Isaac Newton provided the mathematical solution that predicted the paths of two bodies (e.g., planets) orbiting each other, their paths predictable depending upon their relative mass and distance. Adding only one additional mass to the interacting orbits renders the problem mathematically insoluble. Clausewitz's theory on war, a book that still profoundly influences modern militaries, fundamentally presents war as a two-body problem. He begins with the dynamic interaction of two competing agents, each seeking to impose its will on the other. His theory progresses to a three-body problem *within* each of the competing sides (the trinity of the people, the government, and the military). But as British military officer and analyst Emile Simpson has quite reasonably pointed out, war is often defined by more than two competing wills. The war in Afghanistan is not a binary war between the United States plus the Afghan government against the Taliban. Politically speaking, especially at local levels, there are many more armed players, each pursuing their own interests, in a constant dynamic with the other players. Furthermore, even if not a direct party to the conflict, international audiences affect the outcome. These "politics" are far more complex than those in Clausewitz's famous dictum that "war is a continuation of politics with an intermingling of other means." To a very large degree, as discussed in Chapter 1, winning in these conflicts is about more than violently imposing one's will; it is about having, as Simpson says, a "more appealing strategic narrative of what the conflict is about." Strategy becomes persuasion, of which destruction of the enemy armed forces is merely one kind or branch of argumentation.[12] In this strategic environment, it is not clear if more would ever produce more.

Trauma and the Civil–Military Gap

All this makes it harder to generate a successful "strategic narrative" in a complex, multi-polar conflict. Asymmetry and confusion dominate. And that shapes the lives and afterlives of those who experienced it. Life after combat is an exceedingly complex subject and we cannot do justice to it here, but we can make some suggestions. There is a common assumption that American soldiers returning from the war in Vietnam were more traumatized than other veterans because of that lack of a clear narrative. World War II and even the Korean War were fundamentally bipolar: Axis versus Allies, North Korea and China versus the United Nations. Those wars generated a comprehensible "good war" narrative. Veterans of Vietnam, as well as Iraq and Afghanistan, struggled (and still struggle) to convey both the nature and the meaning of their experience. Against Germany, progress could be measured in miles from Berlin. In the guerrilla wars, ground fought for and died over was just as quickly abandoned. Micheal Clodfelter, an infantryman in Vietnam, later reflected on the lack of clarity generated by Vietnam compared to America's earlier wars, admitting that he might "have come out of any war disillusioned. Even when fought for the most glorious cause." Unfortunately, "the only war offered our generation was Vietnam, surely the most disillusioning war ever fought by Americans."[13]

Do intercultural wars produce greater trauma? Suicide rates among veterans of Afghanistan and Iraq outpace the rate in the general population, reflecting a statistical reality that these wars produced unseen wounds, but Manila and Monongahela are hard to gauge in this respect.[14] There are no statistical measures available, but as discussed in the introduction, at least some of the survivors of Monongahela thought it the worst fight they had ever seen. In the eighteenth century, though, there was little notion of the psychic wounds of war, and certainly not one that found support in the wider culture.[15] For the single battle at Manila we can say almost nothing at all, though the wider war with the Filipinos convinced at least some doctors and other observers that the nature of the fight there had caused psychological damage. Writing in 1902, Dr. Henry Rowland opined that American soldiers were suffering from clinical "nostalgia" that produced discontent and even atrocity.[16]

Experts have tried to pinpoint the source of this enhanced sense of trauma in the wars against others, some assigning it to the radical dissonance between the soldiers' expectations of combat and their actual experience, or to the seeming lack of strategic purpose, direction, or success. Almost all have emphasized the post-deployment experience: the disconnection from friends, family, and society in general. In Vietnam this alienation worsened in the later years of the war as the anti-war movement vilified or at least ostracized soldiers as "baby killers." As we discussed in the introduction, the alienation resulted from the soldiers' personal narratives of war not aligning with the public expectations. To Clodfelter, the impact of the Vietnam War on his family and friends was "similar to that made by a pebble dropped into the depths of the ocean."[17] Literary critic and World War II veteran Paul Fussell explored this phenomenon even for the relatively symmetrical World War II experience, pointing out how soldiers and civilians generated separate (and dissonant) languages to describe their wartime experiences.[18] That dissonance widens in an intercultural war, as it was no doubt wider in the conventional war against a Japanese enemy in World War II. In the words of veteran E. B. Sledge, after describing another Marine using his knife to remove the gold teeth of a still struggling Japanese soldier: "The war . . . made savages of us all. We existed in an environment totally in-comprehensible to men behind the lines—service troops and civilians."[19] But the gap widens even further in a multi-polar conflict that lacks a clear strategic narrative.

Today, the American public, hoping to avoid the divisions of the Vietnam era, shows bipartisan gestures of support. First Lieutenant Eric Yates, who was killed at Makuan, was honored recently at his alma mater, Western Kentucky University, by a memorial 5K run and by a ceremony at a foot-ball game announcing a scholarship in his name. As part of that ceremony, Yates's mother quoted his last letter: "What I'm trying to say is, I don't want to be forgotten."[20] But forgetting is inevitable, and the phrase "Thank you for your service" becomes increasingly hollow.[21]

Preparing for the Expected War

The so-called civil-military gap has important strategic consequences. One is that it makes it easier for the institutional military to "forget" intercultural wars and focus on the conventional ones. As argued in the introduction to this book, Americans have almost always prepared for the next war based not on the last war (despite the popular adage) but rather on the assump-tion that the next war will involve someone like themselves.[22] Braddock prepared to confront the French in a conventional positional siege, not a mobile Indian army in the woods. American soldiers and officers at Manila expected only to have to fight the Spanish, not a Filipino independence movement. And Americans prior to 2001 never imagined insurgencies in places they have a hard time finding on a map. Crucially, this expectation is often paired with the "lesser included" fallacy: the belief that handling the bigger conflicts makes handling the smaller ones easy. This was clearly Braddock's assumption. However much he might have wanted allied Indian assistance, he was assured in his belief in the superiority of European tactical techniques.

There is a painful irony here when viewed over the long haul of American history. Nadia Schadlow, a political scientist closely involved in writing the 2018 United States National Security Strategy, also wrote a book that reminds us that that every war in American history, not just the intercultural ones, has required a military role in post-conflict governance, in peacekeeping and policing.[23] The irony is that the more institutionalized and professional the military became, the *easier* it became to ignore the lessons of the unexpected wars and the undesirable missions. Despite the military schools and the written doctrine and the accumulation of "lessons learned," the more modern the army, the more readily it has forgotten them. The Virginians accompanying Braddock knew what they were getting into, and local militia forces on the frontier retained that kind of knowledge over the decades that followed. The old soldiers of 1899 had accumulated years of informal lore about how to fight Indians, and they put that unwritten knowledge to work in the Philippines. In contrast, by the outset of the war in Afghanistan, the military had spent three decades consciously forgetting the lessons learned in Vietnam.[24]

Because of the debacle in Iraq after the 2003 invasion, by the time of the fight at Makuan in 2010 the institutional ship had slowly turned, and a great deal of experience had been accumulated at both the tactical and strategic levels. The Department of Defense's 2006 joint publication on planning, for example, created a more formal construct for "phases" of an operation, including a "phase IV" that dealt with activities after "major combat operations" had ended.[25] That same year, a new manual to instruct Army and Marine forces on counterinsurgency (FM 3-24) was released.[26]

It remains to be seen whether any of those changes will lead to the ultimate policy goal of a stable and friendly regime in Afghanistan. What is clear now, however, is that the reduction of U.S. forces in that country (and in counterinsurgency missions elsewhere) has created an institutional backlash. Some officers in the U.S. Army began referring to those officers seemingly focused on counterinsurgency as "COINdinistas." There is no doubt a need to refresh the Army's ability to fight large-scale conventional war. It is a complex skill that needs practice. But the turn away from recent experience, as the soldiers who have fought in Afghanistan and Iraq will tell you, has been abrupt and radical. The next war had better be the expected war.[27]

Why It Matters

In the summer of 2019, despite a five-year high in U.S. military casualties in Afghanistan and a breakdown of peace negotiations with the Taliban, the U.S. Army pivoted its attention. After almost two decades of fighting insurgent conflicts in Afghanistan and Iraq, the Army turned its focus to large-scale combat operations (LSCO) against adversaries such as China, Russia, Iran, or North Korea. Lieutenant General Michael D. Lundy, the commanding general of the Combined Arms Center and commandant of CGSC at Fort Leavenworth, Kansas, explained in 2018 that the threat of war from great powers demanded that the Army "adapt to the realities of a world where large-scale ground combat against a peer threat is more likely than at any time in recent history." In the same year, the updated National Defense Strategy validated the Army's institutional overhaul, instructing the joint force to shift from an emphasis on irregular war to great power competition, just as it had done after the Vietnam War.[28]

To steer the LSCO transition, the Army updated its doctrine, training, organization, and education. The 2017 publication of FM 3-0, *Operations*, emphasized that division, corps, and field army operations would prevail "during large-scale ground combat." At the Army's force-on-force combat training centers in Germany, Louisiana, and California, rotating units were subjected to a training environment that eschewed counterinsurgency, stability operations, and combating terrorism. Furthermore, the Army took steps to jettison its brigade-based modular force structure, which it had adopted in the late 1990s to counter non-state threats and actors, in favor of a division-centric organization. At Fort Leavenworth's CGSC, senior leaders also implemented an "evolutionary shift" in the education of field-grade officers. FM 3-0 served as the "primary driver" of the revamped curriculum; as a result, historical studies of counterinsurgency and contingency operations largely vanished from the curriculum. As CGSC's Colonel Robert A. Law III quipped, "Gone are the days of CGSC teaching brigade-level operations in a counterinsurgency environment; the curriculum has been realigned to the division fight—the great nation fight."[29] The Army has even stood down whole organizations created and designed to help it fight asymmetrically, not least, in late 2020, the Asymmetric Warfare Group and the Rapid Equipping Force (the latter sought off-the-shelf technologies to solve unexpected problems encountered in combat).[30]

Preparing for this new LSCO-centered future required a host of modernization efforts and organizational changes. In 2017, the Army prioritized six new conventional capabilities: long-range precision fires, the "next-generation combat vehicle," future vertical lift, the Army network, air and missile defense, and soldier lethality. In short: "more." On August 24, 2018, the Army also activated a new four-star command, U.S. Army Futures Command, in Austin, Texas, to streamline and guide its new ambitious modernization and acquisitions program. The current U.S. Army Chief of Staff, General James C. McConville, tweeted on October 15, 2019, that "America's Army will never be out-gunned, it will never be out-ranged, and it will never be over-matched."[31] This replicates precisely the spirit of Vietnam-era officers who claimed that the Americans had won all of the battles.

All of these developments suggest that the Army, as in the past, lacks the introspective spirit necessary to study, apply, and codify its rich experiences with low-intensity, asymmetric, and usually, intercultural conflict. Rather, it has aligned itself for a future conflict that its own history suggests was the exception rather than the norm, and in which culture will somehow be less relevant: the "great nation fight." The future seems a more comfortable place than the recent past.[32] History suggests otherwise. The other face of battle will likely again be the face America sees.

Abbreviations

Add.Mss.	Additional Manuscripts, British Library
ADM	Admiralty Papers, The National Archives
(UK)ANOM Archives	Nationales d'Outre-Mer, Aix-en-Provence, France
BL	British Library
CO	Colonial Office Papers, The National Archives (UK)
DRCHNY	E. B. O'Callaghan, and Berthold Fernow, eds., *Documents Relative to the Colonial History of the State of New York*, 14 vols. (Albany, 1855)
GWP-C	Papers of George Washington, Colonial Series
GWR	Fred Anderson, ed., *George Washington Remembers: Reflections on the French and Indian War* (Oxford, 2004)
JBO	Journal of a British Officer, in Charles Hamilton, *Braddock's Defeat* (Norman, 1959), 39–58
JSCL	Sir John St. Clair Letterbook, John Forbes Papers, University of Virginia
MANA	Stanley Pargellis, ed., *Military Affairs in North America, 1748–1765* (New York: Archon Books, 1969)
MPCP	Samuel Hazard, ed., *Minutes of the Provincial Council of Pennsylvania*, 16 vols. (Philadelphia, 1852)
RCB	Journal of Captain Robert Cholmley's Batman, in Charles Hamilton, *Braddock's Defeat*(Norman, 1959), 5–36
SWJP	James Sullivan et al., eds., The Papers of Sir William Johnson, 14 vols. (Albany, 1921–1963).
TNA	The National Archives, United Kingdom
WO	War Office Papers, The National Archives (UK)

Notes

INTRODUCTION

1. Alfred A. Cave, *The Pequot War* (Amherst: University of Massachusetts Press, 1996), 69–108.
2. Underhill in Charles Orr, ed., *History of the Pequot War: The Contemporary Accounts of Mason, Underhill, Vincent and Gardener* (Cleveland, OH: Helman Taylor Co., 1897), 51 (quote); for his earlier life, see the *Oxford Dictionary of National Biography*, s.v. Underhill, John, online edition, https://doi.org/10.1093/ref:odnb/27999.
3. Underhill in Orr, *History*, 60.
4. Philip L. Barbour, ed., *The Jamestown Voyages Under the First Charter, 1606–1609* (Cambridge: Cambridge University Press for the Hakluyt Society, 1969), 1:50–51.
5. These themes are explored in John Grenier, *The First Way of War: American War Making on the Frontier, 1607–1814* (Cambridge: Cambridge University Press, 2005) and Wayne E. Lee, *Barbarians and Brothers: Anglo-American Warfare, 1500–1865* (New York: Oxford University Press, 2011).
6. Donald M. Snow, *National Security*, 7th ed. (New York: Routledge, 2020), chap. 9.
7. This crucial reimagining of American military history is at the center of Fred Anderson and Andrew Cayton, *The Dominion of War: Empire and Liberty in North America, 1500–2000* (New York: Viking Penguin, 2005).
8. We are aware that Monongahela was part of the beginning of what would become a very large and important war indeed (the Seven Years' War), but in 1755 that was not yet obvious.
9. An interesting exception in modern films, television, and some literature is the near-fetishization of special operations forces of various kinds. Doing so highlights only very specific kinds of combat and divorces those combat portrayals from any meaningful strategic consequences. It also tends to diminish the significance of the combat experience of other veterans. See Paul B. Rich, *Cinema and Unconventional Warfare in the Twentieth Century: Insurgency, Terrorism and Special Operations* (New York: Bloomsbury, 2018).
10. Alexander Hunter, "A High Private's Sketch of Sharpsburg: Paper No. 2," *Southern Historical Society Papers* 11, no. 1 (Jan. 1883): 18.

11. James M. McPherson, *For Cause and Comrades: Why Men Fought in the Civil War* (New York: Oxford University Press, 1997), chap. 11.

12. Quoted in Stephen W. Sears, *Landscape Turned Red: The Battle of Antietam* (New York: Ticknor & Fields, 1983), 280.

13. Duncan Cameron, *The Life, Adventures, and Surprizing Deliverances of Duncan Cameron, Private Soldier in the Regiment of Foot, Late Sir Peter Halkett's* (Philadelphia: James Chattin, 1756), 12–13.

14. "Before the Manila Battle," *Chicago Daily Tribune*, Feb. 20, 1899.

15. Quoted in Christian G. Appy, *Patriots: The Vietnam War Remembered from All Sides* (New York: Penguin Books, 2003), 365.

16. Cathal Nolan is the latest in a long line of historians to note this long-standing predilection. Cathal J. Nolan, *The Allure of Battle: A History of How Wars Have Been Won and Lost* (New York: Oxford University Press, 2017).

17. Underhill in Orr, *History*, 78–81.

18. Taylor Murphy, personal communication with Anthony Carlson, Oct. 10, 2016.

19. Jason Motlagh, "The Afghan War: Why the Kandahar Campaign Matters," *Time*, Monday Oct. 18, 2010. http://content.time.com/time/world/article/0,8599,2026158,00.html.

20. Shakespeare, *Henry V*, Act 4, Scene 8, lines 112–13.

21. Daniel Bolger, *Why We Lost: A General's Inside Account of the Iraq and Afghanistan Wars* (Boston: Houghton Mifflin Harcourt, 2014), 284.

22. See the discussion of gigantism in Alex Roland, *War and Technology: A Very Short Introduction* (Oxford: Oxford University Press, 2016).

23. To be clear: European and American soldiers also learned to scalp, but even as they did so, they protested Indians' use of it as evidence of their innate savagery.

24. Emile Simpson, *War from the Ground Up: Twenty-First-Century Combat as Politics* (Oxford: Oxford University Press, 2018), 22, 23, 27, 31, 36, 38, 58, 73.

25. See the discussion and the sources cited in Interlude II, "Fighting 'Small' Wars."

26. Wikipedia's list of American wars is quite reasonable. We exclude domestic insurrections and non-military interventions abroad. Some of the more recent interventions in Iraq and Syria overlap substantially, but the main point is the scale. "List of Wars Involving the United States," Wikipedia, https://en.wikipedia.org/wiki/List_of_wars_involving_the_United_States, accessed Dec. 5, 2018.

27. It is worth considering the extent to which centralization and institutionalization of the American military *worsened* the mismatch of preparation. Local militias and state forces in the eighteenth and nineteenth centuries, for example, retained irregular skill sets typically dismissed in regular army training.

28. The nature of the SFAB organization is only slowly becoming clear in public documents. Some relevant discussions can be found here: Gary Sheftick, "New Academy Will Train Security Force Assistance Brigades," U.S. Army, Feb. 17, 2017, https://www.army.mil/article/182572; C. Todd Lopez, "Security Force Assistance Brigades to Free Brigade Combat Teams from Advise, Assist Mission," U.S. Army, Sept. 18, 2017, https://www.army.mil/article/188004/

security_force_assistance_brigades_to_free_brigade_combat_teams_from_advise_assist_mission.

29. Sean D. Naylor, "After Years of Fighting Insurgencies, The Army Pivots to Training for a Major War," *Small Wars Journal*, Oct. 31, 2018, http://smallwarsjournal.com/blog/after-years-fighting-insurgencies-army-pivots-training-major-war; Lieutenant General Michael Lundy and Rich Creed, "The Return of U.S. Army Field Manual 3-0, *Operations*," *Military Review* 97, 6 (Nov.–Dec. 2017): 14–21.

30. Quote from Jon Harper, "TRADOC Unveils 'Big Eight' Modernization Priorities," *National Defense*, Mar. 16, 2016, https://www.nationaldefensemagazine.org/articles/2016/3/16/tradoc-unveils-big-eight-modernization-priorities; Sydney J. Freedberg Jr., "Cyber/EW, Aviation, Air Defense, Artillery: CSA Milley's Priorities," *Breaking Defense*, January 12, 2017, https://breakingdefense.com/2017/01/cyberew-aviation-air-defense-artillery-csa-milleys-priorities.

31. The combat experience of pilots or anti-aircraft gunners aboard ships could be included here, but our primary analytical lens is ground combat.

32. Data on number of living veterans from "Veteran Population," National Center for Veterans Analysis and Statistics, https://www.va.gov/vetdata/Veteran_Population.asp, accessed Aug. 6, 2019; active duty force size from "Demographics of the U.S. Military," Council on Foreign Relations, accessed Aug. 6, 2019; https://www.cfr.org/article/demographics-us-military. Also James Fallows, "The Tragedy of the American Military," *The Atlantic*, Jan.–Feb. 2015, https://www.theatlantic.com/magazine/archive/2015/01/the-tragedy-of-the-american-military/383516.

33. John Keegan, *The Face of Battle* (New York: Penguin Books, 1978), 36.

34. Two recent examples that survey the American experience in battle are Christopher Hamner, *Enduring Battle: America's Soldiers in Three Wars, 1776–1945* (Lawrence: University Press of Kansas, 2011) and Alexander Rose, *Men of War: The American Soldier in Combat at Bunker Hill, Gettysburg, and Iwo Jima* (New York: Random House, 2015).

35. The problem of accessing the voices of colonized others while questioning the "what really happened" claims within the sources of the dominant powers is now a common thread in history. See Edward W. Said, *Orientalism* (New York: Pantheon Books, 1978); Gyan Prakash, "Subaltern Studies as Postcolonial Criticism," *American Historical Review* 99, no. 5 (1994); and Amar Singh et al., *Reversing the Gaze: Amar Singh's Diary: A Colonial Subject's Narrative of Imperial India* (Boulder, CO: Westview Press, 2002).

36. Quoted in Robin Braithwaite, *Afgantsy: The Russians in Afghanistan 1979–89* (Oxford: Oxford University Press, 2011), 335.

37. Russell Worth Parker, "I'm Prepared to Talk About the Things I Did in Iraq. Are People Ready to Listen?," *New York Times Magazine*, Jan. 17, 2019, https://www.nytimes.com/2019/01/17/magazine/iraq-marine-phraselator.html.

CHAPTER 2

1. David L. Preston, *Braddock's Defeat: The Battle of the Monongahela and the Road to Revolution* (Oxford: Oxford University Press, 2015), 217–21, 226; Thomas Gage to Lord Albemarle, July 24, 1755, BL, Add. Mss. 32857, ff. 338–39.

2. Journal of Captain Robert Orme, in Winthrop Sargent, *The History of an Expedition Against Fort Duquesne in 1755* (Philadelphia: J. B. Lippincott, 1856), 354; RCB, 27-28; JBO 49. *Writings of George Washington*, ed. Jared Sparks (Boston: John B. Russell, 1833), 2:469 (spectacle).

3. John R. Alden, *General Gage in America* (Baton Rouge: Louisiana State University Press, 1948), chap. 1; Preston, *Braddock's Defeat*, 187–94.

4. *Expedition of Major-General Braddock to Virginia; with the Two Regiments of Halket and Dunbar* (London: H. Carpenter, 1755), 28; Preston, *Braddock's Defeat*, 221, 226–29. Robert Hunter Morris to Sir Thomas Robinson, July 1, 1755, CO 5/16, ff. 19–20, discusses Braddock's letter written while he was at Bear Camp, dated June 21, 1755, of his plan to invest Fort Duquesne on July 10, 1755.

5. Adam Stephen to John Hunter, Fort Cumberland, July 18, 1755, BL Egerton Mss. 3429, ff. 277–82; Preston, *Braddock's Defeat*, 226–30.

6. RCB, 28; George Croghan, quoted in Paul E. Kopperman, *Braddock at the Monongahela* (Pittsburgh: University of Pittsburgh Press, 1977), 184; "Seaman's Journal," in Sargent, *History of an Expedition*, 388; [Harry Gordon], "Journal of Proceedings," July 23, 1755, and "Anonymous Letter on Braddock's Campaign," July 25, 1755, in *MANA*, 106, 113, 117.

7. [Cameron, Duncan], *The Life, Adventures, and Surprizing Deliverances of Duncan Cameron, A Private Soldier in the Regiment of Foot, Late Sir Peter Halket's* (Philadelphia: James Chattin, 1756), 12–13.

8. Matthew Leslie, quoted in Kopperman, *Braddock*, 204.

9. Thomas Birch to Lord Royston, August 30, 1755, BL Add. Mss. 35398, Hardwicke Papers, Vol. L, ff. 280–82; Spencer Phips to Sir Thomas Robinson, August 4, 1755, TNA CO 5/16, ff. 143–44, Colonel John Winslow to William Coffin, August 22, 1755, in *Collections of the Nova Scotia Historical Society* 3 (1885): 72; George Washington to Robert Jackson, August 2, 1755, *GWP-C*, 1:350.

10. N. Darnell Davis, ed., "British Newspaper Accounts of Braddock's Defeat," *Pennsylvania Magazine of History and Biography* 23 (1899): 319. William Smith, *Discourses on Public Occasions in America* (London: A. Millar, 1762), 97.

11. Catherine Desbarats, "The Cost of Early Canada's Native Alliances: Reality and Scarcity's Rhetoric," *William and Mary Quarterly* 52 (October 1995): 609–30; Preston, *Braddock's Defeat*, 14–22.

12. Marquis Duquesne, quoted in Preston, *Braddock's Defeat*, 15; see appendices in Louise Dechêne, *Le peuple, l'état et la guerre sous le régime français* (Montreal: Éditions Boreal, 2008), 468–509.

13. Douglas MacGregor, "The Shot Not Heard Around the World: Trent's Fort and the Opening of the War for Empire," *Pennsylvania History* 74 (Summer 2007): 354–73; Jason Cherry, *Pittsburgh's Lost Outpost: Captain Trent's Fort* (Charleston, SC: History Press, 2019); Charles Morse Stotz, *Outposts of the War for Empire: The French and English in Western Pennsylvania: Their Armies, Their Forts, Their People, 1749–1764* (Pittsburgh: Historical Society of Western Pennsylvania, 1985), 80–87.

14. Preston, *Braddock's Defeat*, 17–18, 26–29; Preston, "The Trigger: A Just-Discovered Account Provides Startling New Evidence That It Was George Washington Who Fired the Shot That Sparked the French and Indian War," *Smithsonian Magazine* 50, no. 6 (October 2019): 30–41, 78.

15. Preston, *Braddock's Defeat*, 29–30.

16. WO 47/44, f. 207 ("Expedition to Virginia"); *MANA* 45–54 (Braddock's instructions); Preston, *Braddock's Defeat*, 29–41.

17. Braddock to Morris, April 15, 1755, in *Pennsylvania Archives*. 9 series, 138 vols. Philadelphia and Harrisburg, 1852–1949), 1st ser., Vol. 2: 290; *Benjamin Franklin's Autobiography*, ed. Joyce E. Chaplin (New York: W. W. Norton, 2012), 127; Preston, *Braddock's Defeat*, chap. 3.

18. Thomas More Molyneux, *Conjunct Expeditions: or Expeditions That Have Been Carried on Jointly by the Fleet and the Army* (London: R. & J. Dodsley, 1759); Preston, *Braddock's Defeat*, 32, 46–47, 74.

19. *The Political Mirror*, 1776, 29.

20. Lee McCardell, *Ill-Starred General: Braddock of the Coldstream Guards* (Pittsburgh: University of Pittsburgh Press, 1958); Preston, *Braddock's Defeat*, 43–49.

21. Sir Thomas Robinson to Newcastle, Sept. 22, 1754, BL Add. Mss. 32736, Newcastle Papers, Vol. LI, ff. 563–64; Preston, *Braddock's Defeat*, 50–52.

22. Stephen Saunders Webb, *Marlborough's America* (New Haven, CT: Yale University Press, 2013); Preston, *Braddock's Defeat*, 54–68.

23. J. A. Houlding, *Fit for Service: The Training of the British Army, 1715–1795* (Oxford: Oxford University Press, 1981); "State and Condition of His Majesty's Hired Transports," January 10, 1755, ADM 1/2292: Captains' Letters, 1755, Section 9; Preston, *Braddock's Defeat*, 67–68.

24. "Petite-Guerre," in George Smith, *An Universal Military Dictionary* (London: J. Millan, 1779), Eighteenth Century Collections Online ed.; Peter E. Russell, "Redcoats in the Wilderness: British Officers and Irregular Warfare in Europe and America, 1740 to 1760," *William and Mary Quarterly* 35 (October 1978): 629–52; John Grenier, *The First Way of War: American War Making on the Frontier* (Cambridge: Cambridge University Press, 2005), chap. 3.; Armstrong Starkey, *European and Native American Warfare 1675–1815* (London: UCL Press, 1998), 46–51.

25. Preston, *Braddock's Defeat*, 60–63; Murray Pittock, *Culloden* (Oxford: Oxford University Press, 2016), emphasizes the conventional nature of the Jacobites' organization, tactics, and weaponry at Culloden.

26. Loudoun to Cumberland, October 2, 1756, *MANA*, 234; Sir John St. Clair to Lord Loudoun, January 12, 1756, Loudoun Papers, Huntington Library, San Marino, California, LO 753; Preston, *Braddock's Defeat*, 36–37.

27. JBO, 50 (Mawhawking [i.e., tomahawking]); "Inquiry into the Behaviour of the Troops at the Monongahela, Albany, Nov. 21, 1755," TNA, WO 34/73, ff. 45–46; Dunbar, in Kopperman, *Braddock*, 188; RCB, 29–30.

28. Preston, *Braddock's Defeat*, 32–33.

29. George Washington to Earl of Loudoun, January 10, 1757, *GWP-C*, 4:90. Preston, *Braddock's Defeat*, 32–36, 39–40. See also Stephen Eames, *Rustic Warriors: Warfare and the Provincial Soldier on the New England Frontier, 1689–1748* (New York: New York University Press, 2011).

30. "Sketch of an Order about the Rank &ca of the Provincial Troops in North America," November 12, 1754, *MANA*, 43–44; Dinwiddie to Horatio Sharpe, June 20, 1754, in Robert Alonzo Brock, ed., *The Official Records of Robert Dinwiddie* (Richmond: Virginia Historical Society, 1883–1884), 1:213. "Gentleman volunteer" was a contemporary term designating an ambitious or zealous civilian who served in a military capacity, often with the intent of gaining formal rank and commission.

31. Preston, *Braddock's Defeat*, 32–36. 39–40; Journal of Captain Robert Orme, 312; James Titus, *The Old Dominion at War: Society, Politics, and Warfare in Late Colonial Virginia* (Columbia: University of South Carolina Press, 1991); William A. Foote, "The American Independent Companies of the British Army, 1664–1764," Ph.D. diss., UCLA, 1966.

32. See John Demos, *The Unredeemed Captive: A Family Story from Early America* (New York: Alfred A. Knopf, 1994); Matthew Ward, *Breaking the Backcountry: The Seven Years' War in Virginia and Pennsylvania, 1754–1765* (Pittsburgh: University of Pittsburgh Press, 2003), 46; Ian K. Steele, *Setting the Captives Free: Capture, Adjustment, and Recollection in Allegheny Country* (Montreal: McGill-Queen's University Press, 2013); see James Smith, *Scoouwa: James Smith's Indian Captivity Narrative*, ed. John J. Barsotti (Columbus: Ohio Historical Society, 1996) for British terminology.

33. Julia Osman, "Pride, Prejudice, and Prestige: French Officers in North America During the Seven Years' War," in *The Seven Years' War: Global Views*, ed. Mark Danley and Patrick Speelman (Leiden: Brill, 2012): 192.

34. Gilles Havard, *The Great Peace of Montreal of 1701: French-Native Diplomacy in the Seventeenth Century*, trans. Phyllis Aronoff and Howard Scott (Montreal: McGill-Queen's University Press, 2001); Jon Parmenter, *The Edge of the Woods: Iroquoia, 1534–1701* (East Lansing: Michigan State University Press, 2010).

35. Quoted in D. Peter MacLeod, *The Canadian Iroquois and the Seven Years' War* (Toronto: Dundurn Press, 1996), 64.

36. MacLeod, *The Canadian Iroquois*, xv. For Native decisions during the 1745 expedition, see "Journal de la campagne de Sarastaugué, 1745," Schuyler Papers, Reel 41, New-York Historical Society.

37. George Washington to Robert Dinwiddie, March 10, 1757, *GWP-C*, 4:113; Preston, *Braddock's Defeat*, 151–55; Christian Ayne Crouch, *Nobility Lost: French and Canadian Martial Cultures, Indians and the End of New France* (Ithaca, NY: Cornell University Press, 2014).

38. Liénard de Beaujeu, "Journal de la Campagne du Détachment de Canada à l'Acadie et aux Mines, en 1746–47," in *Le Canada Français* 2 (1889): 66–67; Preston, *Braddock's Defeat*, 131–34; on the 1745 Saratoga raid, see David Preston, *Colonial Saratoga: War and Peace on the Borderlands of Early America* (Washington, DC: National Park Service, 2019).

39. Preston, *Braddock's Defeat*, 155–59.

40. Preston, *Braddock's Defeat*, 149–51, 159–63.

41. "Major William Sparke Along the Monongahela: A New Historical Account of Braddock's Defeat," ed. Sheldon Cohen, *Pennsylvania History* 62 (October 1995): 550; Preston, *Braddock's Defeat*, 170 (British officers); Charles Lee to Sidney Lee, June 18, 1756, *The Charles Lee Papers* (New York: Collections of the New-York Historical Society, 1871–1874), 1:3.

42. Houlding, *Fit for Service*, 195; Preston, *Braddock's Defeat*, 75–85. See also Timothy J. Shannon, *Indians and Colonists at the Crossroads of Empire: The Albany Congress of 1754* (Ithaca, NY: Cornell University Press, 2000), for the general contours of intercolonial cooperation and imperial politics.

43. St. Clair to Braddock, February 9, 1755 and St. Clair to Sir Peter Halkett, April 17, 1755, JSCL, Box 1, 16–17, 105.

44. Franklin, *Autobiography*, 127; Preston, *Braddock's Defeat*, chap. 3; Alan Houston, ed., "Benjamin Franklin and the 'Wagon Affair' of 1755," *William and Mary Quarterly* 66 (April 2009): 235–86; Albert Louis Zambone, *Daniel Morgan: A Revolutionary Life* (Yardley, PA: Westholme Press, 2018).

45. Preston, *Braddock's Defeat*, chap. 5; Copy of an Order to Lt. Spendelowe, March 14, 1755, ADM 1/480, Box 2, Part 3, ff. 610–15.

46. Preston, *Braddock's Defeat*, 135–41.

47. Preston, *Braddock's Defeat*, 141–48.

48. Thanks to Wayne Lee for his thoughts on Native logistics, and his forthcoming essay "'The Indians Are Hunting': Native American Expeditionary Logistics and the Problem of Territorial Conquest"; James H. Merrell, "'Their Very Bones Shall Fight': The Catawba-Iroquois Wars," in Daniel K. Richter and James H. Merrell, *Beyond the Covenant Chain: The Iroquois and Their Neighbors in Indian North America, 1600–1800* (Syracuse, NY: Syracuse University Press, 1987), 115–33.

49. [Chevalier James Johnstone], *A Parallel of Military Errors, of Which the French and English Armies Were Guilty, During the Campaign of 1759, in Canada* (Quebec: Literary and Historical Society of Quebec, 1887), 29.

50. Braddock to Robinson, April 19, 1755, in Jacob Nicholas Moreau, *A Memorial Containing a Summary View of the Facts, with Their Authorities. In Answer to the Observations Sent by the English Ministry to the Courts of Europe* (New York: H.

Gaine, 1757), 130; Franklin, *Autobiography*, 132; Preston, *Braddock's Defeat*, 35, 119 (Stobo), 109–18.

51. *MPCP* 6:589 (Scaroyady); John K. Rowland, "Treating American Indians as 'Slaves,' 'Dogs,' and Unwanted Allies: George Washington, Edward Braddock, and the Influence of Ethnocentrism and Diplomatic Pragmatism in Ohio Valley Military Relations, 1753–1755," in *A Companion to George Washington*, ed. Edward Lengel (Malden, MA: Wiley-Blackwell, 2012), 32–52; Preston, *Braddock's Defeat*, 119–20, 200–201.

52. George Washington to John Augustine Washington, June 28–July 2, 1755, *GWP-C*, 1:321; Preston, *Braddock's Defeat*, 180–85.

53. "Expeditions" and "Coup de Main," in Smith, *An Universal Military Dictionary*.

54. Anonymous Letter, *MANA*, 120; Preston, *Braddock's Defeat*, 130–31 (French complacency).

55. Douglas R. Cubbison, *"The Artillery Never Gained More Honour": The British Artillery in the 1776 Valcour Island and 1777 Saratoga Campaigns* (Fleischmanns, NY: Purple Mountain Press, 2008).

56. Contrecoeur à le marquis de Vaudreuil, le 21 juin 1755, Duquesne to Contrecoeur, February 15, 1755 and April 27, 1755, in Fernand Grenier, ed., *Papiers Contrecoeur et autres documents concernant le conflit anglo-français sur l'Ohio de 1745 à 1756* (Québec: Les presses universitaires Laval, 1952), at 366, 275, 323.

57. Contrecoeur to Vaudreuil, July 14, 1755, *MANA*, 129; Preston, *Braddock's Defeat*, 188–89, 193, 201–2, 205, 209–10.

58. For references to Skowonidous, see *SWJP* 1:544 n. 1 (Skowonidous); cf. *DRCHNY* 7:178 (Showonidous); "Seaman's Journal," 378 ("Jerry Smith"); *SWJP* 1:529 (Delaware lineage).

59. Preston, *Braddock's Defeat*, 187–89; Smith, *Scoouwa*, 24.

60. Contrecoeur à Beaujeu, le 7 juin 1755, et Contrecoeur à le marquis de Vaudreuil, le 21 juin 1755, *Papiers Contrecoeur*, 356–57, 366; Preston, *Braddock's Defeat*, 128, 147, 163, 222–23.

61. Kopperman, *Braddock*, 256 (Beaujeu); Preston, *Braddock's Defeat*, 160–63, 209–10, 355 (assembling); Claude De Bonnault, ed., "Pièces au sujet de M. Landriève," *Bulletin des recherches historiques* 33 no. 8 (August 1927): 497–512.

62. Michel-Pierre-Augustin-Thomas Le Courtois des Bourbes à son cousin Surlaville, 20 octobre 1755, Archives du Calvados, Caen, France, Fonds Surlaville, Série F-1859 (author translation); *Bataille du fort Duquesne defaitte de Bradok*, 1755 map in Library and Archives Canada, NMC 7755; Preston, *Braddock's Defeat*, 222–26. Le Courtois's letter is translated and published in its entirety in Preston, *Braddock's Defeat*, 355–56.

63. Preston, *Braddock's Defeat*, 223–29; Map of Fort Duquesne, in "General Braddock's Military Plans, Captured by the French Before Fort Duquesne," 1755, Huntington Manuscripts 898, Huntington Library, San Marino, California.

64. Le Courtois, quoted in Preston, *Braddock's Defeat*, 356; "Seaman's Journal," 388; Laperière to Contrecoeur, June 1755, Archives du Séminaire de Québec, Fonds Viger-Verreau, Carton 2, no. 135, reel 1 (Courtemanche).

65. St. Clair to Robert Napier, July 22, 1755, *MANA*, 103.

66. See Preston, *Braddock's Defeat*, 228–30 and 285 for a discussion of Stanley Pargellis's arguments, which reflect an ignorance of the actual terrain and of the French and Indian dispositions in the battle.

67. Gage to Albemarle, July 24, 1755, BL Add. Mss. 32857, ff. 338–39; Le Courtois, quoted in Preston, *Braddock's Defeat*, 356; Kopperman, *Braddock*, 254, 259; Francis-Joseph Audet, *Jean-Daniel Dumas: Le héros de la Monongahela* (Montréal: G. Ducharme, 1920), 24–25; Return of Ordnance, July 18, 1755, *MANA*, 97; Preston, *Braddock's Defeat*, 323, 402 n. 35 for British artillery.

68. "Journal of Christian Frederick Post," in *Early Western Journals, 1748–1765*, Reuben Gold Thwaites (Cleveland: Clark, 1904), 1:231; Preston, *Braddock's Defeat*, 234; Kopperman, *Braddock*, 268; *Annual Register of 1759* (London, 1760), 34; Davis, "British Newspaper Accounts of Braddock's Defeat," 319; Winthrop Sargent, "Winthrop Sargent's Diary While with General Arthur St. Clair's Expedition Against the Indians," *Ohio Archaeological and Historical Quarterly* 33 (April 1924): 258 (horse bells).

69. [Ebenezer Denny], *The Military Journal of Major Ebenezer Denny, an Officer in the Revolutionary and Indian Wars* (Philadelphia: J. B. Lippincott, 1859), 68.

70. "Journal of Christian Frederick Post," 1:231; Smith, *Scoouwa*, 162; William Michael Gorman, ed., *A Concise Account of North America, 1765, Originally Published in 1765 by Major Robert Rogers* (Westminster, MD: Heritage Books, 2007), 165–66.

71. Dr. Alexander Hamilton, quoted in Leroy V. Eid, "'A Kind of Running Fight': Indian Battlefield Tactics in the Late Eighteenth Century," *Western Pennsylvania Historical Magazine* 71 (April 1988): 147–71; Preston, *Braddock's Defeat*, 235.

72. Le Courtois, quoted in Preston, *Braddock's Defeat*, 356, 237–38; Franklin Thayer Nichols, "The Braddock Expedition, 1754–1755," Ph.D. diss., 1946, Harvard University, 303 n. 68 (Tatton); Stuart Reid, *1745: A Military History of the Last Jacobite Rising* (New York: Sarpedon, 1966), 39 (Tatton at Prestonpans).

73. *Expedition of Major-General Braddock*, 28; William Dunbar, quoted in Kopperman, *Braddock*, 187; "Seaman's Journal," 388; "Major William Sparke," 551; Horatio Gates, in Kopperman, *Braddock*, 196 (fifteen of eighteen officers); Preston, *Braddock's Defeat*, 238–40.

74. St. Clair to Napier, July 22, 1755, *MANA*, 103; Kopperman, *Braddock*, 170; Preston, *Braddock's Defeat*, 240–41.

75. Robert Orme to Augustus Keppel, July 18, 1755, in "The Keppel Manuscripts Descriptive of the Defeat of Major-General Edward Braddock," ed. Charles Henry Lincoln, *Transactions and Collections of the American Antiquarian Society* 11 (1909): 175; JBO, 50 (crowding twenty to thirty deep); Preston, *Braddock's Defeat*, 245–47.

76. Gage to Albemarle, July 24, 1755; "Keppel Manuscripts," 175; Preston, *Braddock's Defeat*, 248–51.

77. Horatio Sharpe to John Sharpe, August 11, 1755, BL Add. Mss. 32858, f. 111; JBO, 50; "Inquiry," TNA WO 34/73, ff. 45–46; Gage to Albemarle, July 24, 1755; Anonymous Letter, July 25, 1755, *MANA*, 117.

78. "Major William Sparke," 553; JBO, 50; "An Account of the Detachment of Seamen," ADM 1/2009, f. 20.

79. Preston, *Braddock's Defeat*, 243–45, 255; "Journal of Christian Frederick Post," 230.

80. For Captain Cholmley's death, see *London Evening Post*, November 27, 1755, 1; *SWJP* 1:544 n. 1 (Skowonidous); Loudoun to Cumberland, August 20, 1756, *MANA*, 225. See also Richard Hall, "'Storys, Scalping and Mohawking': American Tales, Narratives, Stories—'The Rhetoric of Fear'—and the Defeat of General Edward Braddock," *Journal of Early American History* 5 (September 2015): 158–86.

81. Orme to Keppel, in "Keppel Manuscripts," 175 (pickled); Orme to Franklin, July 27, 1755, in Houston, "Wagon Affair," 284 (leg wound); *South Carolina Gazette*, August 21, 1755 (Morris); George Washington to Mary Ball Washington, July 18, 1755, *GWP-C* 1:336–37 (duty and early timing in battle); Elaine G. Breslaw, ed. "A Dismal Tragedy: Drs. Alexander and John Hamilton Comment on Braddock's Defeat," *Maryland Historical Magazine* 75, no. 2 (1980): 118–44, at 137 (Shirley killed at same time as Halkett).

82. Dunbar, quoted in Kopperman, *Braddock*, 187.

83. St. Clair to Earl of Hyndford, September 3, 1755, JSCL, 169–70; RCB, 29–30; Preston, *Braddock's Defeat*, 248–50, 405 n. 75, citing Dave Grossman's work on the physiology of combat; Davis, "British Newspaper Accounts of Braddock's Defeat," 316. See also Trevor N. Dupuy, *Understanding Defeat* (McLean, VA: NOVA Publications, 1990), and B. A. Friedman, *On Tactics: A Theory of Victory in Battle* (Annapolis: Naval Institute Press, 2017), chaps. 10–11.

84. St. Clair to Robert Dinwiddie, July 23, 1755, JSCL, 142–43; Preston, *Braddock's Defeat*, 250–54.

85. General Court-Martial of Private Martin Lucorney, New York Independent Company of Peter Wraxall, July 13, 1757, WO 71/65, f. 354. Stephen Brumwell first discovered Lucorney's important testimony. "Return of His Majesty's Independant Company of Foot Commanded by Captain Horatio Gates New York 29th: January 1756," Horatio Gates Papers, New-York Historical Society (an unpublished return never previously cited in studies of Gates or of the Monongahela); Preston, *Braddock's Defeat*, 249–53.

86. *GWR*, 19; see Preston, *Braddock's Defeat*, 253–55 and 406 n. 90 for contemporary evidence of Washington's claim.

87. JBO, 51; Gage to Albemarle, July 24, 1755 (giving way).

88. JBO, 52; Preston, *Braddock's Defeat*, 255–57; Admission Books (1755–1764), Royal Hospital, Chelsea, TNA WO 116/5, ff. 4, 8, 20, 25; Archives nationales d'outre-mer, COL E 100, f. 401 (dossier Croisil de Courtemanche).

89. JCB, 30; Preston, *Braddock's Defeat*, 259–60.

90. "Judge Yeates Visit to Braddock's Field," *Hazard's Register* 6 (August 1830): 104–5; Preston, *Braddock's Defeat*, 260–66 and appendix D, 347–49; Smith, *Scoouwa*, 25–26.

91. Attestation of William Johnstone, John Adair, and Robert Stuart, June 26, 1764, TNA WO 4/75A, f. 383 (La Péronie).

92. GWR, 20; Preston, *Braddock's Defeat*, 261–63, 269–82; Lord Barrington to Apothecary General, March 16, 1757, WO 4/53, f. 363 (medicines lost). See also Paul Kopperman, "The Medical Aspect of the Braddock and Forbes Expeditions," *Pennsylvania History* 71 (Summer 2004): 257–84; Erica I. Nuckles, "'Remarks on a March': A Female Perspective on Gender, Rank and Imperial Identities During the French and Indian War," Ph.D. diss., University of Albany, 2018.

93. *A Modest Address to the Commons of Great Britain, and in Particular to the Free Citizens of London; Occasioned by the Ill Success of Our Present* (London: J. Scott, 1756), 9; Preston, *Braddock's Defeat*, 1–10, 282–87.

94. Smith, *Scoouwa*, 162

95. "Captain Thomas Morris's Journal," in *Early Western Journals, 1748–1765*, Reuben Gold Thwaites (Cleveland: Clark, 1904), 1:311; John Craig Deposition, March 30, 1756, Penn Papers Indian Affairs, Vol. 2 (1754–1756), Historical Society of Pennsylvania, 78 (parcel); Preston, *Braddock's Defeat*, 288–302.

96. Johnstone, *A Dialogue in Hades*, 32; Stephen Brumwell, *Redcoats: The British Soldier and War in the Americas, 1755–1763* (Cambridge: Cambridge University Press, 2002), 200–201.

97. GWR, 21; Loudoun to Cumberland, November 22–December 26, 1756, *MANA*, 269.

98. Thomas Gist, quoted in David L. Preston, "'Make Indians of Our White Men': British Soldiers and Indian Warriors from Braddock's to Forbes's Campaigns, 1755–1758," *Pennsylvania History* 74 (Summer 2007): 295; see also Brumwell, *Redcoats*.

99. Adam Stephen to George Washington, August 20, 1757, GWP-C 4:375; Preston, *Braddock's Defeat*, 303–16.

100. Preston, *Braddock's Defeat*, 8–9, 311–14; on British logistics, see David L. Preston, *Colonial Saratoga: War and Peace on the Borderlands of Early America*, National Park Service Historic Resource Study (Washington, DC: National Park Service, 2019), chap. 3.

101. Franklin, *Autobiography*, 134; Bouquet to Duke of Portland, December 3, 1758, in Sylvester K. Stevens, Donald H. Kent, and Louis M. Waddell, eds. *The Papers of Henry Bouquet*, 6 vols. (Harrisburg: Pennsylvania Historical and Museum Commission, 1951–94), 2:620; Preston, *Braddock's Defeat*, 311, 328.

102. Timothy J. Todish and Todd E. Harburn, *"A Most Troublesome Situation": The British Military and the Pontiac Uprising of 1763–1764* (Fleischmanns, NY: Purple Mountain Press, 2006); Martin West, *Bouquet's Expedition Against the Ohio Indians in 1764 by William Smith* (Kent: Kent State University Press, 2017); Charles Brodine, "Henry Bouquet and British Infantry Tactics on the Ohio Frontier, 1758–1764," in *The Sixty Years' War for the Great Lakes, 1754–1814*, ed. David Curtis Skaggs (East Lansing: Michigan State University Press, 2001), 43–61.

103. Brumwell, *Redcoats*, 6; Preston, *Braddock's Defeat*, 316; Matthew Spring, *With Zeal and with Bayonets Only: The British Army on Campaign in North America, 1775–1783* (Norman: University of Oklahoma Press, 2008). See also Houlding, *Fit for Service*, chaps. 3, 5, and 6, for the evolution of light infantry.

104. George Washington to Robert Dinwiddie, March 10, 1757, *GWP-C*, 4:113.

105. Thomas A. Chambers, *Memories of War: Visiting Battlegrounds and Bonefields in the Early American Republic* (Ithaca, NY: Cornell University Press, 2012), chap. 1.

106. Robert K. Wright, *The Continental Army* (Washington, DC: Center of Military History, 1983), 23–24; Preston, *Braddock's Defeat*, 323–31.

107. *Military Journal of Major Ebenezer Denny*, 118.

CHAPTER 3

1. James Kirby Martin and Mark Edward Lender, *A Respectable Army: The Military Origins of the Republic, 1763–1789* (Arlington Heights, IL: Harlan Davidson, 1982); John Shy, "The Military Conflict Considered as a Revolutionary War," in *A People Numerous and Armed*, ed. John Shy (Oxford: Oxford University Press, 1976), 78. To be clear, the British army adjusted its tactics, uniforms, and training systems to fight in heavily wooded North America. They did not fight exactly as they had in Europe, but they nevertheless remained primarily a linear army, producing volleys and charging with the bayonet. Matthew H. Spring, *With Zeal and with Bayonets Only: The British Army on Campaign in North America, 1775–1783* (Norman: University of Oklahoma Press, 2008).

2. The key text here is John Grenier, *The First Way of War: American War Making on the Frontier, 1607–1814* (Cambridge: Cambridge University Press, 2005). Armstrong Starkey argues that such units were not as effective as often claimed; see his *European and Native American Warfare, 1675–1815* (Norman: University of Oklahoma Press, 1998). Contrarily, Guy Chet argues that real decisiveness depended on sticking with European linear tactics that Indians struggled to overcome, in *Conquering the American Wilderness: The Triumph of European Warfare in the Colonial Northeast* (Amherst: University of Massachusetts Press, 2003). It is worth mentioning that ranger units often fought directly alongside units of allied Native Americans, or were even heavily composed of them. See Brian D. Carroll, "'Savages' in the Service of Empire: Native American

Soldiers in Gorham's Rangers, 1744–1762," *New England Quarterly* 85, no. 3 (2012): 383–429.

3. Brian McAllister Linn, *The Echo of Battle: The Army's Way of War* (Cambridge, MA: Harvard University Press, 2007), 10–37.

4. J. P. Clark, *Preparing for War: The Emergence of the Modern U.S. Army, 1815–1917* (Cambridge, MA: Harvard University Press, 2017), 25–29; Joseph T. Glatthaar, *The American Military: A Concise History* (New York: Oxford University Press, 2018), 25–27.

5. Colin G. Calloway, *The Victory with No Name: The Native American Defeat of the First American Army* (New York: Oxford University Press, 2015); William Hogeland, *Autumn of the Black Snake: George Washington, Mad Anthony Wayne, and the Invasion That Opened the West* (New York: Farrar, Straus and Giroux, 2017).

6. Wayne E. Lee, *Barbarians and Brothers: Anglo-American Warfare, 1500–1865* (New York: Oxford University Press, 2011), 219–30; Antulio J. Echevarria II, *Reconsidering the American Way of War: US Military Practice from the Revolution to Afghanistan* (Washington, DC: Georgetown University Press, 2014), 93–97; Peter Maslowski, "The 300-Years War," in *Between War and Peace: How America Ends Its Wars*, ed. Matthew Moten (New York: Free Press, 2011), 144–49; Andrew J. Birtle, *U.S. Army Counterinsurgency and Contingency Operations Doctrine, 1860–1941* (Washington, DC: Center of Military History, 1998, 2009), 67–69.

7. Maslowski, "The 300-Years War," 144.

8. David D. Smits, "The Frontier Army and the Destruction of the Buffalo: 1865–1883," *Western Historical Quarterly* 25, no. 3 (1994): 312–38; Wayne E. Lee, "'The Indians Are Hunting': Native American Expeditionary Logistics and the Problem of Territorial Conquest," article in preparation; Robert M. Utley, *Frontier Regulars: The United States Army and the Indian, 1866–1891* (New York: Macmillan, 1973), 423 n. 20.

9. Wayne E. Lee, "Plattsburgh 1814: Warring for Bargaining Chips," in *Between War and Peace: How America Ends Its Wars*, ed. Matthew Moten (New York: Free Press, 2011), 61; Maslowski, "The 300-Years War," 152.

10. William B. Skelton, *An American Profession of Arms: The Army Officer Corps, 1784–1861* (Lawrence: University of Kansas Press, 1993); Clark, *Preparing for War*.

11. Linn, *Echo of Battle*, 20–21.

12. Michael A. Bonura, *Under the Shadow of Napoleon: French Influence on the American Way of Warfare from the War of 1812 to the Eve of World War II* (New York: New York University Press, 2012).

13. Birtle, *U.S. Army Counterinsurgency, 1860–1941*, 86–87.

14. Walter E. Kretchik, *U.S. Army Doctrine: From the American Revolution to the War on Terror* (Lawrence: University Press of Kansas, 2011), 81–84; Utley, *Frontier Regulars*, 45–57.

15. Clark, *Preparing for War*, 183–87.

16. Wayne E. Lee, *Waging War: Conflict, Culture, and Innovation in World History* (New York: Oxford University Press, 2015), 376–81.

CHAPTER 4

1. Japan is an obvious exception, though even here, the Japanese were treated in the same essentialist fashion as Native Americans, Filipinos, and so on. They too found themselves overwhelmed by the United States in World War II.
2. Katharine Bjork, *Prairie Imperialists: The Indian Country Origins of American Empire* (Philadelphia: University of Pennsylvania Press, 2019), chaps. 5–6.
3. John Bowe, *With the Thirteenth Minnesota in the Philippines* (Minneapolis: A. B. Farnham, 1905), 82–83.
4. Brian McAllister Linn, "The Long Twilight of the Frontier Army," *Western Historical Quarterly* 27, no. 2 (Summer 1996): 141–67.
5. Despite being blamed by an American inquiry after the catastrophe, the Spanish do not seem to have had anything to do with the *Maine's* explosion. Instead, the most convincing theory is that a buildup of coal gas in the ship's bunkers exploded. See Hyman George Rickover, *How the Battleship Maine Was Destroyed* (Washington, DC: Naval History Division, Dept. of the Navy, 1976).
6. Jose S. Arcilla, "The Fall of Manila: Excerpts from a Jesuit Diary," *Philippine Studies* 37, no. 2 (1989): 194.
7. Volker Schult, "Revolutionaries and Admirals: The German East Asia Squadron in Manila Bay," *Philippine Studies* 50, no. 4 (Winter 2002): 496, 501.
8. Thomas A. Bailey, "Dewey and the Germans at Manila Bay," *American Historical Review* 45, no. 1 (October 1939).
9. Alexander Leroy Hawkins, *Official History of the Operations of the Tenth Pennsylvania Infantry, USV, in the Campaign in the Philippine Islands* (San Francisco: Hicks-Judd, 1899), 2–3.
10. Hawkins, *Tenth Pennsylvania*, 2–3.
11. Hawkins, *Tenth Pennsylvania*, 2–3.
12. "General Wesley Merritt," *Journal of the Illinois State Historical Society* 3, no. 4 (1911): 130–33.
13. Edward M. Coffman, *The Hilt of the Sword: The Career of Peyton C. March* (Madison: University of Wisconsin Press, 1966), 14.
14. Richard R. Poplin, "The Letters of W. Thomas Osborne: A Spanish-American War Soldier of Bedford County," *Tennessee Historical Quarterly* 22, no. 2 (1963): 156.
15. Poplin, "Letters," 156.
16. Ernest C. James, *The First, Sixth, Seventh and Eighth California Volunteer Regiments and the California Heavy Artillery in the Spanish American War and Philippine Insurrection, 1898–1899* (Sacramento: Ernest C. James, 1996), 11.
17. Hawkins, *Tenth Pennsylvania*, 3.
18. Arcilla, *Fall of Manila*, 213.

19. Alexander Laist, *Official History of the Operations of the First Montana Infantry, USV, in the Campaign in the Philippine Islands* (San Francisco: Hicks-Judd, 1899), p. 10.

20. David Silbey, *War of Frontier and Empire: The Philippine-American War, 1899–1902* (New York: Hill & Wang, 2007), 46.

21. Kenneth Ray Young, *The General's General: The Life and Times of Arthur MacArthur* (Boulder, CO: Westview Press, 1994), 194.

22. Aguinaldo did have some notice of the plan. An August 10 telegram from del Pilar warned Aguinaldo that the Spanish planned to surrender to the Americans, who were going to "deceive" the Filipinos. Del Pilar to Aguinaldo, August 10, 1898, in John R. M. Taylor, *The Philippine Insurrection Against the United States: A Compilation of Documents with Notes and Introduction* (Pasay City, Philippines: Eugenio Lopez Foundation, 1971), 1:10.

23. James, *California Volunteer*, 49.

24. Hawkins, *Tenth Pennsylvania*, 9.

25. Charles Maybey, *The Utah Batteries: A History* (Salt Lake City: Daily Reporter, 1900), 37.

26. Elwell S. Otis, *The Indian Question* (New York: Sheldon, 1878), 221.

27. William Thaddeus Sexton, *Soldiers in the Sun: An Adventure in Imperialism* (Harrisburg, PA: Military Service Publishing, 1939), 64.

28. William L. Luhn, *Official History of the Operations of the First Washington Infantry, USV, in the Campaign in the Philippine Islands* (San Francisco: np, 1899), 8.

29. James, *California Volunteer*, 79.

30. James, *California Volunteer*, 79.

31. *History of the Operations of the First Nebraska Infantry, USV in the Campaign in the Philippine Islands* (n.p.: n.p., 1899), 14.

32. John R. M. Taylor, *Report on the Organization for the Administration of Civil Government Instituted by Emilio Aguinaldo and His Followers in the Philippine Archipelago* (Washington, DC: Government Printing Office, 1903), 54–55.

33. Telegram to Aguinaldo, January 10, 1899, in Taylor, *Philippine Insurrection*, 39.

34. Jeffrey J. McLean, "The MacArthurs and the Mitchells: Wisconsin's First Military Families," *Wisconsin Magazine of History* 94, no. 2 (2010): 9.

35. Sexton, *Soldiers in the Sun*, 78.

36. Sexton, *Soldiers in the Sun*, 87.

37. Laist, *First Montana*, 7.

38. Sexton, *Soldiers in the Sun*, 84.

39. Sexton, *Soldiers in the Sun*, 84.

40. Maybey, *Utah Batteries*, 47–48.

41. Frederick Jackson Turner, "The Significance of the Frontier in American History," *Annual Report of the American Historical Association*, 1893, 199–229.

42. Kristin L. Hoganson, *Fighting for American Manhood: How Gender Politics Provoked the Spanish-American and Philippine-American Wars* (New Haven, CT: Yale University Press, 1998), chaps. 6–7.

43. Poplin, "Letters," 164.

44. "Before the Manila Battle," *Chicago Daily Tribune*, February 20, 1899.

45. Murat Halstead, *The Story of the Philippines: The El Dorado of the Orient* (Chicago: Barber, 1898), 7.

46. Rudyard Kipling, "The White Man's Burden" (1899), http://historymatters. gmu.edu/d/5478.

47. Halstead, *Philippines*, 39.

48. Quoted in Paul A. Kramer, "Race-Making and Colonial Violence in the US Empire: The Philippine-American War as Race War," *Diplomatic History* 30, no. 2 (2006): 173.

49. Halstead, *Philippines*, 174.

50. "Before the Manila Battle."

51. Laist, *First Montana*, 16.

52. Elwell Otis, *Annual Report of Major General E. S. Otis, US Volunteers, Commanding, Department of the Pacific and 8th Army Corps, Military Governor in the Philippine Islands* (Washington, DC: Government Printing Office, 1899), 42.

53. "Forty Were Killed in Battle," *Washington Post*, February 7, 1899.

54. Earl Pearsall of the 1st Nebraska complained of the lack of these daily visits in January 1899 in *First Nebraska*, 189.

55. Quoted in Sean McEnroe, "Painting the Philippines with an American Brush: Visions of Race and National Mission Among the Oregon Volunteers in the Philippine Wars of 1898 and 1899," *Oregon Historical Quarterly* 104, no. 1 (2003): 39.

56. McEnroe, "Painting," 47.

57. Quoted in McEnroe, "Painting," 39.

58. *Report of a Tour Through Luzon*, 1898, quoted in Kramer, "Race-Making," 179.

59. Quoted in A. B. Feuer, ed., *America at War: The Philippines, 1898–1913* (Westport, CT: Praeger, 2002), 89.

60. Clayton D. Laurie, "The Philippine Scouts: America's Colonial Army, 1899–1913," *Philippine Studies* 37, no. 2 (1989): 179–80. The United States would later advantage of that mistrust by recruiting Filipinos from multiple groups to fight on the American side, among other strategies. Laurie, "Philippine Scouts," 182.

61. John A. Larkin, "Philippine History Reconsidered: A Socioeconomic Perspective," *American Historical Review* 87, no. 3 (1982): 616.

62. Sexton, *Soldiers in the Sun*, 85.

63. Rene Escalante, "Collapse of the Malolos Republic," *Philippine Studies* 46, no. 4 (1998): 455. Luna, the son of a traveling tobacco salesman, had a Ph.D in pharmacy and a hasty temper. He had some skill as a general, but nowhere near what it was magnified into in Philippine public memory during the twentieth century. He was assassinated at Aguinaldo's orders in late 1899 because Aguinaldo feared him as a political rival.

64. I.e., MacArthur's testimony about the number of unarmed people in the Philippine Army who were clearly carriers rather than soldiers, but whom he took as soldiers. Quoted in Sexton, *Soldiers in the Sun*, 86.

65. Brian McAllister Linn, *The Philippine War, 1899–1902* (Lawrence: University Press of Kansas, 2000), 42.

66. Jose Amiel Angeles, "As Our Might Grows Less: The Philippine-American War in Context," Ph.D. dissertation, University of Oregon, 2014, 214.

67. Marrion Wilcox, *Harper's History of the War in the Philippines* (New York: Harper & Brothers, 1900), III.

68. Mariano Lunera to Emilio Aguinaldo, August 7, 1898 in Taylor, *Philippine Insurrection*, 9–10.

69. Roughly translates to "ammunition factories." Quoted in Angeles, "Our Might," 201.

70. Quoted in Grant K. Goodman, "Filipino Secret Agents, 1896–1910," *Philippine Studies* 46, no. 3 (1998): 382.

71. Angeles, "Our Might," 212.

72. Christine Doran, "Women in the Philippine Revolution," *Philippine Studies* 46, no. 3 (1998): 367.

73. August 3, 1898, quoted in Angeles, "Our Might," 206.

74. Sexton, *Soldiers in the Sun*, 87.

75. Angeles, "Our Might," 187–88. Reported by whom is not clear.

76. Angeles, "Our Might," 189.

77. Coffman, *Hilt*, 14.

78. Angeles, "Our Might," 206.

79. Angeles, "Our Might," 222–23.

80. Sexton, *Soldiers in the Sun*, 89.

81. Frederick Funston, *Memories of Two Wars : Cuban and Philippine Experiences* (New York: Scribner's Sons, 1911), 175–76.

82. Wilcox, *Harper's History*.

83. Sexton, *Soldiers in the Sun*, 88.

84. Quoted in Sexton, *Soldiers in the Sun*, 91.

85. Quoted in Sexton, *Soldiers in the Sun*, 91.

86. *First Nebraska*, 16–17.

87. Terpsichore being the Greek muse of music and dance. Diary of Santiago Barcelona, February 4, 1899, at http://philippinediaryproject.com/category/diary-of-santiago-barcelona/page/4.

88. Aguinaldo, "True Version of the Philippine Revolution" (1899), chap. XIX, http://www.authorama.com/true-version-of-the-philippine-revolution-20.html.

89. Angeles, "Our Might," 220.

90. *First Nebraska*, 17.

91. *First Nebraska*, 17.

92. Wilcox, *Harper's History*, III.

93. Laist, *First Montana*, 16.

94. Otis, *Annual Report*, 516.

95. Funston, *Two Wars*, 179.

96. Funston, *Two Wars*, 179.

97. Funston, *Two Wars*, 181.

98. Funston, *Two Wars*, 181.

99. Theo Mortimer and James J. Loughrey, "James J. Loughrey's Diary of the Wars in the Philippines 1898/1899," *Dublin Historical Record* 56, no. 1 (2003): 78–97.

100. James, *California Volunteer*, 8–9.

101. Laist, *First Montana*, 17.

102. Laist, *First Montana*, 16.

103. *First Nebraska*, 18.

104. Madison Stoneman, *Official History of the Operations of the First Battalion Wyoming Infantry, U.S.V., in the Campaign in the Philippine Islands* (San Felipe Neri: First Wyoming Infantry, 1899), 18.

105. *First Nebraska*, 18.

106. Karl Irving Faust, *Campaigning in the Philippines: Illustrated* (San Francisco: Hicks-Judd, 1899), 137.

107. Faust, *Campaigning*, 137.

108. Hawkins, *Tenth Pennsylvania*.

109. Wilcox, *Harper's History*, 124.

110. Funston, *Two Wars*, 196.

111. Faust, *Campaigning*, 136.

112. Arthur C. Johnson, *Official History of the Operations of the First Colorado Infantry, U.S.V.* (n.p.: n.p., 1900), 13.

113. Johnson, *First Colorado*, 13.

114. Johnson, *First Colorado*, 13.

115. Stoneman, *Wyoming*, 17–18.

116. Maybey, *Utah Batteries*, 39.

117. Funston did not specify what the difference in noise between a young and old cyclone was. Funston, *Two Wars*, 180.

118. Funston, *Two Wars*, 179–80.

119. Funston, *Two Wars*, 182.

120. Linn, *Philippine War*, 106. Linn is describing a later battle, but the phrase is an important and common one.

121. Maybey, *Utah Batteries*, 43.

122. Maybey, *Utah Batteries*, 43.

123. Maybey, *Utah Batteries*, 43.

124. Maybey, *Utah Batteries*, 40.

125. The Krag-Jørgensen round weighed about 10 grams and had a muzzle velocity of about 2,000 feet per second. The 3.2-inch gun shell only went about two-thirds of that speed but weighed 6 kilograms, about 600 times as heavy. Weights and speeds approximate.

126. The bursting charge in the shell was approximately 150 pounds, which created an overpressure of around 10 psi in the immediate vicinity. See "Ordnance and Gunnery," *Proceedings of the United States Naval Institute* 38, no. 2 (1912): 783 (bursting charge); Michael Chipley et al., "Explosive Blast," in *Reference Manual to Mitigate Potential Terrorist Attacks Against Buildings* (Washington, DC: Federal Emergency Management Authority, 2003), 17.

127. Angeles, "Our Might," 221.

128. Funston, *Two Wars*, 187, 217.

129. Maybey, *Utah Batteries*, 40.

130. Funston, *Two Wars*, 185.

131. Taylor, *Organization*, 55.

132. "Filipino Version of Battle," *New York Times*, February 12, 1899. Note that the Filipinos claimed that the defensive stance was the result of deliberate orders from Aguinaldo, but he does not seem to have actually issued such an order.

133. Quoted in Young, *General's General*, 222.

134. Nicholas Murray, "The Second Anglo-Boer War," in *The Rocky Road to the Great War: The Evolution of Trench Warfare to 1914*, ed. Hew Strachan (Lincoln: University of Nebraska Press, 2013), 81–122.

135. Funston, *Two Wars*, 181.

136. *First Nebraska*, 16.

137. Mark D. Van Ells, "Assuming the White Man's Burden: The Seizure of the Philippines, 1898–1902," *Philippine Studies* 43, no. 4 (Winter 1995): 616.

138. Poplin, "Letters," 162.

139. Sexton, *Soldiers in the Sun*, 97.

140. Funston, *Two Wars*, 200.

141. Otis, *Report*, 435.

142. Sexton, *Soldiers in the Sun*, 93.

143. Wilcox, *Harper's History*, 113.

144. Sexton, *Soldiers in the Sun*, 94.

145. Luhn, *First Washington*, 9–10.

146. Faust, *Campaigning*, 138.

147. Luhn, *First Washington*, 9–10.

148. Luhn, *First Washington*, 9–10.

149. Sexton, *Soldiers in the Sun*, 87–88.

150. Luhn, *First Washington*, 9–10.

151. Faust, *Campaigning*, 136–37.

152. Wilcox, *Harper's History*, 120.

153. McEnroe, "Painting the Philippines," 45.

154. McEnroe, "Painting the Philippines," 45.

155. Leonard Adams letter, February 14, 1899, published in the *New York Times*, April 14, 1899, 8.

156. Funston, *Two Wars*, 186.

157. Faust, *Campaigning*, 137.

158. Otis, *Report*, 102.

159. Funston, *Two Wars*, 176.

160. Funston, *Two Wars*, 176.

161. Funston, *Two Wars*, 183.

162. Barcelona diary, February 4, 1899, http://philippinediaryproject.com/1899/02/04/february-4th-1899.

163. Peter C. English, *Shock, Physiological Surgery, and George Washington Crile: Medical Innovation in the Progressive Era* (Westport, CT: Greenwood Press, 1980); Kim Pelis, "Taking Credit: The Canadian Army Medical Corps and the British Conversion to Blood Transfusion in WWI," *Journal of the History of Medicine and Allied Sciences* 56, no. 3 (2001).

164. Quoted in Warwick Anderson, *Colonial Pathologies: American Tropical Medicine, Race, and Hygiene in the Philippines* (Durham, NC: Duke University Press, 2006), 32.

165. Quoted in Anderson, *Colonial Pathologies*, 30.

166. Quoted in Anderson, *Colonial Pathologies*, 30.

167. Quoted in Anderson, *Colonial Pathologies*, 31.

168. Funston tells of such a Filipino who recounted his wound at a later time. Funston, *Two Wars*, 192.

169. Funston, *Two Wars*, 197–98; Angeles, "Our Might," 226.

170. Otis, *Report*, 99.

171. Luhn, *First Washington*, 9.

172. Rachel Levandoski, "'The Touchstone of Insanity': Perceptions of the Psychological Trauma of War Within the United States from 1861 to 1918," Ph.D. diss., University of North Carolina, 2018, 66–87. Useful on the twentieth-century evolution of the understanding of PTSD is Ben Shephard, *A War of Nerves: Soldiers and Psychiatrists in the Twentieth Century* (Cambridge, MA: Harvard University Press, 2001).

173. Frank Tennyson Neely, *Fighting in the Philippines* (New York: Frank Tennyson Neely, 1899), n.p.

174. Neely, *Fighting*, n.p.

175. John W. Dower, *War Without Mercy: Race and Power in the Pacific War* (New York: Pantheon, 1987) has a good discussion of such souvenirs in World War II.

176. *New York Times*, April 14, 1899, 8.

177. Quoted in Kramer, "Race-Making," 190.

178. Funston, *Two Wars*, 187.

179. Angeles, "Our Might," 226.

180. Linn, *Philippine War*, 52.

181. "Filipino Version of Battle."

182. Wilcox, *Harper's History*, 117.

183. Funston, *Two Wars*, 190.

184. Taylor, *Organization*, 45.

185. Taylor, *Organization*, 47.

186. E.g., Funston, *Two Wars*, 192–93.

187. Arthur MacArthur, *Annual Report of Major General Arthur MacArthur, U.S. Volunteers, Commanding, Division of the Philippines, Military Governor in the Philippine Islands* (Washington, DC: Government Printing Office, 1901), 2.

188. That he said this in 1900 makes the incomprehension even more impressive. MacArthur, *Report*, 3.

189. Quoted in Russell Roth, *Muddy Glory: America's "Indian Wars" in the Philippines* (West Hanover, MA: Christopher, 1981), 18.

190. MacArthur, *Report*, 3.

191. Quoted in Young, *General's General*, 282.

CHAPTER 5

1. It is important to emphasize that Root embodied and enacted reforms that had long been germinating in the Army, and which also closely paralleled the Progressive Era's modernization of other industries and institutions. Graham A. Cosmas, "Military Reform After the Spanish-American War: The Army Reorganization Fight of 1898–1899," *Military Affairs* 35, no. 1 (1971): 12–18; Benjamin D. Brands, "'Unsatisfactory and Futile': The Officers' Lyceum Program and U.S. Army Reform," *Journal of Military History* 83, no. 4 (2019): 1067–94.

2. Joseph T. Glatthaar, *The American Military: A Concise History* (New York: Oxford University Press, 2018), 51–52.

3. J. P. Clark, *Preparing for War: The Emergence of the Modern U.S. Army, 1815–1917* (Cambridge, Mass.: Harvard University Press, 2017), 217.

4. Andrew J. Birtle, *U.S. Army Counterinsurgency and Contingency Operations Doctrine, 1860-1941* (Washington D.C.: Center of Military History, 1998), 175.

5. David Silbey, "Losing the Insurgent 20th Century: The American Army After the Spanish-American War, 1902–1916," in *Victory or Defeat: Armies in the Aftermath of Conflict, Proceedings of the 2010 Chief of Army's Conference*, ed. Peter Dennis and Jeffrey Grey (Canberra: Australian Army History Unit, 2011), 28.

6. Silbey, "Losing the Insurgent," 28.

7. Brian M. Linn, "Batangas: Ending the Philippines War," in *Between War and Peace: How America Ends Its Wars*, ed. Matthew Moten (New York: Free Press, 2011), 177.

8. War Department, *Field Service Regulations, United States Army* (Washington, DC: GPO, 1905), 206–8, 210, 217; Birtle, *U.S. Army Counterinsurgency, 1860–1941*, 175. Birtle is a little cavalier in saying that the 1905 manual and the 1911 Infantry Drill Regulations "enumerat[e] some of the countermeasures that had proved effective in the past." We do not see even that level of detail.

9. Birtle, *U.S. Army Counterinsurgency, 1860–1941*, 175, 181–82, 208, 239–40, 244, 247; Andrew J. Birtle, *U.S. Army Counterinsurgency and Contingency Operations Doctrine, 1942–1976* (Washington, DC: Center of Military History, 2006), 10–11.

10. Quoted in Birtle, *U.S. Army Counterinsurgency, 1860–1941*, 249.

11. Frederick Funston, *Memories of Two Wars: Cuban and Philippine Experiences* (New York: Charles Scribner's Sons, 1911), 200.

12. Clark, *Preparing for War*, 216–17, 225. Gene Fax provides a short discussion of the "open warfare" problem in "Pershing's 'Open Warfare' Doctrine in the Light of American Military History," *Army History* 113 (Fall 2019): 32–37.

13. Mark Ethan Grotelueschen, *The AEF Way of War: The American Army and Combat in World War I* (Cambridge: Cambridge University Press, 2006).

14. Glatthaar, *The American Military*, 57–58; Peter S. Kindsvatter, *American Soldiers: Ground Combat in the World Wars, Korea, and Vietnam* (Lawrence: University Press of Kansas, 2003), 10–11.

15. Edward A. Gutiérrez with Michael S. Neiberg, "The Elusive Lesson: U.S. Army Unpreparedness from 1898 to 1938," in *Drawdown: The American Way of Postwar*, ed. Jason Warren (New York: NYU Press, 2016), 149.

16. Glatthaar, *The American Military*, 89, 97.

17. The term is common, for example, in E. B. Sledge's memoir, *With the Old Breed* (New York: Ballantine, 2010).

18. John Dower, *War Without Mercy: Race and Power in the Pacific War* (New York: Pantheon, 1986); Peter Schrijvers, *The GI War Against Japan: American Soldiers in Asia and the Pacific During World War II* (London: Palgrave, 2002); Craig M. Cameron, *American Samurai: Myth, Imagination, and the Conduct of Battle in the First Marine Division, 1941–1951* (New York: Cambridge University Press, 1994), esp. 176. John A. Lynn argues against a primarily racist explanation for the war's violence in *Battle: A Cultural History of Combat and Culture* (Boulder, CO: Westview Press, 2003), 219–80, but see Cameron's response in Craig M. Cameron, "Race and Identity: The Culture of Combat in the Pacific War," *International History Review* 27, no. 3 (2003): 550–66.

19. Mark Clodfelter, *The Limits of Air Power: The American Bombing of North Vietnam* (New York: Free Press, 1989); Fred Kaplan, *To Kill Nations: American Strategy in the Air-Atomic Age and the Rise of Mutually Assured Destruction* (Ithaca, NY: Cornell University Press, 2015).

20. President Lyndon Johnson used the quoted phrase, cited in Nick Turse, *Kill Anything That Moves: The Real American War in Vietnam* (New York: Metropolitan Books, 2013), 49. Turse also points to defense secretary Robert McNamara calling North Vietnam a "backward nation," while secretary of state Henry Kissinger called North Vietnam "a little, fourth rate power, later downgrading it to 'fifth-rate' status." He also argues that "such feelings permeated the chain of command and found even more colourful voice among those in the field, who regarded Vietnam as 'the outhouse of Asia,' 'the garbage dump of civilisation,' 'the asshole of the world.'"

21. Birtle, *Counterinsurgency and Contingency Operations Doctrine, 1942–1976*, 134. This was part of a bigger broadening that moved the Army away from a strictly nuclear war outlook and toward limited conventional wars, as well as less

conventional ones. Brian McAllister Linn, *Elvis's Army: Cold War GIs and the Atomic Battlefield* (Cambridge, MA: Harvard University Press, 2016), 298–99.

22. Ingo Trauschweizer, *Maxwell Taylor's Cold War: From Berlin to Vietnam* (Lexington: University Press of Kentucky, 2019), 112–13.

23. Walter E. Kretchik, *U.S. Army Doctrine: From the American Revolution to the War on Terror* (Lawrence: University Press of Kansas, 2011), 183–86; Linn, *Elvis's Army*, 301–02.

24. Robert Buzzanco argues that senior military leaders understood the strategic complexity both before and during the war, and rarely believed that they were actually on the verge of winning. Robert Buzzanco, *Masters of War: Military Dissent and Politics in the Vietnam Era* (Cambridge: Cambridge University Press, 1996), 4–5, 8. Also, H. R. McMaster, *Dereliction of Duty: Lyndon Johnson, Robert McNamara, the Joint Chiefs of Staff, and the Lies That Led to Vietnam* (New York: Harper Collins, 1997), esp. 326–30; Jacqueline L. Hazelton, "The Client Gets a Vote: Counterinsurgency Warfare and the U.S. Military Advisory Mission in South Vietnam, 1954–1965," *Journal of Strategic Studies* 43 (2020): 126–53.

25. Diem is usually seen as hopelessly corrupt, but American Cold War tunnel vision also played a role, as did American orientalist racism, and a profoundly different vision of how to built a new nation in South Vietnam. See Edward Miller, *Misalliance: Ngo Dinh Diem, the United States, and the Fate of South Vietnam* (Cambridge, MA: Harvard University Press, 2013), 8–9, 13, 17–18. But see also Trauschweizer, *Maxwell Taylor's Cold War*, 121.

26. The literature here is enormous. A good review of its outlines is Gary R. Hess, *Vietnam: Explaining America's Lost War*, 2nd ed. (Malden, MA: Blackwell, 2015). A key recent intervention on American preparedness and early war strategy is Gregory Daddis, *Westmoreland's War: Reassessing American Strategy in Vietnam* (New York: Oxford University Press, 2014).

27. North Vietnamese strategists debated the necessity, timing, and tactics for such an attack. See Lien-Hang T. Nguyen, *Hanoi's War: An International History of the War for Peace in Vietnam* (Chapel Hill: University of North Carolina Press, 2012).

28. For discussions of this process of deliberate forgetting, see David Fitzgerald, *Learning to Forget: US Army Counterinsurgency Doctrine from Vietnam to Iraq* (Stanford, CA: Stanford University Press, 2013); Conrad Crane, *Avoiding Vietnam: The US Army's Response to Defeat in Southeast Asia* (Carlisle, PA: SSI, 2002).

29. Robert T. Davis II, *The Challenge of Adaptation: The US Army in the Aftermath of Conflict, 1953–2000* (Ft. Leavenworth, KS: Combat Studies Institute Press, 2008), 54–56.

30. Glatthaar, *The American Military*, 108–110; Brian McAllister Linn, *The Echo of Battle: The Army's Way of War* (Cambridge, Mass.: Harvard University Press, 2007), 193–220; Kretchik, *U.S. Army Doctrine*, 197–212; Birtle, *Counterinsurgency and Contingency Operations Doctrine, 1942–1976*, 479–81; Buzzanco, *Masters of War*, 2–3.

31. Beth L. Bailey, *America's Army: Making the All-Volunteer Force* (Cambridge, MA: Harvard University Press, 2009); James Kitfield, *Prodigal Soldiers: How the Generation of Officers Born of Vietnam Revolutionized the American Style of War* (New York: Simon & Schuster, 1995); John Sloan Brown, *Kevlar Legions: The Transformation of the U.S. Army, 1989–2005* (Washington, DC: Center for Military History, 2011); Robert K. Griffith Jr., *The U.S. Army's Transition to the All-Volunteer Force, 1968–1974* (Washington, DC: Center of Military History, 1997).

32. There is a separate and vibrant history of change in the Air Force and Navy, and of their role in Operation Desert Storm, but that is beyond our scope here.

33. Department of the Army, FM 100-5 (1986) *Operations*.

34. The argument over whether these operations contributed to an informal American Empire is a different book; suffice it to say that the military operations were more similar to imperial constabulary missions than they were to conventional combat.

35. Richard Haass, "Desert Storm: The Last Classic War," *Wall Street Journal*, July 31, 2015; Christopher Gelpi, Peter D. Feaver, and Jason Reifler, "Success Matters: Casualty Sensitivity and the War in Iraq," *International Security* 30, no. 3 (2005): 7–46.

36. Department of Defense, *Joint Pub 3–07, Joint Doctrine for Military Operations Other than War* (Washington, DC: DOD, 1995).

37. Rosa Brooks, *How Everything Became War and the Military Became Everything: Tales from the Pentagon* (New York: Simon & Schuster, 2016), 80.

38. Brown, *Kevlar Legions*, 192–98

39. Kretchik, *U.S. Army Doctrine*, 248–55; Department of the Army, *FM 3–0 Operations* (2001).

40. For the success of the Army's conventional focus on preventing a general war with the Soviets, but also the related inability to fulfill the "lesser included" missions such as counterinsurgency, see Ingo Trauschweizer, *The Cold War U.S. Army: Building Deterrence for Limited War* (Lawrence: University Press of Kansas, 2008), 230–37.

41. Michael D. Gambone, *Small Wars: Low-Intensity Threats and the American Response Since Vietnam* (Knoxville: University of Tennessee Press, 2012), 230, 240–42; Yaniv Barzilai, *102 Days of War: How Osama Bin Laden, Al Qaeda and the Taliban Survived 2001* (Washington, DC: Potomac Books, 2013), 20–29; Annie Jacobsen, *Surprise, Kill, Vanish: The Secret History of CIA Paramilitary Armies, Operators, and Assassins* (New York: Little, Brown, 2019), 341–55; Henry A. Crumpton, *The Art of Intelligence: Lessons from a Life in the CIA's Clandestine Service* (New York: Penguin Books, 2012), 171–215.

CHAPTER 6

1. Quoted in Kevin M. Hymel, "Toe to Toe with the Taliban: Bravo Company Fights in Makuan," in *Vanguard of Valor: Small Unit Actions in Afghanistan Volume*

II, ed. Donald P. Wright (Fort Leavenworth, KS: Combat Studies Institute Press, 2012), 12.

2. Nicholas Williams, communication with the author, Dec. 16, 2018.

3. Jason Motlagh, "The Afghan War: Why the Kandahar Campaign Matters," *Time*, Oct. 18, 2010; Headquarters, 2nd Brigade Combat Team, 101st Airborne Division (Air Assault), *Book of Valor: Combined Task Force STRIKE: Operation Enduring Freedom 10–11* (Fort Campbell, KY: 2nd Brigade Combat Team, 2011), 306. There is no single book-length study of Dragon Strike; in 2012–2013, the U.S. Army's Combat Studies Institute at Fort Leavenworth, Kansas, at the direction of International Security Assistance Force Commander General David H. Petraeus, published a series of tactical studies from the operation, including Hymel's "Toe to Toe," from which many details for this chapter are drawn. See, for instance, Michael J. Doidge, "Flipping the Switch: Weapons Platoon Movement to Contact in Zhari District," in *Vanguard of Valor: Small Unit Actions in Afghanistan*, ed. Donald P. Wright (Fort Leavenworth, KS: Combat Studies Institute Press, 2012), 49–71; Matt M. Matthews, "Disrupt and Destroy: Platoon Patrol in Zhari District, September 2010," in *Vanguard of Valor*, 131–55; Kevin M. Hymel, "Trapping the Taliban at OP Dusty: A Scout Platoon in Zhari District," in *Vanguard of Valor*, 157–78. Also see Anthony E. Carlson, "Operation NASHVILLE: Breaking the Taliban's Stranglehold in Kandahar, 2010," in *16 Cases of Mission Command*, ed. Donald P. Wright (Fort Leavenworth, KS: Combat Studies Institute Press, 2013), 195–204.

4. On President Obama's declaration, see Maeve Reston, "Obama Tells Veterans Afghanistan Is a 'War of Necessity,'" *Los Angeles Times,* Aug. 18, 2009. Prisock estimated that Bravo Company's 130 soldiers were supplemented with roughly 100 attachments, including Marines, Navy Seabees, Air Force personnel, and soldiers drawn from other Army units. In his memoirs, Secretary of Defense Robert M. Gates described the surge's military and political aims: "The December 2009 decisions and related troop surge provided sufficient military forces to break the stalemate by rooting the Taliban out of their strongholds and keeping them out while training a much larger and more capable Afghan army." See, for instance, Robert M. Gates, *Duty: Memoirs of a Secretary at War* (New York: Vintage, 2015), 477, 570–73, quote at 571.

5. Quoted in Laura King, "Taliban Gears Up for Western Offensive in Kandahar," *Los Angeles Times*, May 9, 2010.

6. James Brandon Prisock, communication with the author, Nov. 6, 2018.

7. George W. Bush, "Address to a Joint Session of the 107th Congress," Sept. 20, 2001; *Selected Speeches of George W. Bush, 2001–2008*, 69, available from https://georgewbush-whitehouse.archives.gov/infocus/bushrecord/documents/Selected_Speeches_George_W_Bush.pdf, accessed July 19, 2017.

8. Tommy Franks, *American Soldier* (New York: HarperCollins, 2004), 251; Michael DeLong, *Inside CENTCOM: The Unvarnished Truth About the Wars in Afghanistan and Iraq* (Washington, DC: Regnery, 2004), 22–23. On the Soviet

experience in Afghanistan, see Russian General Staff, *The Soviet-Afghan War: How a Superpower Fought and Lost*, trans. and ed. Lester W. Grau and Michael A. Gress (Lawrence, KS: University Press of Kansas, 2002); Robin Braithwaite, *Afgantsy: The Russians in Afghanistan 1979–89* (Oxford: Oxford University Press, 2011).

9. Donald P. Wright et al., *A Different Kind of War: The United States Army in Operation ENDURING FREEDOM, October 2001–September 2005* (Fort Leavenworth, KS: Combat Studies Institute Press, 2010), 62–64, 71–72, 78.

10. Wright et al., *Different Kind of War*, 71–88.

11. Wright et al., *Different Kind of War*, 3–5, 35–40, 48, 113–74; Richard W. Stewart, *The U.S. Army in Afghanistan: Operation ENDURING FREEDOM, October 2001—March 2002* (Washington, DC: Government Printing Office, 2004), 26–44.

12. Wright et al., *Different Kind of War*, 181–88; 191–96; Ahmed Rashid, *Descent into Chaos: The U.S. and the Disaster in Pakistan, Afghanistan, and Central Asia* (New York: Penguin, 2008), 240–42.

13. Rashid, *Descent into Chaos*, 244–48, 253; Ahmed Rashid, *Taliban: Militant Islam, Oil, and Fundamentalism in Central Asia* (New Haven, CT: Yale University Press, 2000), 1–5; Thomas Barfield, *Afghanistan: A Cultural and Political History* (Princeton, NJ: Princeton University Press, 2010), 24–26, 255–58; Vernon Loeb, "Rumsfeld Announces End of Combat," *Washington Post*, May 2, 2003.

14. Wright et al., *Different Kind of War*, 237–47, 254; Dov S. Zakheim, *A Vulcan's Tale: How the Bush Administration Mismanaged the Reconstruction of Afghanistan* (Washington, DC: Brookings Institution Press, 2011), 170.

15. Wright et al., *Different Kind of War*, 227–28, 254–55, 294; Headquarters, Department of the Army, Field Manual 3-24, *Counterinsurgency* (Washington, DC: Government Printing Office, 2006), 1–13. For the population of Afghanistan, see Barfield, *Afghanistan*, 23. For the combined number of American and NATO personnel deployed to Afghanistan, see "A Timeline of U.S. Troop Levels in Afghanistan since 2001," *Military Times,* July 6, 2016; Ian S. Livingston and Michael O'Hanlon, "Afghanistan Index," Brookings Institution, Sept. 30, 2012, accessed May 1, 2017, 5, https://www.brookings.edu/wp-content/uploads/2016/07/index20120930.pdf.

16. James Brandon Prisock, communication with the author, Nov. 6, 2018.

17. Rashid, *Descent into Chaos*, 353–67. For one example of night letters, see Declan Walsh, "Night Letters from the Taliban Threaten Afghan Democracy," *The Guardian,* Sept. 18, 2004.

18. Rashid, *Descent into Chaos*, 363–64; Bernd Horn, "Lesson Learned: Operation Medusa and the Taliban Epiphany," in *No Easy Task: Fighting in Afghanistan*, ed. Bernd Horn and Emily Spencer (Toronto: Dundurn, 2012), 163–98.

19. Rashid, *Descent into Chaos*, 363–65; FM 3-24, 1-13.

20. Carl Forsberg, *The Taliban's Campaign for Kandahar*, Afghanistan Report 3 (n.p.: Institute for the Study of War, 2009), 27.

21. Murray Brewster, *The Savage War: The Untold Battles of Afghanistan* (Mississauga, ON: John Wiley & Sons Canada, 2011), 113. See also Horn, "Lesson Learned," 190–92.

22. Quoted in King, "Taliban Gears Up"; Forsberg, *The Taliban's Campaign for Kandahar*, 27–29.

23. Forsberg, *The Taliban's Campaign for Kandahar*, 34–35; Anand Gopal, "The Taliban in Kandahar," in *Talibanistan: Negotiating the Borders Between Terror, Politics, and Religion*, ed. Peter Bergen (Oxford: Oxford University Press, 2013), 55.

24. Reston, "Obama Tells Veterans Afghanistan Is a 'War of Necessity'"; "Transcript of Obama Speech on Afghanistan," CNN, Dec. 2, 2009, accessed July 16, 2017.

25. Dianna Cahn, "Rodriguez to Helm New ISAF Command," *Stars and Stripes*, Oct. 10, 2009; Ian M. Terry, "43rd Sustainment Brigade Cases Colors," *The Rough Rider* 1, no. 1 (Mar.–Apr. 2010): 2, https://static.dvidshub.net/media/pubs/pdf_6769.pdf; Roxana Tiron, "$400 per Gallon Gas to Drive Debate over Cost of War in Afghanistan," *The Hill*, Oct. 16, 2009; Larry Shaughnessy, "One Soldier, One Year: $850,000 and Rising," CNN, Feb. 28, 2012.

26. *Book of Valor*, 306.

27. Data for the 1973 and 2010 U.S. militaries was drawn from the annual reports of the Defense Manpower and Data Center, https://www.dmdc.osd.mil/appj/dwp/dwp_reports.jsp, accessed July 1, 2017. See also Paul Taylor, ed., *The Military-Civilian Gap: War and Sacrifice in the Post-9/11 Era* (Washington, DC: Pew Research Center, 2011), 22, 36; Lisa Mundey, "The Combatants' Experiences," in *Understanding the U.S. Wars in Iraq and Afghanistan*, ed. Beth Bailey and Richard H. Immerman (New York: New York University Press, 2015), 177; James Wright, *Those Who Have Borne the Battle: A History of America's Wars and Those Who Fought Them* (New York: PublicAffairs, 2012), 242.

28. Quote from Adrian R. Lewis, *The American Culture of War: The History of U.S. Military Force from World War II to Operation Enduring Freedom*, 2nd ed. (New York: Routledge, 2012), 486, emphasis in original; David R. Segal and Lawrence J. Korb, "Manning and Financing the Twenty-First Century All-Volunteer Force," in *The Modern American Military*, ed. David M. Kennedy (Oxford: Oxford University Press, 2013), 123, 125–26; Defense Manpower and Data Center, "Counts of Active Duty and Reserve Service Members and APF Civilians," Sept. 30, 2010, https://www.dmdc.osd.mil/appj/dwp/dwp_reports.jsp.

29. Headquarters, Department of the Army, Deputy Chief of Staff of Personnel, "FY10 Army Profile," Sept. 30, 2010, http://www.armyg1.army.mil/HR/docs/demographics/FY10_Army_Profile.pdf; Taylor, ed., *The Military-Civilian Gap*, 28, 33.

30. Luke Rella, communication with the author, Dec. 12, 2018.

31. Nicholas Williams, communication with the author, Dec. 16, 2018; Taylor Murphy, communication with the author, Dec. 13, 2018.

32. James Brandon Prisock, communication with the author, Nov. 6, 2018; Nicholas Williams, communication with the author, Dec. 16, 2018. For an account of Bravo Company's sordid 2006 deployment, see Jim Frederick, *Black Hearts: One Platoon's Descent into Madness in Iraq's Triangle of Death* (New York: Crown, 2010).

33. Mapping Militant Organizations, "The Taliban," Stanford University, July 15, 2016, http://web.stanford.edu/group/mappingmilitants/cgi-bin/groups/view/367#note62.

34. Matt Waldman, "Dangerous Liaisons with the Afghan Taliban: The Feasibility and Risks of Negotiations," United States Institute of Peace, Special Report 256, Oct. 2010, 3–4; Andrew Garfield and Alicia Boyd, "Understanding Afghan Insurgents: ivations, Goals, and the Reconciliation and Reintegration Process," *Foreign Policy Research Institute E-Notes*, Apr. 2003, 2–3http://www.fpri.org/docs/garfield_-_understanding_Afghan_insurgents.pdf; Major General Michael Flynn, *State of the Insurgency: Trends, Intentions, and Objectives*, Dec. 22, 2009, briefing, slide 15.

35. C. J. Chivers, "The Weakness of Taliban Marksmanship," *New York Times*, Apr. 2, 2010.

36. Chivers, "The Weakness of Taliban Marksmanship"; Flynn, *State of the Insurgency*, slides 9–10; Mundey, "The Combatants' Experiences," 182.

37. Craig Whitlock, "Soaring IED Attacks in Afghanistan Stymie U.S. Counteroffensive," *Washington Post*, Mar. 18, 2010.

38. Centers for Disease Control and Prevention, "Explosions and Blast Injuries: A Primer for Clinicians," n.d., 1–4, https://www.cdc.gov/masstrauma/preparedness/primer.pdf, accessed Sept. 12, 2019.

39. *Book of Valor*, 306.

40. "Decree of the President of the Islamic Transitional State of Afghanistan on the Afghan National Army," Dec. 1, 2002, https://www.unric.org/html/german/afghanistan/talks2002/decree.pdf; Wright et al., *Different Kind of War*, 261–62.

41. C. J. Radan, "Afghan National Army Update, May 2011," *Long War Journal*, May 9, 2011.

42. Precise guidelines on rules of engagement remain classified. These descriptions are from soldiers' memories.

43. Quoted in Andrew J. Bacevich, *America's War for the Greater Middle East: A Military History* (New York: Random House, 2016), 316; Fred Kaplan, *The Insurgents: David Petraeus and the Plot to Change the American Way of War* (New York: Simon & Schuster, 2013), 343–44.

44. Clint Cox, communication with the author, May 22, 2013.

45. Headquarters, 2nd Brigade Combat Team, 101st Airborne Division (Air Assault), Untitled Briefing, n.d., slide 129 (hereafter cited as CTF Strike Post-Deployment Briefing).

46. CTF Strike Post-Deployment Briefing, slide 57, emphasis in original. The in-
    sertion of "destroy" in the revised mission statement dictated an entirely new
    operational approach. U.S. Army doctrine defined "destroy" as the application
    of "lethal combat power on an enemy capability so that it can no longer per-
    form any function and cannot be restored to a usable condition without being
    entirely rebuilt." See Headquarters, Department of the Army, Field Manual
    3-0, Operations (Washington, DC: Government Printing Office, 2008), 6-9.
    See also, Carlson, "Operation NASHVILLE," 195.

47. Clint Cox, communication with the author, May 22, 2103; CTF Strike
    Post-Deployment Briefing, slide, 57.

48. Hymel, "Toe to Toe," 1; Book of Valor, 47–48; Philip Grey, "Wounded in Body and
    Mind, 'Eagle 7' Lived to Soar Again," Clarksville Leaf Chronicle, June 29, 2014.

49. Hymel, "Toe to Toe," 2–3; Headquarters, Department of the Army, Field
    Manual 3-21.10 (FM 7-10), The Infantry Rifle Company (Washington, DC:
    Government Printing Office, 2006), 1-11, 1-13; Headquarters, Department of
    the Army, Field Manual 3-21.8 (FM 7-8), The Infantry Rifle Platoon and Squad
    (Washington, DC: Government Printing Office, 2007), 1-11–1-12.

50. Nicholas Williams, communication with the author, Mar. 9, 2017; Hymel, "Toe
    to Toe," 2–3.

51. Hymel, "Toe to Toe," 3; Johnny Davis, communication with the author, June
    29, 2017.

52. FM 3 (2008) 3-8; Forsberg, Counterinsurgency in Kandahar, 24; John Boone,
    "Kandahar Braces Itself for a Bloody Summer Offensive," The Guardian, May
    9, 2010; Nick Schifrin and Matt McGarry, "Battle for Kandahar, Heart of
    Afghanistan's Taliban Country," ABC News, May 25, 2010.

53. Gopal, "The Taliban in Kandahar," 36, 44; Forsberg, Counterinsurgency in
    Kandahar, 23.

54. Gopal, "The Taliban in Kandahar," 36–37, 44; CTF Strike Post-Deployment
    Briefing, slide 48.

55. Ali Ahmad Jalali and Lester W. Grau, The Other Side of the Mountain: Mujahideen
    Tactics in the Soviet-Afghan War (Quantico, VA: United States Marine Corps
    Studies and Analysis Division, 1999), 42–46, quote at 45.

56. Forsberg, Counterinsurgency in Kandahar, 23.

57. Forsberg, The Taliban's Campaign for Kandahar, 11; Daniel P. Bolger, Why We
    Lost: A General's Inside Account of the Iraq and Afghanistan Wars (New York:
    Houghton Mifflin Harcourt, 2014), 344–46.

58. Daniel F. Plumb, communication with the author, Oct. 9, 2016; Daniel Luckett,
    communication with the author, Oct. 16, 2016.

59. Luke Rella, communication with the author, Oct. 7, 2016; Daniel Luckett,
    communication with the author, Oct. 16, 2016. The combat uniform's crotch
    busting problem proved a common phenomenon throughout the theater of
    operations. During his visits to Afghanistan, Secretary of Defense Gates rou-
    tinely heard soldiers complain about the design flaw. See, for instance, Gates,

Duty, 479. For soldier remedies, see Kevin Hymel, *Strykers in Afghanistan: 1st Battalion, 17th Infantry Regiment in Kandahar Province 2009* (Ft. Leavenworth, KS: Combat Studies Institute Press, 2014), 73.

60. Taylor Murphy, communication with the author, Oct. 10, 2016.

61. Daniel F. Plumb, communication with the author, Oct. 9, 2016; Luke Rella, communication with the author, Oct. 7, 2016; Nick Christensen, communication with the author, June 5, 2017.

62. "Black Hearts," National Public Radio, video posted July 23, 2010, on YouTube, https://www.youtube.com/watch?v=QiyGgIBrNCA.

63. Daniel F. Plumb, communication with the author, Oct. 9, 2016; "Black Hearts."

64. Nicholas Williams, communication with the author, Mar. 9, 2017.

65. Marvin "Trae" C. Morgan III, communication with the author, July 13, 2017.

66. Mandy Clark, "Operation Dragon Strike Targets Taliban Hometown," CBS News, Sept. 27, 2010; "Afghanistan: Operation Dragon Strike," ABC News, Sept. 25, 2010; Rod Nordland, "American and Afghan Troops Begin Combat for Kandahar," *New York Times*, Sept. 26, 2010.

67. Jeffrey M. Jones, "Voters Rate Economy as Top Issue for 2010," Gallup, Apr. 8, 2010; Jeffrey M. Jones, "In U.S., New High of 43% Call Afghanistan War a 'Mistake,'" Gallup, Aug. 3, 2010.

68. Craig Whitlock, "IED Casualties in Afghanistan Spike," *Overseas Civilian Contractors*, Jan. 26, 2011, https://civiliancontractors.wordpress.com/2011/01/26/ied-casualties-in-afghanistan-spike; Tony Perry, "Marine Assault Vehicles Key to Afghan Strategy," *Los Angeles Times*, Jan. 31, 2010; Alfred de Montesquiou, "Marines Push 'The Breacher' Against Taliban lines," *Seattle Times*, Feb. 12, 2010; "Assault Breacher Vehicle (AVB)," Global Security, n.d., https://www.globalsecurity.org/military/systems/ground/abv.htm, accessed July 3, 2017; "ABV Assault Breacher Vehicle," Army Recognition, Dec. 23, 2018, https://www.armyrecognition.com/united_states_army_heavy_armoured_vehicles_tank_uk/abv_assault_breacher_vehicle_engineer_armoured_vehicle_tank_data_sheet_description_information_uk.html; Ammunition Program Executive Officer, *PEO Ammunition Systems Portfolio Book 2012–2013* (Picatinny, NJ: Picatinny Arsenal, 2011), 75, accessed April 4, 2016, http://www.dtic.mil/dtic/tr/fulltext/u2/a567897.pdf.

69. Hymel, "Toe to Toe," 2–3; Headquarters, 1st Battalion, 502nd Infantry Regiment, 2nd Brigade Combat Team, 101st Airborne Division (Air Assault), "Talon Overview," Feb. 18, 2011, Briefing, slide 44 (hereafter cited as Talon Overview); Nicholas L. Morgans, communication with the author, May 14, 2018; Carl von Clausewitz, *On War*, ed. and trans. Michael Howard and Peter Paret (Princeton, NJ: Princeton University Press, 1976), 119.

70. Nicholas Williams, "17 Sept 2010," unpublished manuscript, n.d., 1–2; Talon Overview, slide 43; Hymel, "Toe to Toe," 5.

71. Talon Overview, slide 43.

72. Taylor Murphy, communication with the author, Oct. 10, 2016, and Dec. 13, 2018; Nicholas Williams, communication with the author, Mar. 9, 2017.

73. Talon Overview, slide 43; Hymel, "Toe to Toe," 6–7.

74. Talon Overview, slide 43; Hymel, "Toe to Toe," 7–8.

75. Nicholas Williams, communication with the author, Dec. 16, 2018; Talon Overview, slide 43; Hymel, "Toe to Toe," 7–8.

76. Hymel, "Toe to Toe," 9–10.

77. Talon Overview, slide 43; Hymel, "Toe to Toe," 9–10.

78. Anthony Bower, communication with the author, July 15, 2017; Nicholas Williams, communication with the author, Dec. 16, 2018; Hymel, "Toe to Toe," 9–11.

79. Quoted in Hymel, "Toe to Toe," 12.

80. Hymel, "Toe to Toe," 13; "Black Hearts."

81. Johnny Davis, communication with the author, June 29, 2017; Headquarters, Department of the Army, Army Doctrine Reference Publication 3-0, *Operations*, (Washington, DC: Government Printing Office, 2017), 3-13.

82. Quoted in Wesley Morgan, "Afghanistan: The Problems with Partnering," *New York Times*, Oct. 14, 2010. As Secretary Gates later commented, "Effectively training a sizable Afghan security force was the exit strategy for all of us." Gates, *Duty*, 477.

83. James Brandon Prisock, communication with the author, July 15, 2017.

84. Williams, "17 Sept 2010," 1.

85. Williams, "17 Sept 2010," 1.

86. Williams, "17 Sept 2010," 1; Hymel, "Toe to Toe," 14.

87. Williams, "17 Sept 2010," 2.

88. Williams, "17 Sept 2010," 2; Luke Rella, "Another Life Changed," unpublished manuscript, n.d., 14; Hymel, "Toe to Toe," 15–16.

89. Williams, "17 Sept 2010," 2; Nick Christensen, communication with the author, June 10, 2017; Hymel, "Toe to Toe," 15–16.

90. Taylor Murphy, communication with the author, Oct. 10, 2016; Hymel, "Toe to Toe," 18. For a sampling of the literature on imperial policing, see Georginia Sinclair, *At the End of the Line: Colonial Policing and the Imperial Endgame 1945–80* (Manchester: Manchester University Press, 2007); David E. Omissi, *Air Power and Colonial Control: The Royal Air Force 1919–1939* (Manchester: Manchester University Press, 1990). For indigenous force training, see Jacob Stoil, "Command and Irregular Indigenous Combat Forces in the Middle East and Africa: A Historical Perspective on a Current Reality," *MCU Press* 7 (Fall 2016): 58–76; Jacob Stoil, "'Friends' and 'Patriots': A Comparative Study of Indigenous Force Cooperation in the Second World War," D.Phil. thesis, University of Oxford, 2015; Jacob Stoil, "Martial Race and Indigenous Forces in the Levant and Horn of Africa: A Legacy of the Indian Army Manifest?," in *The British Indian Army: Virtue and Necessity*, ed. Rob Johnson (Newcastle upon Tyne: Cambridge Scholars Publishing, 2014), 58–76.

91. Williams, "17 Sept 2010," 2; James Brandon Prisock, communication with the author, Nov. 6, 2018; Hymel, "Toe to Toe," 16–18.

92. James Brandon Prisock, communication with author, Nov. 6, 2018; Taylor Murphy, communication with the author, Oct. 10, 2016; Hymel, "Toe to Toe," 19–20.

93. Williams, "17 Sept 2010," 2; Taylor Murphy, communication with the author, Oct. 10, 2016; Rella, "Another Life Changed," 14; Hymel, "Toe to Toe," 18–19.

94. Paul Huston, communication with the author, June 15, 2018; "Black Hearts." I am grateful to U.S. Army Major Brian M. Downs for describing the basic procedures and processes of treating wounded personnel.

95. Paul Huston, communication with the author, June 15, 2018; "Black Hearts."

96. Nicholas L. Morgans, communication with the author, May 14, 2018.

97. Nicholas L. Morgans, communication with the author, May 14, 2018.

98. Talon Overview, slide 42; Williams, "17 Sept 2010," 3; Hymel, "Toe to Toe," 15–16.

99. *Book of Valor,* 307; Bolger, *Why We Lost,* 364; Department of the Army, U.S. Army Human Resources Command, "Permanent Order 299-16," Oct. 25, 2012; Steve Coll, *Directorate S: The C.I.A. and America's Secret Wars in Afghanistan and Pakistan* (New York: Penguin, 2018), 490–91.

100. Carlotta Gall, "Coalition Forces Routing Taliban in Key Afghan Region," *New York Times,* Oct. 20, 2010; Ben Gilbert, "Journalist Embeds Canceled in Afghanistan," NPR, Oct. 18, 2010.

101. Rajiv Chandrasekaran, *Little America: The War Within the War for Afghanistan* (New York: Alfred A. Knopf, 2012), 283–85; Carlotta Gall, *The Wrong Enemy: American in Afghanistan, 2001–2014* (New York: Houghton Mifflin Harcourt, 2014), 228–40, quote at 238.

102. Sune Engel Rasmussen and Aziz Ahmad Tassal, "'150,000 Americans Couldn't Beat Us': Taliban Fighters Defiant in Afghanistan," *The Guardian,* Oct. 31, 2017.

103. United Nations General Assembly Security Council, "Special Report on the Strategic Review of the United Nations Assistance Mission in Afghanistan," Aug. 10, 2017, 4; Special Inspector General for Afghanistan (SIGAR), *Quarterly Report to the United States Congress,* Oct. 30, 2017, 106; SIGAR, *Quarterly Report to the United States Congress,* Jan. 30, 2018, 2.

104. Headquarters, Department of the Army, Field Manual 3-0, *Operations* (Washington, DC: Government Printing Office, 2017), foreword, 1-2, 1-3; "Army Chief: Future War Is 'Almost Guaranteed,'" Association of the United States Army, Oct. 4, 2016, https://www.ausa.org/news/army-chief-future-war-almost-guaranteed; "Large-Scale Combat Operations," *Military Review: The Professional Journal of the U.S. Army* 98 (July–Aug. 2018): 137. The operational concept of unified land operations was unveiled in Headquarters, Department of the Army, Army Doctrine Publication 3-0, *Unified Land Operations* (Washington, DC: Government Printing Office, 2011).

105. James Brandon Prisock, communication with the author, Nov. 6, 2018.

106. Luke Rella, communication with the author, Dec. 12, 2018.

107. Nicholas Williams, communication with the author, Dec. 16, 2018.

CHAPTER 7

1. Anil K. Seth, "Our Inner Universes," *Scientific American* 321, no. 3 (September 2019): 42.

2. Craig M. Cameron, *American Samurai: Myth, Imagination, and the Conduct of Battle in the First Marine Division, 1941–1951* (Cambridge: Cambridge University Press, 1994), 185–86.

3. Wayne E. Lee, "Subjects, Clients, Allies, or Mercenaries? The British Use of Irish and Amerindian Military Power, 1500–1815," in *Britain's Oceanic Empire: Atlantic and Indian Ocean Worlds, c. 1550–1850*, ed. H. V. Bowen, Elizabeth Mancke, and John G. Reid (Cambridge: Cambridge University Press, 2012), 179–217.

4. Andrew J. Birtle, *U.S. Army Counterinsurgency and Contingency Operations Doctrine, 1860–1941* (Washington, DC: Center of Military History, 1998), 69–70.

5. David Silbey, *A War of Frontier and Empire: The Philippine-American War, 1899–1902* (New York: Hill and Wang, 2007), 165; Brian McAllister Linn, *Guardians of Empire: The U.S. Army and the Pacific, 1902–1940* (Chapel Hill: University of North Carolina Press, 2007), 14, 32–33, 40.

6. The issue has been widely covered in the media. William McGurn, "Operation Lost in Translation," *Wall Street Journal*, May 22, 2015; Golnar Motevalli, "Afghan 'Terps' Risk Lives to Work with U.S. Forces," Reuters, Apr. 23, 2009; Dan De Luce, "Only 2 Iraqi Translators Who Worked with U.S. Troops Got U.S. Visas Last Year," *Washington Times*, Aug. 23, 2019; Phil Klay, "The Soldiers We Leave Behind," *New York Times*, Nov. 9, 2019.

7. This is not to diminish the role or the courage of CIA and special operations forces on the ground. But key to their successes was the ability to provide precision targeting information for other weapons platforms.

8. Sean Naylor, *Not a Good Day to Die: The Untold Story of Operation Anaconda* (New York: Berkley Books, 2005), 130–32, 137, 148, 194, 267, 270–72, 370–71.

9. Naylor, *Not a Good Day to Die*, 271

10. Andrew J. Bacevich, *America's War for the Greater Middle East: A Military History* (New York: Random House: 2016), 316–17.

11. Mujib Mashal, "Homes Lost and Lives Trampled, Rural Afghans Urgently Want Peace," *New York Times*, March 5, 2019.

12. Emile Simpson, *War From the Ground Up: Twenty-First-Century Combat as Politics* (Oxford: Oxford University Press, 2018), 22, 23, 27, 31, 36, 38, 58, 73. The "polarity" problem is summarized on 57 and 67. This multi-polarity of the conflict is one reason so-called high-value target hunting, without a real sense of the consequences of a decapitation strategy, remains a problematic solution to the

"war on terror" or to the conflict in Afghanistan. See Steven Metz, "Strategic Decapitation: The Dynamics of High Value Targeting in Counterinsurgency," unpublished paper, 2008; Jenna Jordan, *Leadership Decapitation: Strategic Targeting of Terrorist Organizations* (Stanford, CA: Stanford University Press, 2019); Max Abrahms and Jochen Mierau, "Leadership Matters: The Effects of Targeted Killings on Militant Group Tactics," *Terrorism and Political Violence* 29, no. 5 (2017).

13. Michael Hunt, ed., *A Vietnam War Reader: American and Vietnamese Perspectives* (New York: Penguin, 2010), 198.

14. "In 2017, Veterans accounted for 13.5% of all deaths by suicide among U.S. adults and constituted 7.9% of the U.S. adult population. In 2005, Veterans accounted for 18.3% of all deaths by suicide and represented 11.3% of the U.S. adult population." Department of Veterans Affairs, "2019 National Veteran Suicide Prevention Annual Report," https://www.mentalhealth.va.gov/docs/data-sheets/2019/2019_National_Veteran_Suicide_Prevention_Annual_Report_508.pdf. (Note that we distinguish here between "combat fatigue"—mental and physical exhaustion while in combat—from post-redeployment experiences of depression or remembered trauma.) See the historical data on Army suicides in Jeffrey Allen Smith, Michael Doidge, Ryan Hanoa, et al., "A Historical Examination of Military Records of US Army Suicide, 1819 to 2017," *Journal of the American Medical Association Network* 2, no. 12 (2019): e1917448.

15. Yuval Harari has analyzed this difference in "Martial Illusions: War and Disillusionment in Twentieth-Century and Renaissance Military Memoirs," *Journal of Military History* 69 (2005): 43–72. Contrast Adam N. McKeown's analysis of English Renaissance poetry: *English Mercuries: Soldier Poets in the Age of Shakespeare* (Nashville, TN: Vanderbilt University Press, 2009). John Resch tried to measure the impact of trauma on Revolutionary War veterans' postwar success, but there was very little contemporary discussion of the issue. John Resch, *Suffering Soldiers: Revolutionary War Veterans, Moral Sentiment, and Political Culture in the Early Republic* (Amherst: University of Massachusetts Press, 2000).

16. Rachel J. Levandoski, "'The Touchstone of Insanity': Perceptions of the Psychological Trauma of War Within the United States from 1861 to 1918," Ph.D. diss., University of North Carolina at Chapel Hill, 2018, 76–82, quote on 80.

17. Hunt, *Vietnam War Reader*, 199. See also the discussion on alienation from the war and from fellow citizens in Christian G. Appy, *Working-Class War: American Combat Soldiers and Vietnam* (Chapel Hill: University of North Carolina Press, 1993), 250–55, 292, 296, 299–321.

18. Paul Fussell, *Wartime: Understanding and Behavior in the Second World War* (New York: Oxford University Press, 1989).

19. E. B. Sledge, *With the Old Breed* (New York: Ballantine, 2010), 120–21.

20. Krista Garrison, "Community Celebrates the Life of a Fallen Soldier," WNKY News, September 19, 2019.

21. *Thank You For Your Service* (dir. Jason Hall, 2017). This is an impressionistic sense of following servicemembers on Twitter, blogs, and other internet platforms. For one example, see James Kelly, "Why Saying 'Thank You for Your Service' Offends Some Veterans," American Military University Edge, Feb. 3, 2019, https://inmilitary.com/why-saying-thank-you-for-your-service-offends-some-veterans. Compare Sebastian Junger's discussion, which blames alienation at home, more than "trauma" in war, for veterans' sense of psychic wounds from war, in *Tribe: On Homecoming and Belonging* (New York: Twelve, 2016), esp. 90–91.

22. Donald Stoker makes a strong case that the American military and policy community has failed in the modern era to understand the nature of *limited* war. This is a separate argument, albeit related to the one we make here about the probability of the next war involving an enemy we neither expect nor understand. See his *Why America Loses Wars: Limited War and US Strategy from the Korean War to the Present* (Cambridge: Cambridge University Press, 2019).

23. Nadia Schadlow, *War and the Art of Governance: Consolidating Combat Success into Political Victory* (Washington, DC: Georgetown University Press, 2017).

24. It is important to say "mostly," because the special operations community within the services retained a focus on "small war" and counterinsurgency missions (as well as insurgency assistance). See Chapter 5 for more on this process of forgetting.

25. A 2002 version of the doctrine included a phasing construct, but the 2006 version greatly increased the emphasis on the phases after combat, including a phase IV, "stabilizing activities," and a phase V, "enabling civil authority activities." It is of note that this phasing structure has recently been removed from planning doctrine. JP 5-0, *Joint Operation Planning*, Dec. 26, 2006, IV-34, and JP 5-00.1, *Joint Doctrine for Campaign Planning*, Jan. 25, 2002, II-16. See also Thomas E. Ricks, *Fiasco: The American Military Adventure in Iraq* (New York: Penguin Press, 2006) and David P. Cavaleri, "'Stay the Course': Nine Planning Themes for Stability and Reconstruction Operations," *Military Review* 85, no. 4 (July–Aug. 2005): 32–38. Thanks to Chuck Chappell and James Lacey for discussions on the history of "phasing" in doctrine.

26. A whole separate and crucial discussion could be made here about the shift to emphasizing a so-called counterterror strategy that relied on drone strikes and/or kill-capture raids against key militant leaders. But that type of "combat" represents yet a different face of battle.

27. Almost as if to compensate, the U.S. Army created a whole new type of unit: the security force assistance brigade, designed to capture the experience of senior NCOs and officers and put them into an assistance role for local forces, mostly providing training. The exact equipment for this organization is unclear, but recent reports suggest that the army is having trouble manning the

units, since it is perceived within the service as not especially career enhancing. Christopher Woody, "The Army Wants to Send Its Newest Units Worldwide, but the Top Watchdog in Afghanistan Says It's Struggling to Find Enough Troops to Do the Job," *Business Insider*, Sept. 5, 2019.

28. Michael D. Lundy, "Meeting the Challenge of Large-Scale Combat Operations Today and Tomorrow," *Military Review*, special edition, September–October 2018, 111; Headquarters, Department of the Army, Field Manual 3-0, *Operations* (Washington, DC: Government Printing Office, 2017), foreword; *Summary of the 2018 National Defense Strategy of the United States of America* (Washington, DC: Department of Defense, 2018). For a critical voice on this reemphasis, see John Vrolyk, "Insurgency, Not War, Is China's Most Likely Course of Action," *War on the Rocks*, Dec. 19, 2019, https://warontherocks.com/2019/12/insurgency-not-war-is-chinas-most-likely-course-of-action.

29. Lundy, "Meeting the Challenge," 111–13; Bill Ackerly, "CAC Commander Lt. Gen. Lundy Discusses Large Scale Combat Operations at Army Leader Exchange," U.S. *Army*, Feb. 6, 2018, https://www.army.mil/article/200187/cac_commander_lt_gen_lundy_discusses_large_scale_combat_operations_at_army_leader_exchange; Robert A. Law III, "Major Changes to the Command and General Staff Officer's Course Curriculum," Jan. 28, 2019, https://www.army.mil/article/216667/major_changes_to_the_command_and_general_staff_officers_course_curriculum.

30. Todd South, "The Army Is Shutting Down Its Highly praised Asymmetric Warfare Group," *Army Times*, Oct. 2, 2020.

31. Gen. James McConville, "America's Army will never be out-gunned, it will never be out-ranged, and it will never be over-matched," Twitter, Oct. 15, 2019, 1:54 p.m., https://twitter.com/ArmyChiefStaff/status/1184165768939888641.

32. "Army Futures Command Activated in Austin," Association of the United States Army, Aug. 24, 2018, https://www.ausa.org/news/army-futures-command-activated-austin; United States Government Accountability Office, "Army Modernization: Steps Needed to Ensure Army Futures Command Fully Applies Leading Practices," A Report of the Committee on Armed Services, House of Representatives, GAO-19-132, January 2019, introduction, 3.

Index